Ex Líbris

Randy Manning

© APCo

The Cause Lost
Myths and Realities
of the Confederacy

William C. Davis

The Cause Lost

Myths and Realities

of the Confederacy

University Press of Kansas

Published by the University Press of Kansas (Lawrence, Kansas 66049),
which was organized by the Kansas Board of Regents and is operated
and funded by Emporia State University, Fort Hays State University,
Kansas State University, Pittsburg State University, the University of Kansas,
and Wichita State University

Library of Congress Cataloging-in-Publication Data

Davis, William C., 1946–
　　The cause lost : myths and realities of the Confederacy /
　　William C. Davis.
　　　　　　　　　p.　　cm.　—　(Modern war studies)
　　　　Includes bibliographical references and index.
　　ISBN　0-7006-0809-5
　　　　1. Confederate States of America—History
　　　　I. Title. II. Series.
　　E487.D276 1996
　　973.7'13—DC20　　　　　　　　　　　　　　　96–14237

British Library Cataloguing in Publication Data is available.

Printed in the United States of America

10 9 8 7 6 5 4 3 2 1

Contents

List of Illustrations   *vii*

Introduction   *ix*

Part One: **Jefferson Davis and His Generals**

1 Jefferson Davis: The Mystery of the Myth   *3*

2 Davis, Johnston, and Beauregard:
The Triple Play That Crippled the Confederacy   *15*

3 Davis and Lee: Partnership for Success   *35*

Part Two: **Forgotten Wars**

4 The Siege of Charleston   *53*

5 A Different Kind of War: Fighting in the West   *71*

6 Forgotten Wars: The Confederate Trans-Mississippi   *93*

Part Three: **Excuses, Turning Points, and Defeats**

7 Lost Will, Lost Causes   *111*

8 The Turning Point That Wasn't:
The Confederates and the Election of 1864   *127*

9 John C. Breckinridge and Confederate Defeat   *148*

Part Four: **The Confederacy in Myth and Posterity**

10 Stonewall Jackson in Myth and Memory   *161*

11 Myths and Realities of the Confederacy   *175*

12 The Civil War and the Confederacy in Cinema   *191*

Notes   *207*

Index   *219*

Illustrations

Jefferson Davis as president of the Confederacy   4

Joseph E. Johnston   17

P. G. T. Beauregard   19

"Beauregard Mess"   23

Robert E. Lee just after the war   37

Lee monument in Richmond   46

An almost demolished Fort Sumter   63

Charleston's Meeting Street after disastrous fires   69

General Edmund Kirby Smith   79

General Sterling Price   80

Porter's ironclad fleet waiting for the water to rise   83

General Albert Pike   85

Brigadier General Ben McCulloch   96

Destruction, rather than loss of will, defeated the South   118

Gallego Mills in Richmond   123

Lincoln before his election   128

Major General George B. McClellan   143

Major General John C. Breckinridge   149

Lieutenant General Thomas J. "Stonewall" Jackson   163

Admiral Raphael Semmes   176

John C. Calhoun's grave   181

Slave pens of Alexandria   183

The war on film   192

Introduction

WE HAVE COME A LONG WAY in interpreting the Confederacy since the days when people spoke of "slave power" conspiracies. Reflecting from the vantage of more than a century, we can see today how trapped the leaders of the South felt in 1860. That the snare was only partially genuine, and partially in their imaginations and fears, made it no less real to them at the time. They had to act on the basis of what they knew and believed, and the fact that subsequent events and detached dispassionate study reveal that some of their belief was chimerical does not signify. We dare not judge their failures in hindsight's light unless we are ready to stand in that same glare ourselves.

A look at the Confederacy is a look at Americans in the act of nation-building. Thanks to a cornucopian abundance of sources, we can view these Americans in a depth and detail denied to our vision of those earlier revolutionaries of 1776. Consider the Confederacy's president, Jefferson Davis. More than 50,000 pieces of his personal and official correspondence have survived, more than enough to allow us some profound insights into his mind and character, wherein lies much of the fate of the Confederacy. Nothing so reveals some of the bedrock weaknesses of the Southern move for independence as the problems Davis had with some of his generals and they with him. They were all men of their time and place, at least some of which foredoomed them to clash, while for the rest circumstances and their own very human weaknesses well account. That Davis forged such a strong relationship with one of them, Robert E. Lee, however, shows a side of the president and the general that biographers and critics of both have often ignored.

Now, too, we can see what people of the time, even the Confederates, failed to see—that there was a large war out there beyond the confines of Virginia. It is only in our century that historians have finally come to appreciate the extent of the conflict west of the Appalachians, and only more recently still has the decisive nature of that region been recognized. Yet there are backwaters either ignored or doomed to dwell in the greater shadows cast by the armies of Virginia and Tennessee. The faraway Trans-Mississippi affords a look at warfare at its worst, perhaps even at its most pointless, yet it was all too real to those who fought it. And even under the umbrella of the stellar eastern theater there were forgotten places like Charleston that endured war in a degree known nowhere else on the continent.

From the first, of course, the Confederates hoped to win, and for thirteen decades since they lost, they and their partisans—including many historians—have been trying to find a way they could have won or to agree on the precise moment when they lost. The "turning point" and "what if" school of Civil War history flourishes today, generally more enthused than informed, and even some of our better historians still take too much for granted without question. A cold, hard look at some of those watershed moments in the Confederacy's brief life can produce an entirely different outcome. What did Antietam *really* mean on the world stage? What if Lincoln *had* lost his bid for reelection? Did the Confederates lose because they lost their will to continue, and if not, then when did their leaders *really* know it was all over?

Most interesting of all, perhaps, is our perspective now on how that cause lost became the Lost Cause. One thing more and more Civil War historians are still learning is just how consciously former Confederates molded their story for posterity. Indeed, Southern historians today speak almost as of the loss of old friends when they talk about the latest time-honored memoir whose fictions are discovered. Mythology about the South and its leaders—and the Civil War as a whole, incidentally—commenced the moment the war ended, if not before. The growth of that mythology has been nurtured ever since thanks to the self-interest of participants, the defensiveness of their descendants, and the craving of all of us for a good story. Mortals like Stonewall Jackson have been meta-morphosed into demigods. Causes and effects of the war have been manipu-lated and mythologized to suit political and social agendas, past and present. And the whole story of the Confederacy and the conflict has been filtered through the camera's lens to give us yet another view of it on the screen. The impact of all of that on the truth at the heart of the Confederate experience has been profound, making it vital that we try to identify and preserve that truth, even while appreciating and enjoying the myth that encrusts it now.

These essays were written over a period of twenty years, and from the ear-liest dealing with John C. Breckinridge, to the most recent covering the election of 1864, there has been some inevitable maturation of my thoughts (or there should have been). One thing that has not changed, however, is my continuing fascination with these would-be founding fathers, their idealism—yes, they were idealists of a sort—their naïveté, their folly, and their courage. In all of their elements, for better and worse, they were much more than a regional phenomenon. Their every act revealed not how Southern they were but how American. Theirs was to be the new "cittie on a hill," or so they thought, but they failed. The fault was not in their Stars and Bars but in themselves.

A few acknowledgments are in order. The University of Nebraska Press has graciously allowed the reuse of the essay "Davis and Lee: Partnership for Success," which first appeared in Gary Gallagher, ed., *Lee the Soldier* (1996). Lynda Crist, coeditor of *The Papers of Jefferson Davis,* who deserves acknowledgment just for being delightful, helped with an elusive citation. My old friend Albert Castel offered substantial comments on Chapters 5 and 6 especially that have taken my foot out of my mouth. And most of all, thanks must go to a whole generation of Civil War scholars and enthusiasts who have heard or read these essays over the years and whose response has played no small role in their evolution. Quite likely, the thoughts here expressed will continue to develop over time, and so what follows may perhaps best be regarded as ideas "in progress."

Part One

Jefferson Davis and His Generals

Jefferson Davis: The Mystery of the Myth

I N SPRING 1863 Clement Clay of Alabama wrote to William L. Yancey of his friend Jefferson Davis. "He is a strange compound which I cannot analyze," noted Clay: "Inscrutable, and the more I see of him the less I understand him."[1] In time Clay came to regard Davis as "the Sphinx of the Confederacy," and generations of students and historians alike have followed in his wake. Indeed, throughout our own century and right to the present our most distinguished interpreters of the Confederate experience have echoed Clay's bewilderment. Scholars such as Bell I. Wiley, Frank Vandiver, and the late Thomas L. Connelly comment so uniformly upon Davis' incomprehensible character that quite independently they even settle upon the same terse definitions of the man. He is, they say, "an enigma."[2]

Even when we put aside the chief question of whether Davis really does present an enigma to the historian, there can be no doubt that the question is one of paramount importance. No other figure in the Confederacy exerted so profound an influence upon the course of its short life. The story of the Confederate States of America cannot be separated from that of the man who led it, and the former defies full comprehension without an equal grasp of the latter.

And so we return to the original question: Was Jefferson Davis an enigma, and if so, what is it about him that his friend Clay and those who followed have found so mysterious? In fact, of course, Davis presented a host of character and personality traits that taxed the patience even of his closest friends and family and that certainly present a discordant feast for historians to digest. From earliest years he exhibited a hot temper that at times became ungovernable, its first known manifestation being his unsuccessful attempt to ram a pocketknife onto a powder charge in his squirrel rifle to fire at another boy who had angered him.[3] Davis later confessed that "in my youth I was overwilling to fight," and at that he was being easy on himself, for he remained hot-tempered well into his fifties.[4] On at least eight recorded occasions he engaged in arguments that led to near-duels or challenges, the first being with his close friend William S. Har-

Jefferson Davis as he looked as president of the Confederacy.
Alabama Department of Archives and History, Montgomery, Ala.

ney over what started as a friendly horse race.[5] Only the intercession of friends prevented later duels with Robert Toombs and Judah P. Benjamin, both men destined to serve one day in Davis' cabinet.

Temper exhibited at so early an age is probably an inherited trait. But Davis offers a host of other elements for study that allow us to speculate on their formation and evolution. Certainly we work at a disadvantage in attempting to psychoanalyze figures from the past, for we do so in ignorance of relevant facts now lost to history. We are also not entirely fair, for the subject can hardly look up from the "couch" to say us nay. Conscious of these limitations, we may still draw some important conclusions about the development of Davis' character, conclusions that may dispel the mystery supposedly surrounding the man. All we need are common sense and the realization that people of a century ago, whether great or small, are not so different from us today.

The litany of shortcomings that associates and observers found and still find in Davis is a long one, though it is all too often forgotten that each has a positive obverse. Yes, he was obstinate, but he was also determined. He was oversensitive to criticism, yet able to cope with mind-numbing pressures. His indecisiveness went hand in hand with a commendable reluctance to be hasty. Certainly he was hot-tempered and impulsive, but he was also impervious to fear. He demonstrated a consistently poor judgment of character but was also trusting to a fault. Very susceptible to sycophants, he nevertheless stimulated genuine love and admiration in those who knew him intimately. Obsessed with detail, he also possessed a phenomenal grasp of legal and military minutiae, and to his equal obsession with always being right must be matched the diligent effort he made in forming conclusions that to his mind were right. In all of these pairings, the former are not traits to make a man endearing. But that does not mean that there is anything either unusual or mysterious about them.

Jefferson Davis spent much of his life looking for a father. He lost his birth father in 1824 when only seventeen. Samuel Emory Davis was neither a cold nor a cruel parent, but he was a distant one. "My father was a silent, undemonstrative man," the son declared in later years. Among the few things he recalled of his father were his "grave and stoical character" and the fact that, though he was capable of emotion, "he sought to repress the expression of it whenever practicable." Indeed, so effectively did Samuel withhold such expression that his son later remembered as remarkable a single occasion when his father had hugged him.[6] Even before Samuel's death, young Jefferson had come to look more and more to his older brother Joseph as a model, and once their father was gone, the elder Davis quickly became a surrogate parent. This began a pattern that would see Jefferson Davis repeatedly form a reverence for older men that lasted almost all of his life. First it was Andrew Jackson, whom he met while still a boy, then later Martin Van Buren, John C. Calhoun, Franklin Pierce, Zachary Taylor, John Quincy Adams, and more. In every case Davis offered an almost unquestioning affection and respect, just as he had never questioned his father. Even with men like Adams, whom Davis opposed politically, he was able to rationalize his way around differences that with other men often precluded even friendship.

Significantly, even Davis' most revered friends were men at least slightly older than himself and first met in circumstances that resulted in him looking up to them. His deep affection for Albert Sidney Johnston is well known to anyone even passingly familiar with Davis' life. The Mississippian practically worshiped Johnston, whom he regarded to the end of his days as his closest friend. Yet after their days together at West Point, where the older Johnston befriended Davis, there is no evidence that they saw each other again for fully twenty years, until the Mexican War briefly reunited them. After that they apparently did not meet again until fall 1861. Neither did they correspond so far as we can surmise. Despite the survival of roughly 50,000 pieces of Davis' correspondence, not a single personal or nonofficial letter between them is to be found. Yet in 1862 Davis would assert, "I knew Sidney Johnston, I believe, better than I know any other man." If so, then his statement illustrates not how well he knew Johnston but how little he knew everyone else, for in fact the man whom Davis so revered to the end of his life was largely a stranger to him.[7]

It was this kind of blind loyalty to those he admired, combined with Davis' palpably poor judgment of character, that enabled him to adhere so tenaciously to men such as Leonidas Polk, Theophilus Holmes, and Braxton Bragg, whose shortcomings as commanders during the Civil War were so obvious to others. Wrapped up in this phenomenon is another element of Davis' character, his susceptibility to sycophants. Davis regarded loyalty as a paramount virtue. Just as he gave it without reservation, so he expected it in return, unquestioningly, and there were many lesser men like these who retained the president's goodwill and favor because they never challenged him. Usually Davis could spot a blatant flatterer, but the more subtle Judah Benjamin became an independent power in the Confederate cabinet by attuning himself carefully to Davis' prejudices. Even the more obvious John Bell Hood could play on those prejudices to obtain command of an army.

There is nothing too mysterious about a man being receptive to syco-phants. Like so many of the traits manifested by Davis, this one sprang from in-security. In his case it lay grounded in an obsession with being right that, in turn, sprang from a considerable streak of indecision. In regard to the latter, a look at the major events of his first fifty years reveals an illuminating pattern. We may assume that in his boyhood Davis obeyed his dour father without ques-tion. It was Samuel who decided that Jefferson would go away to boarding school in Kentucky when still a child. Certainly it was Samuel who decided to send Jefferson to Transylvania University as a young man of sixteen. When Samuel died, Jefferson wanted to finish at Transylvania and then study law at the University of Virginia. However, Joseph Davis decided otherwise, and his brother went to the United States Military Academy instead. "It was no desire of mine to go," Jefferson Davis recalled. Four years later, however, he believed that the academy had made him into a soldier for life. But a year after that he was anxious to resign if he could find anything else to do.[8]

Instead Davis remained in the military, but three years later he wanted to leave once more to try railroading in Mississippi. Joseph persuaded him against it. Three years later when Jefferson was about to marry Sarah Knox Taylor, he submitted his resignation in such fashion that he gave himself fully six weeks to change his mind. Once more Joseph made his brother's decision for him, setting him up with a plantation of his own and the slaves and money to work it now that he was to be a married man. Following Sarah's tragic death just after their 1835 marriage, Joseph sent his brother to Cuba to recuperate. For two years thereafter Jefferson worked his plantation, but in 1837 when he learned of two new infantry regiments to be raised, he tried unsuccessfully to get back into the army again, even though he had left it under acrimonious circumstances over pay.

Then came politics. In 1843 friends selected him as a convention delegate, and then he allowed himself to be nominated for a seat in the Mississippi leg-islature. In this, as in every other political race in his career, Davis was an en-tirely passive participant. Of course, the ethic of the time dictated that the man did not seek office but that the office sought the man. Nevertheless, backdoor politicking and maneuvering by candidates were the rule, despite their public poses. Not for Davis, however. Certainly he looked upon public service as a duty if called, but to a degree that, in this as in all his other contests, he left some of his major life's decisions in the hands of others.

That same year Joseph began to manage another area of his brother's life when he first introduced Jefferson to Varina Howell and thereafter encouraged the match. In 1845, without his own involvement, Davis was nominated for a congressional seat, which he subsequently won. Then came the war with Mexico, and barely weeks after first taking his seat in Congress, he started politicking actively to get command of a regiment of Mississippi volunteers. When he got the commission, however, he tried to hold onto his House seat, too, once more submitting a resignation in such a fashion that he might withdraw it if the war should end too quickly. The resignation went through, however, but as soon as he returned from the Battle of Buena Vista a hero in 1847, politics arose once more. He repeatedly declined entreaties to run for the governorship but accepted an appointment to the U.S. Senate to fill a seat left vacant by the death of the incumbent. Then President James K. Polk gave him an appointment as brigadier general of volunteers, and it took Davis two weeks and consultation with his former father-in-law, General Zachary Taylor, to make up his mind to decline.

Davis won election to the Senate in his own right in 1848, but then three years later, despite all his earlier refusals, he accepted a nomination for the governorship that required resigning his Senate seat. Defeated, he retired to private life, only to be offered a cabinet post in 1852 by President-elect Franklin Pierce. Davis declined and then three months later changed his mind to become secretary of war. When he left that portfolio in 1857, he stepped immediately into his old Senate seat once more, only to resign at Mississippi's instruction in January 1861. A few weeks later he was chosen president of the Confederacy, despite his having issued an equivocal preference not to be considered for the office.

What emerges is a consistent portrait of indecision, of a man unable or unwilling to commit himself to anything for long and repeatedly willing to assume at best a minority voice in determining his own destiny. Davis protested over and over again of how much distaste he felt for public office and as late as summer 1862 mused on how strange it was that a man with his dislike of politics should have spent so much of his life in the calling. Yet not once did he decline permanently a nomination or an appointment. Significantly, also, not once did he ever serve out a full term in any of his elective offices. This is the indecisiveness that so many complained of in the president of the Confederacy. It took painfully long for him to make up his mind. "By all who have ever been associated with him in public affairs," lamented Secretary of the Navy Stephen Mallory just after the Confederate collapse, "he is probably known to be singularly cautious, if not dilatory in these respects."[9]

There is little to be wondered at in such a trait in a man whose youth and young manhood were governed by a father like Samuel and a domineering brother like Joseph. Indeed, Joseph continued to influence much of Jefferson Davis' affairs well into middle age. Moreover, this indecision is the more readily understood when measured along with another of Davis' most dominant traits, his inability to admit error. The more difficult it is for an individual to come to a decision or conclusion, the more obstinately that person will cling to it once made. Davis evidenced such a trait very early in life when court-martialed at West Point for drinking beer against regulations at the off-limits tavern of the notorious Benny Havens. Not only did Davis steadfastly deny that of which he was most certainly guilty, but he also pettifogged in his defense by trying to convince the court that, strictly speaking, beer and porter were not alcoholic beverages. Thereafter in his life he would go to any lengths to defend the correctness of his own position or behavior. Court-martialed again in 1835 for insubordination, he actually came down to hairsplitting over the proper definition of the exclamation *hum*, and his subsequent resignation from the service owes as much to the court's failure to exonerate him wholly of blame as it does to his engagement to Sarah Taylor. Indeed, so much did the court's equivocal finding wound him that he never afterward spoke of it, apparently not even to his second wife and lifelong companion, Varina.[10]

This trait grew more developed as the years went by. When a word or action appeared to reflect criticism of any kind, his mind took on a single purpose, to prove himself right, even if in his conviction of rectitude he overlooked, discounted, or misstated views and evidence to the contrary. Certainly this trait manifested itself in his public life, where Davis would more than once address an issue with what he called "the assurance that I am right." During the debate over the 1850 compromise measures in Congress, a Wisconsin senator observed of Davis that he spoke "with an air . . . which seems to say, 'Nothing more can be said'—'I know it all'—'it must be as I think.'" Davis did not deny it, explaining his attitude by saying simply that "I am very certain."[11] This obstinacy led him into his disgraceful letter-writing feud with General Winfield Scott while Davis was secretary of war and contributed to similar future imbroglios with several others. Even in the dying days of the Confederacy, Davis would take time from more pressing matters to write long lecturing letters to men such as Alexander H. Stephens, pointing out in painful detail their errors and his own inevitable correctness.

It also led to problems in his second marriage. He and Varina suffered difficulties during their courtship and then again within months after their wedding. Again in 1847, upon his return from Mexico, the problems arose, as they would occasionally for years to come. Davis found her "querulous" and complained to her that "I cannot bear to be suspected or complained of, or misconstrued after explanation." When he went to take his new Senate seat that fall, he left her behind in Mississippi, speaking of "a necessity for separation." They would be separated again in their lives together, and in the end it is quite probable that the only reason the marriage lasted as long as it did is that Varina finally was willing to subordinate her own strong will to her husband's. Davis could not even handle being questioned by his own wife. To paraphrase Henry Clay, he would rather be right than be married. It was often noted of Davis by friends and contemporaries that he got along best with women, children, and blacks, slave and free. Unsaid is that in his time and place all were the social inferiors of a white adult male. On that basis of unquestioned authority, he could be open and easy with them. His feuds, many and celebrated, were all with other white males of strong will and independent mind, a mold of man that Jefferson Davis never learned to tolerate, much less manage.[12]

Such an exaggerated fixation on being right may be out of the ordinary, but it is hardly mysterious given Davis' background and the one great error of his life that he could never admit to himself or anyone else. The riverbanks of the lower Mississippi were a dangerous place in those times. Davis had lost members of his family to the malarial fevers that raged each summer. Indeed, when he graduated from West Point in June 1828, he delayed going directly home until October, even getting an extension of his furlough in order to avoid a summer visit to Mississippi that he said would be "unsafe for me." But seven years later he seemingly forgot that. Engaged to Sarah Taylor, Davis appears originally to have planned a fall marriage in Kentucky in order to avoid the fever season in Mississippi. But in late May or early June, fresh from the sting of his rebuke in the court-martial that contributed to his resignation from the army, Davis changed his mind. Anxious to start his new life as a planter and undoubtedly anxious to begin his married life with Sarah after a troubled two-year courtship, he persuaded her against the advice of others that his acreage on Davis Bend near Vicksburg would be perfectly healthy. In short, in the irrepressible enthusiasm of youthful love, he asked Sarah to take a risk that seven years earlier he had been unwilling to take himself. He wanted Sarah for his wife now, his wife in his bed, and his bed at Brierfield, his new plantation. Sarah loved him, believed him, took the risk, and in less than three months lay dead of malaria.[13]

A mosquito may have been the active agent of the tragedy, but Sarah's death lay heavily on Jefferson Davis' conscience. He had made a hasty decision, taken an impulsive risk, and it cost him probably the greatest love of his life. Many of the ensuing years of solitude in which he lived must have been spent in bitter reflection and in battle with the guilt he felt. In the end, as do most humans, he must have found a way to rationalize his conduct that freed him from the onerous burden of responsibility. Yet such freedom comes at a price. Most often, in instances like Davis', that cost is a subsequent inability to cope with or admit of error, a compulsion to be right at all costs, for fear that admission of mistake in some small thing may open the door to forced recognition of that great, overriding error that in Davis' case had cost him so much.

Is it any wonder, then, that such a man would be susceptible to sycophants? Just as his own family surely told him after Sarah's death that it was not his fault, in after years, working from such a tenuously grounded sense of his own rectitude, Davis needed to have his conviction reinforced repeatedly. This meant a dependence upon at least a few members of his court, such as Benjamin, General Samuel Cooper, and Lucius B. Northrop, who did not question him and who told him what he needed to hear. It also meant that he had to either overpower or banish those who would not yield to him. He saw these matters as questions of loyalty and simple right and wrong, not as the psychological and emotional needs they were in reality.

Surely Davis' much-vaunted obsession with detail springs from this same insecurity. He did, indeed, immerse himself in a mountain of trivial matters as U.S. secretary of war, and later as Confederate president, so much so that most of those around him complained of it—though never to his face. Especially during the Confederate years, when the mistakes of any subordinate commander in the government or military could eventually find their way up the chain of command to roost where the "buck" then, as now, stopped, Davis felt positively obsessed with being in command of everything that came into or left the executive office. He worked himself literally to distraction handling uncounted thousands of minor matters or paperwork, even down to the appointments of obscure captains and lieutenants. Worse, he would not decide immediately upon the best way of dealing with a document. Rather, he would send it to an already overburdened cabinet officer and require an investigation and a report, sometimes repeating the process with other departments so that the same document might pass back and forth across his desk half a dozen times. Even then, after all that bother, Davis might decide in the end simply to file it without action. Better to make no decision than to risk the wrong one.

Just as frustrating to his associates, Davis could not or would not change his mind once he had settled it in a matter. Thomas Watts of Alabama, his last attorney general, found him to be "deliberate in the formations of his conclusions, and when formed, rarely changed." Postmaster General John H. Reagan observed of the president that once he had reached a conclusion, "the matter was settled with him." Mallory went further, lamenting that when Davis "indulge[d] an erroneous estimate it generally continued to govern his actions." "It was ever difficult for him to change an opinion."[14] The reason for this attitude is hardly difficult to fathom. With the emotional stake that Davis had in making the correct decision, the effort it took to overcome his natural indecisiveness, and the enormous effort he put into marshaling all the facts available to form a conclusion, he simply could not face the abandonment of a position once adopted. As a result, examples of him changing his mind or being persuaded to abandon an opinion are so few as to be almost nonexistent.

Thus, too, was his judgment of men influenced. Not only did Davis fall susceptible to sycophants. He was also the victim of a peculiar axiom of his own that, in the context of the man, is perfectly understandable. The less a man complained, the less he boasted, the more self-effacing he was, the more Davis was inclined to trust him and to entrust him with high responsibility. When Theophilus Holmes, with every justification, protested that he was not equal to the command of the vast Trans-Mississippi Department of the Confederacy, Davis replied that in his experience men who doubted their capabilities were usually the most capable.[15] It was a ridiculous maxim that he stated again and again in persuading doubting officers to accept promotion and command, and almost without exception they proved to be failures. Yet these were men who did not argue with him and did not challenge his authority or his rectitude, men who fit the need he had for docile subordinates. But in his mind he was exercising sound judgment in elevating them, as he did in sustaining the likes of Bragg, John C. Pemberton, and Northrop. Indeed, Davis always prided himself on being an excellent judge of character, which meant, in fact, only that he was a good judge of the kind of man with whom he could get along.

It was this support of lesser men, of course, that not only allowed Davis to indulge his penchant for involving himself in minutiae beneath his station but also required it at times. Nevertheless, Davis' interference in the conduct of military affairs has been overblown and overcriticized. In fact, he did little more than offer suggestions to his campaigning generals in the field and almost never overrode one. Indeed, this is the more remarkable when we consider that he even maintained this restraint in dealing with the operations of his two implacable foes, Joseph E. Johnston and P. G. T. Beauregard. When in command, each was left almost entirely to himself, and if Davis erred with them—as he certainly did—it was on the side of restraint, especially in the case of Johnston, who consistently failed to keep his commander in chief informed and just as consistently evidenced an unwillingness to commit himself and his army to action.

The list of Jefferson Davis' quirks of character and personality can go on much longer and with it the informed speculation on their origins, but enough has been discussed by now to suggest several conclusions. He presents a consistent portrait of insecurity as people of the twentieth century define that term. Indecisive, sensitive to criticism, obstinate, unable to admit error, prone to overwhelm himself with detail, and all the rest, he manifested these traits as evidence of his own deeply rooted doubts about himself, doubts at which he hinted from time to time but could never openly confess. In and of themselves these traits are all too common, everyday occurrences. They exist in millions, and one or more are probably to be found in every one of us. Indeed, it would not be at all difficult to gather a couple dozen people in one room and "assemble" Jefferson Davis by selecting elements from those present.

Our quirks will likely never come under public scrutiny, however, unless we achieve a considerable degree of celebrity. What makes these traits seem unusual in Jefferson Davis is that, unlike the overwhelming majority of us, he was called on to assume a very public role in leading one-third of America in a bid for independence. Most of us will blissfully go through life unaware of such foibles in one another and therefore find and offer no cause to be regarded as enigmatic by our fellows. But Jefferson Davis was under the penetrating gaze of millions in his own time and since, with his every act and motive subjected to intense scrutiny. Thus, we can all too easily see in him an exaggeration, a man whose character faults grow larger than life because of the influence they exerted, when what we should see is simply a man of quite ordinary weaknesses thrust into quite extraordinary circumstances.

In the 1980s industrial psychologists posited what they called "the imposter complex" in high corporate officers. In brief, it is the inner turmoil faced by men and women who within themselves know or *believe* that they have been elevated beyond their capacity and beyond their deserts. They manifest a host of symptoms that would be very familiar to anyone who has studied Jefferson Davis. Moreover, these are symptoms with which everyone is familiar. Who has not known an employer or supervisor who consistently favors old cronies despite manifest failings that are obvious to others? Who has never encountered someone in authority who is susceptible to flattery? Who has not known a supervisor whose motto is "If you want it done right, do it yourself," even when that involves doing the jobs of others for them? Historians above all others should be more than familiar with temperaments that form conclusions so confident that there can be no room for admission of error, no successful persuasion to an alternative viewpoint. We have but to look at the friendships ended by a critical book review to see examples of well-intentioned criticism that is misinterpreted as disloyalty or enmity.

In short, we have all known Jefferson Davis and known him very well in bits and pieces of others and of ourselves. He is around us everywhere, just as he will always be present when humans gather. He was not a great man as we normally judge such things. He certainly possessed elements of greatness and a host of positive qualities that are not the province of this discussion but that ought not be forgotten. But it is for his weaknesses that he is regarded as an enigma. People like him have manifested weaknesses, to be sure. To the extent they achieve greatness, it is by their mastering those failings. But Davis, all too often, was mastered by his weaknesses. If he deserves to be accorded a degree of greatness by us, it is because he kept trying despite his limitations and his own self-doubts. "I love approbation," he confessed in 1862, "and will toil on though it be through evil report, to deserve, with the hope that I may gain it."[16]

History has not given him its approbation. Instead it has branded him a mystery, an enigma, merely because he exhibited very ordinary failings on an extraordinary stage that covered half a continent. Ironically, there were few things that Jefferson Davis craved from the public as much as simple understanding. Certainly it is presumptuous of anyone to assert that he or she truly understands another, much less someone dead now more than a century. Yet to that degree that we reveal enough to allow others to truly know us, we can understand Jefferson Davis, strip away the myth of the mystery surrounding him, see him for what he was, and comprehend the impact of his character upon American history. We can even sympathize with him. To whatever extent we are capable of understanding each other, and ourselves, we can understand him.

Davis, Johnston, and Beauregard:
The Triple Play That Crippled the Confederacy

MAJOR CHAPMAN ROOT GRANT, grandson of Ulysses S. Grant, was himself a West Point graduate, a cavalryman with John J. Pershing in the expedition against Pancho Villa, and a veteran of longtime service in the U.S. Army. Grant used to tell a story of a sort of legend in the pre–World War II military. It was about the outbreak of the Spanish-American War in 1898. In the sudden rush to arms more officers were needed than were available, and a number of very junior lieutenants found themselves suddenly elevated to captains, majors, and even lieutenant colonels. When the war was done, these men remained in their new grades but with little experience behind them and little to do. As Major Grant put it, "They sat on their butts in swivel chairs" until 1916, acquiring nothing but seniority. Then came another war, another sudden need for officers, and these fellows now became colonels and even brigadiers, and with the relentless operation of the seniority system, after 1918 they continued to advance in rank in the days prior to World War II. This happened in spite of almost no real battlefield experience and often in spite of demonstrable incompetence. According to Major Grant, he and his fellow officers came to refer to these high-ranking bumblers as the "Crime of '98."[1]

Thirty-seven years earlier, as the new Confederacy rushed to arms, President Jefferson Davis might well have applied a similar term to the situation facing him, only he would have perhaps called it the "Crime of '61." The seniority system was just as relentless then as later. Advancement provided in the earlier Mexican War had a profound impact upon the future careers of men who later became ranking officers in the Confederacy. Thus in 1861 when Davis was forming his officer corps, seniority and the inevitable logic of giving high command to the men with the most experience and highest Old Army rank almost tied Davis' hands in his selections. Not that he minded. He believed in seniority.

Jefferson Davis and His Generals

Nevertheless, it did not serve him well. With the one shining exception of Robert E. Lee, it might have been challenging to assemble a greater assortment of unproven talents and demonstrated inadequacies than those found in the other seven full-rank generals of the Confederacy. Samuel Cooper could not even take the field. Sidney Johnston, in his brief time in command, did little to justify the exalted reputation he enjoyed then and later. Of Braxton Bragg little needs to be said. Even if his reputation is currently undergoing a modest rehabilitation, he still has light years to go to assume any stature as a commander. Yet consider that of all the Confederate Army commanders, Bragg led more offensives than any other except Lee. This says little about Bragg but volumes about the others. Kirby Smith repeatedly politicked and begged for promotion and broader responsibility but then immediately ran away from it every time he got it. John Bell Hood, of course, for all his bravery, simply was not smart enough to command more than a corps.

In many ways they sound like characters from the land of Oz. If so, then the Lion and the Tin Man of the piece are the two remaining full generals of the Confederacy, Joseph E. Johnston and P. G. T. Beauregard. Seniority accounts for the former and public acclaim, the latter. Collectively, these two and their relationships with Jefferson Davis dominated the course of the Southern cause west of the Appalachians and, indeed, much of it in the east. Well could Davis have called these two the "Crime of '61." In the pride, the pettiness, the vanity, and a host of other failings of all three men was born much of the eventual doom of the Lost Cause.

Davis, of course, did not know how to deal with men whom he could not overawe either with his logic or his authority, and thus he was probably destined to come to loggerheads with these two in any event. He and Johnston were somewhat more than passingly acquainted and had been for more than thirty years prior to the war. Johnston was just one year behind Davis at West Point, and there was a post–Civil War story—almost certainly apocryphal—that they had been rivals for a young woman's affections while there, even coming to blows.[2] (One does not study Johnston for long before coming to the conclusion that he would not have fought for anything, even a woman.) They seem not to have crossed paths again during their Old Army careers until the mid-1850s, when Davis was secretary of war and Johnston had charge of running snag boats on the Mississippi and Arkansas Rivers for the Corps of Engineers. They had a very minor, and amicably settled, dispute over the handling of some funds by Johnston, and Davis later came to his defense in the matter. When Davis invited Johnston to his Washington home in 1855, the officer accepted, he said, "with great pleasure."[3]

But then arose a harbinger of what was to come: rank. Johnston had briefly held a temporary commission as a lieutenant colonel during the war in Mexico but lost the rank when his unit mustered out of regular service in 1848. He

Joseph E. Johnston as he appeared early in the war.
Courtesy the Valentine Museum, Richmond, Va.

Jefferson Davis and His Generals

reverted to his permanent rank of captain. When Secretary of War Davis created the First United States Cavalry in 1855, he made Johnston its lieutenant colonel, a handsome promotion that certainly showed goodwill. But Johnston only complained. He maintained that his seniority as lieutenant colonel should date to 1847 when he originally—if only briefly—held that position and not to his new 1855 commission. The reason was painfully obvious. Davis had made Edwin V. Sumner colonel of the First Cavalry, promoting him from a lieutenant colonelcy he had held since 1848. If Johnston's original 1847 lieutenant colonelcy were recognized for seniority purposes, then he would have been Sumner's senior and therefore presumably entitled to the full rank of colonel and command of the new regiment. Davis ruled against Johnston, but he did not accept the judgment and was still pursuing his claim in 1860, to no avail. But then Davis again did something for him, this time supporting Johnston for the post of quartermaster general, which carried with it the staff rank of brigadier. Davis later claimed that he was instrumental in securing Johnston's confirmation against heavy opposition, though the fact that the Senate confirmed Johnston by a vote of 31 to 3 shows that there was no opposition at all. Nevertheless, Davis, now a senator, did vote for Johnston despite the competing candidacy of beloved friend Albert Sidney Johnston.[4]

Their wives were good friends, too, though some rumored that Mrs. Johnston thought Davis detested her husband, a charge that clearly appears unfounded. By 1861, if the two were not close friends, there certainly was no outward hostility on Davis' part. And when Davis became president of the Confederacy, one of his first actions after Virginia seceded was to wire Governor John Letcher to inquire of Johnston's whereabouts and intentions. The officer had extensive combat experience—along with an unlucky habit of getting wounded—and with his staff rank of brigadier he stood very high in seniority. Davis wanted him for a top position wearing the gray. He commissioned Johnston a brigadier general in the Confederate Regular Army—the highest rank then available. So far, so good.

At the same time, circumstances, not seniority, dictated another new general. Davis and Beauregard had only a passing acquaintance prior to the war, and there is little to suggest what they thought of each other in 1860 when the crisis came to a head. Though the Louisiana Creole had risen no higher than major in the Old Army, Davis made him a brigadier in the Confederate Provisional Army on March 1, 1861, and immediately assigned him to the forces surrounding Fort Sumter. Beauregard was Davis' best available experienced engineer officer at the moment, and it needed an engineer to reduce Sumter, or so Davis thought. And after the fall of the fort, Beauregard was so popular in the South that Davis had almost no alternative but to assign this—his winning—general to the next anticipated crisis point, northern Virginia.

Here they started to clash immediately. Both were at fault, and it is difficult to say with certainty who began the sniping. For a start, almost certainly the

P. G. T. Beauregard toward the end of the war.
Courtesy, National Archives

president felt some jealousy of the general. After all, Davis had hoped to be in a military, rather than civil, command in the new nation. Moreover, until the fall of Fort Sumter, Davis himself had been the South's greatest living military hero, going all the way back to his performance at Buena Vista in Mexico in 1847. But now Beauregard was the name on all lips, and Davis would not have been human had he not felt envious. He loved praise, as he himself admitted. A corporal's guard could have taken Fort Sumter, but in the euphoria of the moment a minor achievement made Beauregard the toast of the Confederacy.

Then when the two became more closely associated in Virginia, their personalities came into play. Beauregard—bombastic, egotistical, politically naive—produced one impractical plan after another for grand combined movements into the North to win the war at a single stroke. Davis wisely rejected all of them, for they were all-or-nothing schemes that would likely have led to utter ruin if not successful. Davis had continental concerns to look after; Beauregard could never see beyond the enemy in his front and his dreams for his own reputation. He did not take well to Davis rejecting his grand schemes, and as early as June 1861 he was already referring privately to the president as "a stupid fool" in front of friends and staff officers. For his own part, Davis bristled at Beauregard's haughty and imperious attitude and made fun of his equally self-important staff. "Whoever is too fine, that is, so fine we do not know what to do with him," Davis said to James Chesnut, "we send him to Beauregard's staff." Unfortunately, Chesnut himself was on Beauregard's staff, and the foolish remark undoubtedly got back to the general.[5]

In July Beauregard and Johnston combined forces, under the overall command of the latter, to win the exciting contest along Bull Run. It was to be the only time those two generals would cooperate, and the victory owed much to Davis, too, who funneled troops and matériel from the rest of the South to sustain the armies in northern Virginia. Davis himself rushed to the battlefield, arriving only after the Yankee rout was well under way. He met Johnston first and learned of the victory from him. They rode over the field, then that night met with Beauregard to decide on the future. Davis pressed for an immediate pursuit, but Johnston passively sat still and did not speak, contributing nothing to the conversation, it seems, until later discussion suggested that a pursuit should be postponed until the morning. When Davis wrote a telegram to be sent to Richmond announcing the victory, he signed it himself, rather than having Johnston or Beauregard do so, leading the latter to suspect that Davis was thereby trying to take credit for the victory himself. "My conclusion was," said the Creole, "that we had to deal with an ambitious man."[6] That meeting at Manassas on the evening of triumph revealed the basic tenor of their relationships and behavior for the rest of the war: Davis pressing for advance and initiative, Johnston unwilling to move or act on his own or even to communicate his thoughts, Beauregard terrified that someone might steal his glory and diminish his reputation.

Tragically, it was a matter of only weeks before open warfare broke out among them. It started first with Johnston and predictably over the old bugbear of rank. On May 16 Congress approved a new rank of full general. Davis appointed four under that legislation. Cooper was senior of all, to act as adjutant and inspector general just as he had in the U.S. Army until 1861. Then came Sidney Johnston—who was not even in the Confederacy yet but was in the far-away west. Then came Robert E. Lee and finally Joseph E. Johnston. Davis would make Beauregard a full general later, dating his commission from July 21 and the Manassas victory.

Immediately Davis made a seeming mistake. The legislation called for all of these appointments to be made effective from the same date. Thus, no general at this grade would be senior to any other. Davis wisely sidestepped that since otherwise any time two or more of them should happen to combine forces, there would be no way to determine which was to assume overall command. Foreseeing this same potential problem, Congress had provided that in any such case the man who had been senior in the Old U.S. Army should command. Even then, as events revealed, there still would have been a problem. Joseph E. Johnston immediately broiled, asserting that he should be the senior general of all. Sidney Johnston had been only a colonel, and a brigadier by honorary brevet, in the Old Army. Lee had been a full colonel. Cooper had been but a lieutenant colonel. Johnston, however, had been a brigadier as quartermaster general. Therefore, he should rank them all.

Davis quickly dubbed Johnston's complaints "insubordinate," but then Johnston wrote him a long, lecturing letter—the worst thing anyone could do with Jefferson Davis—and Johnston's arguments were logical, according to the letter of the law. Davis brusquely responded, saying that these arguments were "one-sided" and the "insinuations as unfounded as they are unbecoming." That ended the argument, or so it seemed, for they never spoke of the matter again, but Johnston had caught Davis, who years later sought to rationalize and justify what was, in fact, inconsistent action on his part.

He claimed that Johnston's brigadiership was only a staff position in the

Jefferson Davis and His Generals

Old Army—as indeed it was—and therefore did not count in the apportioning of seniority for field commanders, though the enabling legislation allowed for no such distinction. Davis argued, therefore, that for field grade ranking, Johnston could be considered only by his prewar field grade of lieutenant colonel and thus was junior to Lee and Sidney Johnston. There was a sort of consistency in this, but according to his own logic, Davis should have made Cooper—now the senior general of the whole army—junior to all of them since his staff rank in the Old Army had been only that of a lieutenant colonel and his field rank had been but a mere captaincy. And the most senior field officer of all to join Southern ranks was Brigadier General David E. Twiggs, who outranked all of them by any measure before the war. But Davis made him only a major general, subordinate to all the others.[7]

Davis' reasons are easily fathomed. All these commissions and rankings were done between May and July 1861, months before his old friend and boyhood idol Albert Sidney Johnston finally reached Richmond to join the cause. From the first, Davis had intended for this Johnston to be the premier field commander of the Confederacy, and the only way to achieve this was to circumvent the congressional acts by inventing the distinction between field and staff ranks held in the Old Army. That was the only way to make the one Johnston senior to the other. Davis could ignore Cooper since as adjutant and inspector general he was going from a staff position in the U.S. Army to the same one in the Confederate states service.

Relations with Joseph E. Johnston were never wholly open or cordial again, though he dropped the controversy itself. Davis may even have forgotten the episode, probably because he was almost immediately embroiled in another controversy, this time with Beauregard. He knew how to talk to the press and politicians, especially those inimical to Davis, and was soon criticizing the War Department for a variety of ills. Davis actually tried to soothe him at first, even when Beauregard said he could have taken Washington but for hindrance from Richmond—which was a manifest lie. Then Beauregard submitted more wildly impractical plans for campaigns using his own and Johnston's forces combined, and it became clear that, even though Johnston, as senior, nominally commanded, he was almost completely overawed by the persuasive Beauregard. When Davis visited with them in northern Virginia to try agreeing on a new plan of action, all he found was that two of his four ranking generals were both politically naive and militarily impractical, unable to see the implications of their actions beyond their own armies. Worse, Johnston, the senior, was reticent and very much under the influence of Beauregard and his crony Gustavus W. Smith.

When Davis rejected these new fantasies, Beauregard asked to be assigned elsewhere. Davis refused, but in cordial terms, and even tried to flatter the general by saying how much he was needed in Virginia. Then Beauregard quarreled with Secretary of War Judah P. Benjamin. Davis tried to intervene, but when Beauregard haughtily asserted that the secretary of war should not tie

These Texans in Virginia in the winter of 1861–1862 named their quarters for the hero of Sumter and Manassas. Jefferson Davis might have thought that "Beauregard Mess" referred to the man's generalship.
Courtesy of Herb Peck Jr.

the hands of a general in the field with rules, Davis brought him up short with a stern rebuke, saying, "You certainly did not mean to inform me that your army and yourself are outside of the limits of the law."[8] Beauregard backed down immediately and almost obsequiously, but then came the matter of his report of the battle at Manassas. It appeared in the press before Davis ever saw it, a clear breach of etiquette. Worse, the report played down Davis' important role as one of the architects of victory and implied that it was Davis who had prevented a pursuit, when in fact the president was the only one who had pressed for it. Davis responded with vehemence, and again Beauregard backed down, denying he had intended any such construction of his words or that he had authorized the report's publication.[9]

In fact, neither Johnston nor Beauregard would ever attempt directly to stand up to the president. Rather, from here on they would fight him behind his back by currying the press and carrying on long correspondence with influential members of Congress. For all of Davis' manifest flaws, when it came to character, he was undeniably senior to both. It did not help that the generals had few friends in the cabinet. Benjamin especially detested Beauregard and would come to feel the same about Johnston. So did Secretary of the Navy Stephen Mallory, who called the two generals "self-sufficient, vain, army idiots." According to Mallory, Benjamin's favorite theme in cabinet discussions was the "want of capacity" of the two officers.[10]

Davis finally assigned Beauregard to the west as second in command to Sidney Johnston. Davis probably did so just to get rid of the troublesome commander, but this action certainly did not end their controversies. Instead it only led to their renewal. Beauregard soon came to exert a surprising influence on his new commander, Johnston, just as he had on the old one, and when the commander was mortally wounded on the first day of fighting at Shiloh, Beauregard assumed command and almost immediately yielded the initiative, for all his earlier boastfulness. Worse, after the retreat to Corinth, when Beauregard filed a report of the campaign, he mentioned the dead Johnston no more than four times, making it sound as if the dead general had been entirely peripheral to the battle. Defeat was bad enough for Davis. But to see Beauregard deny his hero a preeminent part was unforgivable. It helped that the dead general's son William Preston Johnston served on Davis' personal staff and fed the president's resentment of Beauregard, whom he referred to as "a newspaper hero and a humbug" and, as if it were even worse, "a vain creature and a little Frenchman."[11]

Davis, Johnston, and Beauregard

All the situation needed was for Davis to hear rumors that Beauregard was actually speaking critically of Sidney Johnston, and the president could not sit still. He sent his aide Johnston to investigate Beauregard's army, inviting a conflict of interest on the son's part. Davis entered correspondence with generals in that army who felt little love for the Creole. And he started to plan a press campaign of his own. Davis himself made snide references to associates about Beauregard's lack of initiative. "It is hard to see incompetence losing opportunity and wasting hard gotten means," he complained, and referred to the western army as idly lying in camp "when not retreating under Beauregard." By June he had concluded that the general was one of those, he said, "who can only walk a log when it is near to the ground, and I fear he has been placed to[o] high for his mental strength." Future references to the situation in west Tennessee were not about ground lost to the enemy but about "what Beauregard has abandoned."[12]

Then Beauregard played into Davis' hands when he left his command without notification or permission, going away for four months to recuperate his health. To Davis that was desertion. He formally relieved the general of his command immediately, put Bragg in charge, and gave orders to ignore any instruction from Beauregard or any attempt on his part to resume his command. It was the most severe action Davis ever took against any Confederate general in a major command. For the next two years Beauregard could fight back only in his letter-writing campaign, referring to Davis as "either demented or a traitor" and calling him "that living specimen of gall & hatred."[13]

Meanwhile Joseph E. Johnston had been only a little less disappointing, and he, too, was out of the war for awhile. Davis' initial mistrust of Johnston's judgment and fitness formed in the days after Manassas and grew steadily, with good cause. When asked for his plans for the next campaign, he had none after Beauregard went west. When asked how he proposed to defend northern Virginia, Johnston replied that he did not know the country and could not take responsibility for making such a decision, despite his having had six months in the region to familiarize himself with its geography and resources. This shocked the president. Worse, when Davis met with Johnston to make plans, the two emerged with distinctly different impressions of what they had agreed upon. Davis believed they had agreed to send all baggage, wagons, and other nonvital impedimenta back toward Richmond in case the army had to retire from its line in northern Virginia. Johnston believed that he had authorization or even orders to pull back the army itself.

Here began three recurring themes in the generalship of Joseph E. Johnston—complaints that he could not take responsibility for something, apparent obtuseness at understanding simple orders, and a consistent instinct to fall back without a fight. Johnston did fall back in March 1862, without telling Davis or getting permission, and the president was stunned. Each had failed to communicate adequately with the other, but Johnston's was the great sin for he intentionally failed throughout to keep Davis informed on plans. Davis failed, in the last extremity, to use his authority to compel Johnston to keep him informed. Now as Johnston took up a new line along the Rappahannock, Davis, who had learned something from the mix-up, assigned aides such as young Preston Johnston to keep an eye on the armies and act as a conduit of official information.

In fact, Davis showed considerable restraint with Johnston, revealing that he may not have held a grudge after the rank controversy of the year before. He was, in fact, unusually patient with Johnston, as he had been with very few others in his life. He apparently still had some confidence in the general and abstained from giving him direct orders. But then came George McClellan's landing on the Virginia peninsula with the Union Army of the Potomac. Davis summoned Johnston to Richmond. Again the general had no ideas of his own, so the president ordered him to move himself and his army to stop the Federal threat. But Johnston complained that it was impossible to defend the peninsula—which Lee later showed to be nonsense—and proposed instead to give all of it up to McClellan without a fight and pull back for a stand at Richmond itself. Davis refused, but then Johnston set about creating a self-fulfilling prophecy by asking permission on May 1 to abandon Yorktown and start a retreat, though there had as yet been no real contact between the armies.

Johnston's history on the peninsula is a sad one. Davis could not get a word out of him, and Johnston intended it that way. The president would ask for specific plans; the general either did not reply at all or responded with questions of his own and restatements of the need to retreat. Johnston abandoned Yorktown without anything like adequate preparation, leaving behind tons of vital ordnance and matériel. To learn anything, Davis now rode personally to the army himself almost daily, and still Johnston was secretive. "I could not consult him without adopting the course he might advise" was the general's weak excuse years later.[14] But Johnston had no course of his own to propose except retreat.

On May 18 when he retreated once more, across the Chickahominy and into the suburbs of Richmond itself, he never informed Davis of his intent, and the president only learned of the move when he left for his daily ride to the army and discovered that he did not have to go nearly as far as the day before. The look of surprise on his face appeared to be one of pain to those around him. He demanded an explanation from Johnston, and when he asked if the general intended to give up Richmond itself without a fight, Johnston dodged the question. At this Davis finally lost his patience and his temper and threatened to replace Johnston with a general who would fight, which apparently put a brief bit of starch in the Virginian's spine. Hereafter Davis had his adviser and general in chief Lee deal directly with Johnston, hoping that the two old friends would communicate better, but still Johnston would not talk. By now he was surly, insubordinate, begging for relief and replacement for his actions. Unaccountably, Davis, for once, was too patient, too forgiving, too understanding with someone, perhaps because he had no other general as a replacement. Sidney Johnston was dead, Beauregard was in the west and much out of favor, Cooper was too old, and Lee's 1861 campaign in western Virginia had been a failure. Johnston had at least fought one successful battle (though he exerted almost no control over its planning and course, leaving that to Beauregard, as usual). In short, Davis was stuck with Johnston. Thus, it was a fortunate thing that at Seven Pines a Yankee bullet and a shell fragment put him out of action with serious wounds. Lee took over, and at last a real general emerged. Davis forgot all past animosities and tenderly looked after the wounded Johnston, even offering a room in the executive mansion for his recovery and referring to him as a "poor old fellow."[15]

It is unfortunate that Davis apparently never heard an anecdote about Johnston that made the rounds of the Richmond salons. Hamilton Boykin said of Johnston that "never in his life could he make up his mind that everything was so exactly right, that the time to act had come." Then he told how Johnston, supposedly a crack marksman with a rifle, never actually took a shot at a bird when hunting with friends. The bird was always too high or too far away, or the dogs were too near. "He was too fussy, too hard to please," said Boykin, "too cautious, too much afraid to miss and risk his fine reputation." While everyone else blithely banged away, missing much but occasionally getting a bird, Johnston just made his excuses and returned from the hunt with an unblemished reputation ... and an empty game bag. His generalship was exactly the same.[16]

Perhaps if Davis had ever gone hunting with Johnston, he would have known better than to give Johnston another command. After the failure of Bragg's Kentucky invasion in late 1862, the command situation in the west was in crisis. Confidence in Bragg plummeted, and Davis was asked to replace him. But with whom? Not Cooper, of course. Lee could not be spared from Virginia. Johnston was still recuperating. And Beauregard was almost a deserter and beyond consideration. In the end Davis had to leave Bragg in place, but the president created a "supercommand," called the Department of the West, that encompassed everything from east Tennessee to the Mississippi. He gave the post to Johnston as soon as he reported fit for duty. Its goal was to make maximum advantage of cooperation of the forces in that vast territory to achieve concentration and harmony.

Johnston and Davis both made a mess of the new organization from the outset. Having learned not to trust Johnston to act on his own, the president interfered far more than usual in dictating policy and movements, an understandable interference given Johnston's history. The general, meanwhile, set up yet another self-fulfilling prophecy by declaring that such a command could not work and that it was too much for one man—which really meant that it was too much for him. Certainly he faced great obstacles, with scattered forces, inadequate transportation, and inferior numbers. But Johnston simply never made a serious effort to overcome those handicaps.

For the next eight months Johnston engaged in a correspondence with Davis that must be unique in Civil War annals for its apparent obtuseness. No matter how often and explicitly Davis explained to the general the full range of his authority and prerogatives, Johnston just wrote back yet again asking the same question. He refused to understand that he had full responsibility because he was terrified of full responsibility. When the subject of replacing Bragg arose again, Johnston clearly said that he did not wish to be considered as a replacement himself. And even though Davis repeatedly made it clear that Johnston had the option of assuming personal command immediately of any force within his department—including Bragg's army—the general kept asking for clarification on the point. Now, more than ever, Davis' antipathy toward Beauregard ruled command decisions. If Bragg had to be replaced and Johnston would not do it, there was still no one else left. The only other option would be for Davis to elevate to full general's rank some subordinate, but Lee could not spare any of his lieutenants, who would not know the western army anyhow, while Bragg's lieutenants were almost all tainted by the undercurrents against him that plagued that army's high command. Thus, it was Davis' loathing of Beauregard, filtered through the timidity of Johnston, that actually kept Bragg in command through 1863. This was not really a good way to run an army.

Johnston's failure to coordinate any assistance for the defense of Vicksburg is well known. All that spring and summer, as usual, he either had no plans or would not communicate them. Instead he sat at Tullahoma and watched as everything took place around him. Davis unfortunately let him get away with it and only issued a peremptory order to go take command at Vicksburg on May 9. Johnston, of course, took his time and missed the whole show.

Entirely setting aside their personal differences, Davis had seen more than enough by the time of Vicksburg's fall to conclude that this Virginian simply did not have the capacity for high command. He would not accept responsibility. He allowed others like Beauregard to dominate him. He would not communicate with his commander in chief. And he carped and politicked behind Davis' back and let himself become the unwitting tool of the president's opposition in Richmond. Johnston was slow, and on the face of it obtuse, and he was unable to get cooperation from subordinates. By being patient with him for so long, Davis injured the cause; by being ruled by his hatred of Beauregard, Davis may have done further damage by not restoring the Creole to a field command in the west in 1863, where he might have achieved some good. Beauregard was a pompous, vain blowhard, to be sure. But he was not afraid to risk a fight and almost certainly would have given a better performance than Johnston, who was a man of great personal bravery in a fight but a moral coward when it came to responsibility for an army. Adherence to Joseph E. Johnston would be Jefferson Davis' greatest mistake of 1862–1863 and one of his greatest of the war.

Beauregard's star was somewhat in the ascendant, by the way, which did not exactly please the president. Beauregard fought a successful defense of Charleston in April 1863, but Davis' prejudice against him was so great that as soon as the news of the victory reached Richmond, those around Davis saw that his only fixed intent was to find some evidence that the Creole had done something wrong or failed to do something he ought to have done. In October Davis went personally to Charleston to confer briefly with the general, even sharing a carriage with him in a parade, though the two were noticeably cool. Beauregard refused to attend a dinner for Davis that evening, and in a speech Davis pointedly omitted any mention of the general in the victory but clearly had him in mind when remarking that "he who would attempt to promote his own personal ends" in these times was little more than a traitor.[17] "May God forgive him," seethed Beauregard. "I fear I shall not have charity enough."[18]

A month later the disaster at Chattanooga took Davis' mind back to the perennial problem of Johnston. Bragg had to go after the debacle at Missionary Ridge, and only Johnston and Beauregard were available. Despite repeated entreaties, Lee refused politely but firmly to go west. Kirby Smith was now a full general, but he was in the Trans-Mississippi and had never led more than a division in a real battle. Since Davis hated Beauregard more than he distrusted Johnston, the latter won the prize, but the president would act only after his cabinet formally met on the matter and recommended Johnston. Sharing what the president feared would be the blame at least eased his mind somewhat of the responsibility of making a decision that he feared was doomed to failure, as indeed it was. He gave command of the Confederacy's second most important army to a man whom he detested simply because he could not find anyone else less odious. Thus, Davis continued to prejudice his own chances for success by adhering to a man whose record gave cause to expect anything but success.

The ensuing campaign in Georgia was déjà vu for Davis. Johnston had no plans. He would not communicate with Davis. When the president sent an aide to learn firsthand what was expected, Johnston was cordial but revealed nothing more than that he had no ideas. His corps commanders confessed themselves equally in the dark. When Davis said that he wanted an offensive in the spring, Johnston dragged his feet and then talked instead of withdrawing from his winter position at Dalton, which is what he did. He never stopped withdrawing until he reached the environs of Atlanta. Given the disparity of odds—which were not nearly as one-sided as Johnston disingenuously claimed after the war—fairness requires an admission that there might not have been much else he could have done. What is not to Johnston's credit, however, is that he never *tried* to do anything else. When he was outside Atlanta and the president asked again about his plans, he could only respond that he had none. Davis relieved him immediately, though again only after being seconded by the cabinet. Once more Davis faced an awful decision. Bragg was out of the question. Lee would not take it. Johnston, like the Lion of Oz, lacked courage. Beauregard, like the Tin Man, lacked a heart—a heart for the cause, that is. Beauregard really had his heart only in his own reputation. And so Davis turned to the Scarecrow, John B. Hood, who might well have sung, "If I only had a Brain."

But Johnston would be back again, at the war's end, when Hood had shown how out of his depth he was in army command. One almost has to feel sorry for poor Davis, forced by seniority and what seemed good logic at the time, and by a paucity of good commanders as the war progressed, to keep bouncing back and forth between these woefully insufficient men. For by the time Johnston resumed command of the Army of Tennessee in 1865, Beauregard had succeeded to Johnston's old supercommand, attempting unsuccessfully to manage some sense out of Hood's campaigns. Davis and Beauregard even managed one cordial meeting to discuss what should be done. Beauregard had performed well in the early defense of Petersburg in summer 1864, and Davis seems to have softened toward him in some small degree. But there was nothing Beauregard could do in the situation facing him in fall 1864, and early in 1865 when Johnston resumed command of the Army of Tennessee, Beauregard returned to his old command in South Carolina.

Given the president's preference, Davis probably would have shot Johnston if he could have found an excuse. From the moment of the loss of Vicksburg, that general waged a behind-the-scenes war against the president, first in the press with critical accounts of Pemberton—a favorite of Davis' who was in some fair degree victimized by Johnston's lethargy—and then in Congress, when friends started to call for copies of Davis' correspondence and reports in the case, seeking to embarrass the president. The newspapers printed a steady flow of defamatory letters. Thus, it came all the harder when even his best friends—Lee, Secretary of War John C. Breckinridge, even his own brother, Joseph—told Davis that the only man to take command of the Army of Tennessee was Johnston. Davis only gave in by rationalizing that Lee, who was now general in chief again, had the authority to request the commanders he wanted for any of the field armies of the Confederacy. Yet relations with Lee were somewhat strained for a brief time as a result, and Davis made it clear that Lee was not just to advise Johnston but also to *order* him when and how to act.

The war came full circle for these three troubled men when Richmond was evacuated and Davis and the government fled south through the Carolinas. Beauregard reported to Davis at Greensborough, North Carolina, and made it clear that he believed the cause hopeless. Davis amazed him by evidencing a "visionary hope" that they would still win independence.[19] Then on April 11 Davis met with Beauregard and Johnston in their first joint session since 1861. Once more Beauregard said the war was all over, and Johnston did the same. Davis did not know that the generals had met privately the evening before to agree on their approach with Davis—the last time these two agreed on anything, their hatred of each other being almost as great as their shared loathing of Davis.

In a cabinet meeting that day they argued strenuously for an honorable surrender, and the other cabinet members agreed. Davis finally, agonizingly, allowed Johnston to ask for an armistice with his opponent Sherman to discuss terms, though Davis privately believed that nothing would come of it and that he was therefore really buying time. Johnston got his armistice and then came to far-reaching terms with Sherman that touched on matters beyond either general's authority. Not surprisingly, Washington rejected Sherman's cartel and said he could only accept the surrender of Johnston's own army. Davis had foreseen this. What he did not foresee was that Johnston would then go ahead and surrender without authority from the president. While Davis expected Johnston to start getting his army away to safety, Johnston—as usual—refused to communicate with his president and took it on himself to surrender on April 26. Davis was livid and never ceased to condemn the general for this disobedience of orders, this one last act of "cowardice."

Thus, it all came to an end, though the controversy among these three men would not cease until their deaths. Thirteen years later Johnston shamefully accused Davis of absconding with part of the Confederate treasury.[20] Beauregard called him a "bitter" old man and questioned his sanity. Davis was more restrained but still refused to be present when either of the other two attended a veterans' reunion or a monument dedication. Each wrote memoirs that were self-justifying and largely devoted to showing the hypocrisies of the others (actually, ghostwriters wrote most of Johnston's and Davis' memoirs; Beauregard largely wrote his own but, ironically, put a friend's name on it as author). Lamentably, none save Davis had ever fought the Yankees as effectively or as viciously as the three men had fought one another.

In 1863 Davis had written to his brother, Joseph, that "a *General* in the full acceptation of the word is a rare product, scarcely more than one can be expected in a generation, but in this mighty war in which we are engaged there is need for half a dozen."[21] In the end Davis got only one, Robert E. Lee. What Davis got in Beauregard we may never really know, for his own folly and Davis' enmity denied him a chance to show what he might have become. But the evidence does not suggest that we should expect too much. Beauregard never shook himself of the outmoded Napoleonic notion of winning the war with one decisive battle, nor did he ever become sophisticated enough in his thinking to see the vital interdependency of military and civil policy. He could speak grandly of giving up Tennessee to the Federals in order to concentrate a mass of force elsewhere. Davis could not, knowing that it would be political suicide to willingly yield any inch of the Confederacy. Beauregard could talk of risking everything on a throw of the dice. Davis had to temper all grand designs with the reality of his responsibility to preserve and protect the Confederacy. Properly supervised, Beauregard might have become an effective army commander subordinate to Lee. Beauregard could never have worked with Davis in the long run and probably could not have got on even with Lee in the end, for he would not admit of any authority greater than his own outsized ego. Even Lincoln, that great manager of men, probably could not have made an effective commander of Beauregard any more than he did of McClellan.

As for Joseph E. Johnston, the raw material for command simply was not there. Ironically, his is one of the great reputations of the Civil War, the man spoken of as the great might-have-been of the Confederacy had Jefferson Davis not stood in his way. It is a myth created by Johnston himself and his friends and so persuasively promulgated that even today it is widely argued and accepted. Johnston is the "master of the defensive" and even the man who might have won the war if given the chance. Johnston always spoke to others of what he *would* do, but his claim was like his marksmanship: he never took a shot, and therefore he never failed in his own eyes. Men then and later have interpreted that somehow as greatness. Davis saw the irony of such interpretation in 1864 when he remarked that some men seemed to win commendation for what they were *expected* to do, while dodging blame when they failed to achieve it. That is Johnston through and through. In fact, if we look for positive evidence to support the high opinion that he still enjoys in many circles, we find little more than his postwar boasts of what he would have done; during the war his efforts amounted to little more than avoidance of responsibility and protection of rank.

Jefferson Davis was not cut out to manage men. His own stubbornness, obstinacy, compulsion to have the last word, thin skin, and inability to subordinate or overcome his own human frailties for the greater good of the cause all incapacitated him for such a task. To his credit, especially in 1862 and in the case of Johnston, Davis did master himself for a time and acted almost as Lincoln did with his troublesome commanders. But inevitably his self-mastery could not last, and Davis instead reverted to controversy, to petty letter wars, and to the making of military policy based far too much on his own prejudices.

Jefferson Davis and His Generals

He was too patient with Johnston for far too long and probably not patient enough for long enough with Beauregard.

But for much of the war, they were all Davis had, and the cruel hand of fate intertwined them inextricably in a deadly dance for power and command that spent much of the energy of the Confederacy and much of its blood and in the end only hastened an earlier defeat than might anyhow have been inevitable. In Lee, Jefferson Davis got his one general in a generation, but for the rest he was largely working with munchkins, and for all his trying, Davis simply was not wizard enough to give the Tin Man his heart or the Lion his courage. And thus the Crime of '61 led inexorably toward the Tragedy of '65.

3

Davis and Lee: Partnership for Success

JEFFERSON DAVIS HELPED achieve minor miracles in keeping the Confederacy afloat for four years against overwhelming odds. Indeed, in some of the darkest hours it seemed as if Davis alone sustained the cause and gave it breath. But there was one other. Seven of his top-ranking generals may have been men of limited vision and hampered abilities, but the one exception was the eighth of the full-rank generals of the Confederacy, Robert E. Lee.

They first met in 1825 at the U.S. Military Academy at West Point when Lee entered as a fourth classman. Davis stood a year ahead of him, yet it was Lee who would become the ideal of all cadets. Davis, given during his youth to hero worship, probably looked up to the younger Lee, but only from afar. Lee, after all, came of the bluest of bloods, with a name known in almost every literate household in America. Davis came from next to nothing. Moreover, Lee would be the exemplary cadet, finally graduating second in the class of 1829. Davis, in contrast, was almost the typical "frat" boy. He was court-martialed and dismissed once for being caught at an off-limits tavern, reinstated, and then nearly killed when he fell down a steep slope while sneaking back to the post drunk after another visit to the same tavern. Finally, he narrowly averted irrevocable dismissal and disgrace during the famous "eggnog" riot of 1826 thanks only to his getting too drunk too early and thus being back in his room getting sick while his fellow classmen rioted and threatened to kill a professor. Lee took no part in such revels, earning but a single demerit in his entire four years at the academy. It would not be hard to imagine that Davis, then a fun-loving and irresponsible man that his later contemporaries would hardly recognize, very likely mixed with his almost certain admiration a bit of resentment or even disdain for the gooder-than-good Lee.

When Davis—almost miraculously—graduated in 1828 in the bottom third of his class, he would not see Lee for at least two decades. When war came with Mexico, Davis joined Zachary Taylor's army at Saltillo in January 1847 as colonel of the First Mississippi Rifles. Lee was there at the same time, but if they saw each other, neither ever mentioned it. Nevertheless, Davis did not remain un-aware of Lee during the war or the years that followed. Both emerged from the war as heroes, though Davis' notoriety outstripped Lee's. In 1850, now a sena-tor from Mississippi, Davis was approached by General Narciso Lopez, a Cuban patriot trying to raise an army and mount an invasion of his homeland to free it from its Spanish overlords. He came to Davis, the war hero, to offer him com-mand of the army and the expedition. Davis declined but then suggested Lee for the post. Lee, too, declined, but it is apparent that he already enjoyed both Davis' respect as a man and a not insubstantial degree of regard for him as a po-tential commander.[1] A few years later, in 1855, when Secretary of War Davis cre-ated the Second United States Cavalry, he gave Lee its choice lieutenant colonelcy, just one grade behind its commander, Davis' lifelong hero and idol Albert Sid-ney Johnston.

Lee, for his part, left little to attest to his pre–Civil War opinion of Davis, other than to comment after that war that he had regarded Davis as one of the extremist Southern rights politicians, which only showed either that Lee did not pay that much attention to politics or that he did not have a very sophisti-cated grasp of men and affairs in the 1850s.[2] Davis, in fact, was one of the more moderate leaders, slow to come to secession, and widely suspected of being a reconstructionist even after he was elected and inaugurated president of the Confederacy.

But Davis continued to pay careful attention to Lee. From the new Con-federate capital in Montgomery, Alabama, Davis tried to build an infant army. Just five days after the secession of Virginia, Davis wired Governor John Letcher to ask after Lee's whereabouts, though he had been kept informed of Lee's ac-tivities for some days beforehand. There was never a question in Davis' mind that he wanted Lee with him. When Davis and the government moved to Rich-mond in late May 1861, Lee was one of those he first sought out. Indeed, well be-fore then he had tried to get Lee to come to Montgomery to confer with him, but the growing emergency on Virginia's Potomac front kept Lee in place. Even if so, however, Lee's very first wartime communication to Davis exposed part of the bedrock of their future relationship. Along with other questions in a prior communication from the president, Davis had asked Lee if he felt any unease about the fact that his commission as a major general was in the Virginia state forces, whereas once Virginia was in the Confederacy, he would be super-seded by brigadiers commissioned in the national regular army, such as Joseph E. Johnston and P. G. T. Beauregard. If the question had been asked of Joe John-

Robert E. Lee as he appeared after the close of the war.
Library of Congress, Washington, D.C.

ston, he would have gone apoplectic. Lee simply replied that "my commission in Virginia [is] satisfactory to me."³ When Davis was already starting to have problems with ambitious men seemingly more interested in rank and reputation than in serving their new nation, such modesty and subordination made Lee a man of mark before he had yet heard a gun fired.

During the ensuing months the president and Lee, now made a full-rank general in the national forces second only to Cooper and Sidney Johnston, conferred constantly on the defense of northern Virginia. In the last stages of planning and movement prior to the battle of First Manassas, Davis discovered that he and Lee thought alike strategically, both inclined to reject the grandiose and risky plans submitted by Beauregard.

Nevertheless, at this stage Davis seems not to have thought of Lee as a field commander. Perhaps this was because the seat of war was in Virginia at the moment, and Lee, with his intimate knowledge of the state and its soldiers, could best serve in Richmond in an advisory capacity. Furthermore, Lee had spent much of his Old Army career as an engineer, not a field commander. Thus it was that when Lee finally got his first real assignment, it was to South Carolina, not to lead an army, but to see to its defenses. Lee did well there, even finally pleasing Governor Francis W. Pickens, who had earlier thought that Lee was not at heart with the cause but was merely a man with a fine family name, good looks, but "too cautious for practical revolution."[4]

Davis retained his regard for Lee after he called him back and gave him command in western Virginia, where Lee's first campaign of the war ended with little, if anything, to his credit. Once more Davis made Lee his chief adviser and actually appointed him to the then largely meaningless title of general in chief. During the frustrating spring of 1862, as Joseph E. Johnston, commanding in Virginia, gave increasing evidences of his incapacity for command and his unwillingness either to fight or even to communicate with his commander in chief, Davis turned increasingly to Lee for counsel. Davis also used him as a conduit of communication with Johnston, hoping that the two Virginians and old friends enjoyed a rapport that Davis and Johnston certainly did not. It was a vain effort, but it revealed Davis' steadily growing trust in Lee as a man. As a commander, however, there was still precious little from which to judge, though as a strategist Lee continued to voice opinions in accord with Davis' own. While Johnston repeatedly argued in favor of retreat and abandonment—his two favorite words—Lee and Davis were as one in their determination that the Virginia peninsula could be held in the face of George B. McClellan's landing and advance toward Richmond.

As the situation became more desperate in mid-May, with Johnston repeatedly pulling back without authorization or without even notifying the government of what he was doing, Davis began to include Lee in cabinet meetings in which strategy was discussed. Lee emphatically argued that Richmond should not be abandoned in the face of McClellan. But then he did something that Johnston would never have done. Lee asked the president what *he* thought they should do.[5] Of course, Davis was never hesitant to voice an opinion—which with him was the same as a certitude—but it is significant that Lee was one of the few high-ranking generals in the war who would repeatedly *ask* the president what he thought. Davis was a vain man in many ways, and his military vanity was particularly well developed. Contrary to popular myth, he did not interfere very much with his commanders in the field in their conduct of operations so long as they were doing something. But Lee's apparent humility in asking Davis' opinion touched the president now and would for the rest of the war. It endeared Lee to him, and no doubt Lee—a much better judge of men and character than Davis—knew that Davis would be flattered.

Of course, one of the most propitious Yankee bullets of the war finally relieved Johnston of command on May 29—arguably the only even more propitious Union projectile from a Confederate point of view was the shell that did in Leonidas Polk two years later. Davis may not at first have intended to turn the army over to Lee, but after only a few hours of having General G. W. Smith in command, Davis put Lee in charge. It would be the single best decision of his presidency.

Prior to June 1862 Lee and Davis still had little more than a formal and professional relationship. Very possibly the proud Mississippian may even have resented the Virginian at one time, especially since he had been the leading protégé of Winfield Scott, a man with whom Davis had a long-running feud going all the way back to the Mexican War, when Scott had politically outmaneuvered Davis' personal favorite Zachary Taylor. Then when Davis was secretary of war, he carried on a celebrated—and utterly childish—letter-writing feud with Scott that did no credit to either of them and found its way into the nation's press. Being Scott's favorite was no recommendation in Davis' eyes.

But familiarity during the first year of the war bridged whatever gap there may have been between the two. Davis did not love Lee as he had the now-dead Sidney Johnston, but he respected Lee's ability and believed that he could rely upon and work with him. Lee, for his part, judged his commander in chief brilliantly. He had seen the Scott feud correspondence. He knew of Davis' feuds with other officers during the Pierce administration. He observed firsthand the breakdown in relations between the president and Joseph Johnston and Beauregard as well as others. In none of these disagreements did Davis hold exclusive title to blame, but he owned a good share of it in all of them, and for a man with Lee's keen insight into character, lessons could be drawn. A man could get along with Jefferson Davis if he observed a few simple rules: Do not question him unless he invited criticism. Do not challenge him. Keep him fully informed at all times. Do not assail his friends or cronies. Have nothing to do with the press, and eschew all public controversy. Avoid politicians, especially those in the growing anti-Davis camp. Most of all, remain loyal. This is what Davis required of anyone, especially a subordinate, if they were to get along. No man on earth who enjoyed Davis' friendship would ever have a more loyal friend, but

Davis expected that loyalty to be returned in kind. Happily, in almost every respect these requirements accorded with Lee's own notions of the proper deportment of a general to his commander in chief.

As a result, Robert E. Lee was ideally suited to be Davis' commanding general in the days before Johnston's wounding, and now he was better equipped than any other man in the Confederacy to manage both that army and that president. In short, though he may not have realized it, Lee was a better politician and statesman than Davis. He knew how to subordinate his own pride to the greater goal of getting what he needed from men, whether his subordinates or his superiors. He would even show that he knew how to be a sycophant at times, giving Davis more flattery than did most other generals of the war and on Davis' most prideful topic, his military judgment.

Lee started off in exactly the right way on June 2 as he took over command and finished a strategy meeting with Davis and his other generals. Beauregard would have told the president in the boldest terms what he intended to do. Johnston would have told him nothing at all. Gustavus Smith would have proposed some great and impractical maneuver, then excused himself with a nervous breakdown. But Robert E. Lee asked the president what he would do. That made all the difference, and Davis' aide William Preston Johnston almost immediately felt some stirrings of hope. "The trouble is we have no *Generals,*" he complained to his wife that same day, but now he hoped for much from Lee. "I believe he has more capacity," wrote the colonel, and in answering the general's question, Davis revealed that he felt the same.[6] He agreed with and approved all of Lee's suggestions for turning McClellan back and then wrote to his wife, Varina, that "General Lee rises with the occasion, and seems to be equal to its conception."[7] There had been constant talk of Davis himself taking the field to lead Johnston's army. A week after Lee assumed command, almost all such talk ceased. "You need have no fears that the President will take the field in person," wrote the aide Johnston. "He has perfect confidence in Genl. Lee and sees no good that could arise from assuming the nominal command, especially as Genl. Lee acts in accord with him."[8] By the end of the peninsular campaign, with McClellan safely quivering back at Harrison's Landing and Richmond secure, Davis knew he had his man. When Lee asked for more troops, Davis sent them, even though it weakened the capital defenses, something he would not have done for Johnston. "Confidence in you," said Davis to his general, "overcomes the view which would otherwise be taken of the exposed condition of Richmond."[9] Lee rewarded his trust.

The way in which Lee nurtured his relationship with Davis is worth considering in some detail. Lee, better than anyone else, knew that Joseph E. Johnston's greatest failing was his refusal to communicate with Davis, Johnston's feeble excuse being the fear that if he suggested anything to Davis, he would then be committed to carrying it out whether he wished to or not, and of course, when it came to fighting or responsibility, Johnston, like Bartleby the scrivener, generally would "prefer not to." On June 5, just four days after assuming command of what he would soon style the Army of Northern Virginia, Lee wrote Davis a very full letter outlining all of his thoughts and closing with the comforting expression that "our position requires you should know everything."[10] Better yet, Lee then apologized for troubling Davis with more information than he might want, a brilliant touch. A few days later, as Lee struggled to reinforce Jackson in the Shenandoah, he "proposed" such a movement to Davis, yet asked the president to decide.[11] Henceforward, expressions like "I need not tell you," or "Do you think anything can be done?" or "What do you think of the propriety of . . . ?" or, most humble and flattering of all, "I shall feel obliged to you for any directions you may think proper to give" appeared in many of Lee's letters.[12] These and similar expressions may have been nothing more than sincerely felt questions, but it cannot be denied that by their wording and use they also, whether by chance or premeditation, consistently reinforced Lee's attitude of respect and subordination to the president, at the same time salving Davis' ego and helping, in part, to ease his own frustration over not being at the front, where of all places he would have preferred to be.

Thanks to this attitude of rapidly growing trust, Davis lent an interested and willing ear to Lee's proposal for the fall invasion of Maryland. And once it was under way, for all of the manifest other considerations confronting him, Lee never lost sight of the president's need to know what was happening. Lee wrote him at least one full letter every day, giving full details of his positions and movements and his intentions for movements to come. "When you do not hear from me," Lee had told Davis, "you may feel sure that I do not think it necessary to trouble you." However, Lee would also apologize for writing too often. "I beg you will excuse my troubling you with my opinions," he wrote Davis in August 1862, "but your kindness had led you to receive them without objection so often that I know I am tempted to trespass."[13] It would almost be heresy to say that the great Lee was being obsequious in such expressions, but it can hardly be doubted that he knew how to flatter the president.

Yet Lee would also speak his mind, however diplomatically, in dealing with

Davis. The president earnestly wanted to be with the army as it invaded Maryland. Just as earnestly, Lee did not want him along. Certainly the general believed, as he told Davis, that it would be too arduous and dangerous for Davis to make the trip, even risking capture. But it is hard not to see a subtext in which Lee also did not want his independence to be fettered by having the president looking directly over his shoulder. Exercising considerable powers of persuasion, Lee even sent a special aide back to Richmond, charged to lay out in detail for the president all the hazards at every point along the route, though Lee at the same time covered himself by saying, "I should feel the greatest satisfaction in having an interview with you and consulting upon all subjects of interest."[14] In the end Lee's persuasions worked, and Davis stayed in Richmond. Significantly, too, while Lee was off on his campaign and daily communicating with the president, Davis from Richmond declined to bombard the general with letters and telegrams as he did other generals. He issued no orders or even suggestions. By keeping Davis steadily informed, Lee also kept him off his own back. Indeed, so well did Lee's demeanor suit itself to Davis' psychological needs that when Lee overstepped his military bounds and proposed to Davis' that the time was right to propose peace terms and Confederate independence to Lincoln, Davis did not bristle at such a suggestion touching on his own civil authority, as he would have from almost any other commander in his army.[15] From *this* general Davis would accept much because this general gave him much. It was also a sign of how well Davis could work with a man on the rare occasion when he found one who suited him. When the campaign ended in failure, there was not one word of reproach from Davis and no making of excuses by Lee.

Again during the Fredericksburg campaign, Lee wrote to Davis daily, keeping him fully advised of affairs, even when there was nothing to tell. Davis craved information and had a right to it. Lee's openness proved to be a double blessing now. It relieved much of Davis' natural anxiety, and it gave him renewed confidence in his general, which always meant that the president interfered less and in this campaign not at all. Indeed, so completely did Davis trust Lee's judgment, and his plans as outlined in detail in Lee's correspondence, that during the ensuing campaign, leading up to the largest land battle ever fought on the American continent in terms of numbers engaged, the president wrote to his commanding general only twice and then only to offer more men and guns. Lee, in turn, rewarded Davis with a victory.

Lee did the same during the Chancellorsville operations, and Davis in turn complimented him upon "this addition to the unprecedented series of great victories which your army has achieved."[16] And then when the two met in Richmond late in May 1863 and Lee proposed another invasion of the North, Davis, after some early trepidation, gave his approval. Better yet, he stayed entirely out of the planning and left it all up to Lee.

And then another facet of Lee's character, and of his perfect alignment with Davis' personality, became evident. When Lee failed to achieve complete success in any of his campaigns, as he failed to bag McClellan completely at the end of the peninsula fighting, he took the responsibility squarely onto his own shoulders. "I fear all was not done that might have been done to harass and destroy our enemies," he told Davis, "but I blame nobody but myself." Now following upon the crushing defeat at Gettysburg, Lee took all of the responsibility upon himself and asked to be allowed to resign. Nothing was better calculated to win Davis' undying regard. Lee's letter touched him deeply. It reminded him of his dead hero Sidney Johnston, how he had always said that "success is the test of merit," and how he had born in silence the clamor of uncomprehending critics such as those now blaming Lee for the defeat. "My dear friend," Davis responded, "there is nothing which I have found to require a greater effort of patience than to bear the criticisms of the ignorant." From a greater experience at being the object of calumny, Davis advised Lee to ignore it. As for resignation and replacement, Lee had no equal, he told him, much less a superior. "To ask me to substitute you by someone in my judgment more fit to command," said Davis, "is to demand an impossibility."[17]

Instead of having his confidence in Lee diminished by defeat, Davis only felt it increased. More and more now he thought of Lee when he looked to other theaters of the war where his confidence was sorely tested, if not eradicated. The Army of Tennessee was a trouble spot almost from the beginning of the conflict, thanks chiefly to Braxton Bragg's peculiar unfitness for command. With that army practically in rebellion against its commander by August 1863, and with a campaign against Rosecrans under way, Davis thought of sending Lee west to assume the command. Lee declined on several grounds, and the president accepted. But then later in August he called Lee to Richmond to discuss the matter again, and again Lee declined. Davis was a man who knew what he wanted, but this general held a special place in his affections and his respects, and he resisted exercising his raw authority to compel his best commander to do something against his wishes. Davis did, however, finally send Longstreet to Tennessee, even when Lee asked that it not be done, and when the president

asked once again that Lee go along with Longstreet, Davis took Lee's third refusal as final. And as Lee remained in Virginia, sparring with Meade in the
months of relative inactivity following Gettysburg, Davis visited the army frequently to confer with the general. While there they were often seen going to
church together. The professional relationship was blossoming into a warm
friendship, at least on Davis' part. Interestingly, one searches almost in vain in
Lee's wartime correspondence to find evidences of his personal feelings toward,
or opinion of, the president.

Again in December, after Bragg's disastrous defeat at Chattanooga, Davis
asked Lee to take the western command, and again Lee declined, showing his
own perception of the condition of affairs in that troubled command by saying he feared he would not get cooperation from its officers. Davis spent a full
week putting Lee on the spot in meeting after meeting, sometimes with the secretary of war or other cabinet members present, but Lee held firm. Not only did
Davis yield in the end to Lee's firm resolve, but he also listened to other advice
from Lee, even when it ran against every fiber of judgment he possessed. With
Beauregard in such poor stead with the president that he was lucky even to
have a uniform, Lee suggested that the only available and logical commander
for the Army of Tennessee was Joseph E. Johnston. This, for a change, reveals
that Lee, too, was occasionally capable of abominable judgment of men, but in
the Confederate system of high command at the moment, alternatives were few
or nil. What is significant is that Davis listened to him. Of course, for the good
of the cause perhaps Davis should have ordered Lee to take the command, and
that would have been that. Lee's sense of duty would not have allowed him to
do anything but accept. We may conjecture another time about what changes,
if any, to the outcome of the war in Georgia might have ensued. What matters
here and now is that the relationship between this commander and this commander in chief had developed to such an extent that Davis was unwilling to
order Lee to do that which he did not wish to do.

The following spring, while Davis tried everything but bombs and levers
to get Johnston to move and found himself fighting an action in his rear with
journalists and politicians who used the naive Johnston as a tool in their own
vendetta against the president, Lee continued to be the one bright spot in the
high command. He did not complain. He did not plot. He did not talk to news-
papermen. And even when he did not bring Davis victories, Davis found it impossible to fault the conduct of Lee's campaigns. Often they met daily as spring
1864 wore on toward the inevitable opening of the campaign with Grant and

Meade. As he had for almost two years, Davis found himself leaving things almost entirely in Lee's hands. As he had for two years, Lee told Davis everything, whether there was anything to tell or not. Even while the Army of the Potomac was slowly pushing Lee back during May, Davis felt unbounded confidence in his general and repeatedly expressed that confidence to his cabinet. Secretary of the Navy Stephen R. Mallory recalled that Davis regarded Lee as "standing alone among the Confederate soldiers in military capacity." When Davis spoke of Lee, said Mallory, "all others were, in comparison to him, beginners."[18] This was the only general in the army whom Davis addressed repeatedly as "my dear friend" in his letters. Remembering the loss of other friends and great leaders such as Sidney Johnston, Jeb Stuart, and Stonewall Jackson, Davis also began to worry more and more for this most unloseable of generals. "Don't expose yourself," he told Lee repeatedly.

By the end of 1864, when even Lee had not been able to hold back the legions of the Union and Richmond lay besieged, Davis' popularity within the Confederate hierarchy had fallen to an all-time low. There were calls for his removal, by impeachment if possible, by extralegal means if necessary. And in his place, rumors surfaced suggesting that Lee should take office, even become dictator, in the emergency. Lee refused to countenance such nonsense or even give evidence that he knew of such thoughts. He remained loyal to Davis in the dark days just as Davis had always been loyal to him, though now, for the first and only time in the war, their relationship appears to have suffered a severe strain. It started with that perennial running sore, Joseph E. Johnston. Davis had removed him after it became evident that he would not try to hold Atlanta. His replacement, Hood, failed to do so as well and then almost lost his army in Tennessee. When he had to be replaced, once more, like a recurring nightmare, there was only Johnston. Lee, once more general in chief by February 1865, tried his best to make it easier for Davis to swallow Johnston. On his own authority, he asked to have Johnston assigned to the command but pointedly added that Johnston would be reporting directly to him. Davis saw some hope in this. It relieved him from the odium of acting on his own to reinstate Johnston—he was simply granting his general in chief's request on a matter quite within that general's area of responsibility. Also, he continued to hope that where he and Johnston had failed to be able to work together, perhaps Johnston and Lee could, a vain hope as it proved.

Nevertheless, it cost Davis much inwardly to see his old nemesis once more given the honor of army command, and this left him testy a few days later when he asked Lee to come into Richmond to confer with him on a matter of secondary import at the moment. Lee, himself probably frustrated at Davis' frequent calls for hand-holding conferences, and Davis' increasingly frequent unwillingness to address the realities of the Confederacy's dreadful situation, failed for once to respond as he always had in the past. If sources can be believed, the general replied that he could not spare the time. The response hurt and angered Davis, who shot back a reply that the general might "rest assured I will not ask your views in answer to measures. Your counsels are no longer wanted in

What Lee became. The unveiling of the Lee monument in Richmond shows vividly just where Southerners placed their hero.
U.S. Army Military History Institute, Carlisle, Pa.

this matter." It smacks of nothing so much as the response of a hurt child. Lee immediately sensed that he had hurt the president's feelings. He went to see him after all, and though their correspondence temporarily took on a cooler tone—Davis ceased addressing him as "my dear friend" for awhile—the injury was soon forgotten. Davis just needed to talk to Lee for security and support. He needed to have his friend with him for comfort in those darkening hours.[19]

Lee realized long before Davis that the cause was lost. Indeed, as 1865 wore on, he almost marveled at the president's continuing optimism that somehow a victory would be wrested from the Yankees and freedom achieved. "The president is very pertinacious in opinion and purpose," Lee told an associate then, showing a "remarkable faith in the possibility of still winning our independence."[20] He might better have called it obstinacy, if not retreat from reality. Yet when Davis seized a new potential weapon for winning that independence, the idea of enlisting blacks to fight in Confederate armies, Lee enthusiastically supported him. Indeed, three years later Lee would claim that he had told Davis often and repeatedly as early as 1862 that the slaves should be emancipated. He believed it would strengthen Confederate hopes abroad and weaken the moral arguments advanced by the Union, but Davis "would not hear of it." Perhaps so. Certainly Lee embraced the idea of raising black regiments, but for all of them it was too little, too late.[21]

Finally came the fateful loss of Five Forks and the evacuation of Richmond. Davis and Lee spent some of that last day together, as they had met occasionally during the last days of March, often at the home of Reverend Charles Minnegerode. The minister could not but note that at the dinner table "it was sad to see these two men with their terrible responsibilities upon them and the hopeless outlook." When Lee arrived during one dinner, all the other diners left the room and closed the door behind them, leaving Lee and the president "to consult in lonely conference."[22] That April 1 would be the last time Lee and Davis would see each other for the next year and a half.

We all know what followed for the two of them. For Davis, an attempt to reach the western Confederacy, capture, and two years of imprisonment leading to a trial that was never completed and his release, to wander England and Europe, and then the South for years before finally he settled in Mississippi once more. For Lee, a quiet surrender at Appomattox, a return first to his Richmond home, and then finally a measure of peace in Lexington before his early death in 1870, worn out by the war and its strains on a weakened heart. Never during those years or afterward did Davis utter a single reproachful word about

Lee for Appomattox or for any other episode of his career. Rather, Davis became an enthusiastic contributor to the Lee legend and one of his most ardent defenders. Lee, as he had during the war, largely kept his views of the president to himself. He did speak critically, and in confidence, only twice that we know of. In 1869 he told a painter that, while he admired Davis' sterling qualities of character, he added that the president was, "of course, one of the extremist politicians." And a year earlier, speaking to a confidant, Lee added that, while he thought highly of Davis, he blamed him for being so confrontational with his opponents and thereby failing to unite everyone to the single purpose of the cause. "Mr. Davis' enemies became so many," said Lee, "as to destroy his power and to paralyze the country."[23]

But nothing was said of this at their first meeting after the war—and what would prove to be their last. Lee was called to testify in Davis' trial in the hope that his testimony would help place the full responsibility for all Confederate activities on its former president. Lee refused to play the game. "I am responsible for what I did," he said on the witness stand, "and I cannot now recall any important movement I made which I would not have made had I acted entirely on my own responsibility."[24] That ended any usefulness Lee might have had for the prosecution. And this straightforward, manly acceptance of his own responsibility was to be the last thing Davis ever heard from his beloved general's lips.

In 1863 Davis had written to his brother, Joseph, that "a *General* in the full acceptation of the word is a rare product, scarcely more than one can be expected in a generation, but in this mighty war in which we are engaged there is need for half a dozen."[25] In the end Davis really got only one, Robert Edward Lee. And for whatever the president may be blamed for shortening the war in the decisive western theater by his adherence to Bragg and then his deadly dance of command with Joseph E. Johnston, it is inarguable that in the eastern theater Davis prolonged the war if by no other single fact than his unwavering and unyielding support for Lee. It is often forgotten that Lee came to command with an unenviable war record behind him. Many thought him too timid, others believed him not entirely committed to the cause, and in Virginia and South Carolina especially he had been dubbed derisively "Granny" and "Spades" Lee. Davis was not obliged to give him command of the Army of Northern Virginia and might not have but for his disillusionment with G. W. Smith and Smith's own psychosomatic ailments when under pressure.

But once Lee was in command, Davis quickly realized his worth and stood by him, even when he confided to Varina that on the peninsula Lee had not achieved all that the president had hoped for. Through the near loss of most of the army at Antietam and the crushing defeat at Gettysburg, the president never once wavered in his attachment to Lee. Furthermore, by resisting the clamor to send Lee to the troubled Army of Tennessee—and his own desire to do so—Davis kept in place the one man who knew his army and countryside better than any other. Moreover, Davis listened to Lee, in time taking his counsel almost as if it had come from the lips of Sidney Johnston himself, whom he always believed might have been an even greater general had he lived. Davis did not interfere with Lee's army, gave him the generals he wanted for his corps and divisions, and bent every effort to send him the regiments he needed.

For his part, Lee read his commander in chief brilliantly and showed a maturity and a devotion to cause above self that would have shamed most other high-ranking commanders. While Johnston would whimper over his rank and spend most of the war complaining, and while Beauregard preened and blustered and took every opportunity to politick behind the back of a president who had the audacity to think that he outranked the great Beauregard, Lee consistently subordinated himself to the president's goals. Lee realized that his mission was not to pamper his own ego or advance his reputation. He had a job to get done with his army, and the best way to achieve it was to have the full support and confidence of his commander in chief. If that meant flattering the president, he would do it. If that meant allowing Davis to think that Lee's ideas were sometimes his own, so be it. If that meant taking precious time out while on an arduous campaign to write the president a letter when there was nothing to say, Lee would do it. If that meant simply being a friend and helping a man deal with a crushing burden even greater than Lee's, the general knew what he had to do. Sycophantic at times? Yes. Fawning, even, now and then? Yes. Counterproductive or wasteful of time? Never. Lee's eye was on his mission, and he knew better than anyone how much stronger was his steel if he had the president behind his weapons rather than in front of them.

And thus these two very different men, men who in another time or under different circumstances probably would not—could not—have been friends, achieved a synergy that helped to keep the Confederacy afloat in the east far longer than could have been expected with any of the other full-rank generals of the Confederacy in command. In the understanding and rapport they achieved, and in the way they cooperated, Davis and Lee formed a model civil-military team surpassing any other of the war, even Lincoln and Grant, and matched in our national history only by that between Franklin Roosevelt and George Marshall in World War II.

Lee, alas, lived too short a life. Davis, for the benefit of his own memory, lived too long. Following his release from prison and his European wanderings, his very first public address in the South came on the sad occasion of Lee's death and a memorial service. Weeks earlier, just as he had returned from Europe, Davis had first gotten the news of Lee's death. It struck him almost like the loss of his brother, who had died a few days before. The onetime president could not fully express what or how he felt when he learned of Lee's passing. "He was my friend," Davis wrote in his anguish, "and in that word is included all that I could say of any man."[26]

Part Two

Forgotten Wars

4

The Siege of Charleston

THERE IS AN OLD philosopher's game about a tree falling in the forest. If no one hears its fall, then did it really make a noise? Is sound an elemental part of the crashing timber or merely our own sensory reaction? Much the same can be said of the ironic, particularly in history. The past is laden heavily with it. We seem to find it everywhere. Perhaps it is a genuine condition, or perhaps it is only a matter of our perceiving it to be. Whichever the case, no one can approach the American Civil War without being soon overwhelmed by the incredible coincidence, the delicious irony that inhabit every corner of the story. Even then, some portions of the Civil War experience stand above the rest, so riddled with contradiction, coincidence, and irony that they could only have been conceived by a poet, a madman, or a people making war upon itself. Nowhere is that more evident than in the place where that war began, Charleston, South Carolina, the "Cradle of the Confederacy." Nothing in the story of this city under siege seems to fit, yet viewed within the overall picture of the war, somehow it all makes perverse sense.

It was regarded than and later as the longest siege of the war, 587 days by one count, nearly three years by others, yet Charleston did not undergo one single day of true siege in the accepted military definition of the term. During much of that siege the South entrusted the defense of the city, the "seedbed of secession," to the hands of generals born in New York and Ohio. For a time the Union Army threatening them was commanded by a man from Virginia. Brothers from South Carolina literally made personal war upon each other. In the attacks and defense of the city, the latest technological and military inventions did battle cheek by jowl with weapons of warfare that dated back to the Greeks of antiquity. One day the defense of the city depended upon one of the most noted generals of the age and the next, upon hapless bumblers. For every day of genuine combat, the generals of the North and South spent ten fighting among themselves. There were four regiments designated the First South Carolina, one composed entirely of black soldiers fighting for the Union, and in the very first engagement in Charleston Harbor, one Federal officer defending Sumter hailed from Indiana and answered to the name Jefferson Davis.

Indeed, the ironies of Charleston's siege began even before the so-called siege itself, even before the war. It was November 1860, a month before South Carolina declared its secession from the Union, that Washington sent a new commander to take over the three forts at Charleston: Moultrie, Castle Pinckney, and the still-unfinished Sumter. With the secession crisis imminent, the War Department sent Major Robert Anderson, son of a Revolutionary War officer, a native of Kentucky, a man of Southern antecedents who had married a woman from Georgia, to maintain this Union bastion in the very heart of the South. Anderson did his duty and more, despite his personal views as a slave owner and Southern sympathizer. He and others of Southern sympathy and extraction in his command remained true to their uniforms and their flag throughout the ensuing five months of increasing tension. And when finally offered the ultimate test, the choice between their personal sympathies or allegiance to the Union, every man and officer in Anderson's command did his duty as a soldier. Yet when finally the guns began to speak, adherence to duty was not enough. After thirty-four hours under fire, under a rain of 4,000 or more Confederate shells, with much of the wooden portion of Sumter in flames, Anderson had to yield.

And already the ironies crowded in upon him. Amid the hail of iron, the smoke and flames during the bombardment, Anderson's men were hard put to keep up an answering fire. They did little damage and could work only a few of Sumter's guns. Yet they maintained a desultory answering fire, more as a token of resistance than as the real thing. And the Confederates trying so desperately to blast them out of the harbor, gazing at the smoking fortress in their sights, frequently held their own fire to shout an admiring cheer at the Yankees every time Anderson managed to get off another shot. Anyone looking on should have realized right there that it was going to be a very peculiar war.

Stranger still in the aftermath of the bombardment. Incredibly, Anderson's garrison got through the fight without a single casualty. Yet when the Confederates accepted his surrender, they agreed to allow the Federals to leave the fort with full honors, including a 100-gun salute to the flag they removed from the fort. At the seventeenth round a premature explosion ripped away the arm of Private Daniel Hough, killing him almost instantly and wounding several others. Poor Hough, having survived the terrible bombardment, became arguably the first Union soldier to be killed in the war, only after the fighting had ceased. Even before this tragedy Anderson had received a message of friendship and sympathy from an old friend, Confederate president Jefferson Davis. It was Davis who, as secretary of war in the administration of Franklin Pierce, had got Anderson his promotion to major.

When finally the Federals left the fort and were on their way home, the conquered fortress was occupied first by Charleston's Palmetto Guard, Colonel Roswell Ripley in command. Ripley was a native of Ohio. Anderson, meanwhile, was greeted as a hero at home, and he and most of his officers eventually became Union generals. One of the few who did not was Lieutenant R. K. Meade of Virginia. He did his part during the bombardment, working his gun manfully in firing back at the Rebels. But once he returned to the North after the surrender, he resigned his commission and became a Confederate officer. Just three months later he died in defense of the very cause that he opposed so nobly at Fort Sumter. Even Anderson could not escape a measure of personal irony in the aftermath of Fort Sumter. More than eighty years earlier Charleston had heard guns, this time as the British attacked during the American Revolution. In those days Fort Moultrie had been called Fort Sullivan, and one of the American officers in charge of its defense had been his own father, Major Richard Anderson. He, too, had been forced to yield. Like father, like son.[1]

Yet there were ironies aplenty for the victors as well, and these grew ever greater in the months following the surrender and in the "siege" that followed. For one thing, in the wake of victory many Confederates in and out of Charleston believed that was an end to it. There would be no war. The Yankees, thus chastised, would bother them no more. Armisted L. Burt of Abbeville, South Carolina, believed so strongly there would be no war that he declared he would drink personally all of the blood shed as a result of secession. As irony would have it, almost exactly four years later, with the Confederacy in shambles, Richmond fallen, and Jefferson Davis and his government in flight, it was in Burt's home that Davis and the remnant of his cabinet and generals met for their last council of war. Burt was not an accommodating host, offered them nothing to drink, and certainly no blood. By that time, the South had so little of it left.[2]

War or no, the Confederates of 1861 believed that they had to consolidate their gains at Charleston and prepare and enhance its defenses. Under the guidance of General Pierre Gustave Toutant Beauregard, a diminutive Creole who dyed his hair and did not use the name *Pierre* because he felt it sounded too "foreign," the damage to Sumter was repaired and the work of strengthening the other works about Charleston begun.

Charlestonians then and later entertained a distinctive notion of their hometown. It was located, they said, where the Ashley and Cooper Rivers met to form the Atlantic Ocean. During the Civil War several channels allowed ships access to Charleston, but at the mouth of the harbor the channels all merged into the so-called Main Channel that passed the southern reaches of Sullivan's Island and into the harbor proper. It is here, of course, that Fort Moultrie lay, soon to be augmented with a series of batteries named for Southern heroes. Directly across the channel from Moultrie, a distance of just over a mile, sat Fort Sumter, erected on an artificial island of rubble. Between them their fields of fire effectively covered every inch of the channel. No ship could pass them without risking a deadly crossfire. Meanwhile less than a mile south of Sumter sat the northern tip of Morris Island, Cumming's Point. A variety of batteries went up here, eventually compassed within the overall designation Battery Gregg. Gregg, too, was close enough to the channel to add its fire to that of the other forts, and so was Fort Johnson on the tip of mammoth James Island a mile and a half west of Sumter. Clearly, no Yankee fleet could steam into Charleston Harbor and remain there without first silencing these fortifications. And once inside the harbor, a foe would still have to contend with Castle Pinckney right in the middle of the harbor. The only alternative to that improbable scenario would be to land troops above or below Charleston and move along the coastline or through the interior to take the city from its land side. Beauregard and his successors foresaw that possibility and early began building a series of earthworks that protected Charleston and its forts in every direction.

Happily for the Confederates, the Lincoln administration in Washington gave them plenty of time to work on their defenses. Charleston, though symbolic of the rebellion, was not a high military priority to the Federals in 1861. They were more concerned with the enemy army in Virginia. As a result, Charleston sat unthreatened for seven months after the fall of Fort Sumter, and even then the first Yankee thrust was indirect, really a by-product of an entirely different sort of operation. Lincoln had imposed a blockade on the South, attempting to interdict all traffic in and out of Confederate ports. That called for a massive fleet, and that in turn required a base somewhere on the Atlantic coastline for the blockaders to supply and repair. The Federals selected Port

Royal Sound, some fifty miles distant from Charleston, and in November 1861 a Union fleet led by Flag Officer Samuel F. I. DuPont appeared off the forts guarding the sound and bombarded them into submission.

It was familiar ground to many of those engaged in the battle. Fort Walker, one of the works guarding the sound, lay on the tip of Hilton Head Island. The commander of the Confederates defending Port Royal, Brigadier General Thomas F. Drayton, owned a plantation on the island and had lived there for nearly a quarter century. Also familiar with the area was the general's brother, Percival Drayton, and he was in the battle, too. Only he commanded the USS *Pocahontas,* one of the attacking ships. When a malfunction of his ship's engine caused Drayton to be late getting into the fight, he feared that DuPont might think he delayed intentionally to avoid having to fight against his own brother. As a result, once in the battle, Percival Drayton took the *Pocahontas* closer in toward Fort Walker than any other vessel and maintained such a heavy fire that he made an absolute shambles of the fort's interior. "It is very hard," said the naval Drayton afterward, "but I cannot exactly see the difference between [him] fighting against me and I against [him]." Happily, both brothers survived this little bit of sibling rivalry.[3]

The fall of Port Royal awakened the Confederates to the fact that at last the enemy might take an interest in Charleston. Indeed, even as DuPont was attacking Port Royal, a new Confederate arrived to take command of the defenses of Charleston and South Carolina. It was a difficult post, if for no other reason than the meddlesome governor of the state, Francis W. Pickens. He was one of the original fire-eating secessionists. He was also, like so many politicians of the age, deluded that he possessed no ordinary quotient of military sagacity. He interfered continually with Beauregard in the early months of the war and apparently bore some responsibility for the loss of Port Royal, though after its fall he happily stepped aside to let Beauregard take all the blame. When that general was ordered to Virginia, and shortly thereafter the defense of Charleston fell to the irascible Roswell Ripley of Ohio, Pickens proved equally troublesome to him as well.

But then in November came the new commander, a man not much known of outside the Old United States Army, General Robert E. Lee. Though he had had a distinguished career in the Mexican War and came of an old and honored Virginia family, his part in the present war had not thus far been exemplary. First an adviser to President Davis and commander of the Virginia militia, he then went on an unsuccessful campaign in western Virginia that almost ruined him. Pickens already did not like him, thinking him good looking enough but overrated and too cautious for their cause.[4] The governor had a good deal to learn about Lee, as did the world.

Despite interference from Pickens, Lee spent his four months in South Carolina actively strengthening the state, accomplishing much with few resources. And quickly he and Pickens came to agree on one matter at least—that the defense of Charleston and the state of South Carolina was vital. Pickens promised to make South Carolina an armed camp before winter and to practice a scorched earth policy if the Yankees invaded. When Lee left the South Carolina command in March 1862, he echoed the governor's sentiments. "The loss of Charleston would cut us off almost entirely from communications with the rest of the world and close the only channel through which we can expect to get supplies from abroad, now almost our only dependence," he warned. Hold Charleston, he said, and in words presaging Winston Churchill's future admonition to England in 1940, he added that the defense of Charleston would have to be "fought street by street and house by house as long as we have a foot of ground to stand upon."[5]

With the natural logic that permeates the Civil War, when Lee left South Carolina the defense of it and its principal city was entrusted to a man from Pennsylvania, General John C. Pemberton. He lasted just six months, fought constantly with Ripley and Pickens, and was finally replaced late in 1862 by Beauregard once more. The transition was extremely smooth. In less than a week after assuming command, Beauregard was fighting with Pickens again. But it was apparent that before long there would be another enemy. DuPont was known to be massing a powerful fleet at Port Royal, his intent presumably an attack on Charleston. Beauregard feverishly pressed the work of constructing the city's defenses. He placed obstructions in the main channel to hinder enemy ships and even stretched a wooden boom across the water. But then came twin strokes of good fortune. When DuPont left Port Royal, it turned out that his objective was the coast of North Carolina, not Charleston. And in what Beauregard certainly must have regarded as an even more significant military event, in December 1862 Governor Francis Pickens left office.

It is a measure of the lack of importance that the Federals attached to Charleston that it was not until June 1862, more than a year after Sumter's fall, that the first real military advance was made on the city. Prior to that time Lincoln had been content merely to attempt the closing of the harbor by sending two fleets of old merchant and whaling ships, their holds bulging with granite, to the harbor mouth. There their hapless captains scuttled them and sank the so-called Stone Fleet in the main channel, expecting that the harbor would thus be closed for years to come. They reckoned without the soft mud on the bottom. Within days the Stone Fleet sank deep into the mire, where it rests to this day, leaving the channel quite free for the blockade-running traffic to continue.

But then came an ambitious new Federal commander. Major General David Hunter took control of Union land forces at Port Royal and, in conjunction with DuPont, planned a landing on the southern part of James Island. Hunter is a perversely engaging character, fascinating because of his utter unlikability. The fourth highest-ranking general in the Union volunteer service, he was nearly incompetent in command, yet always managed to shift the blame for his failures to others. He was arguably the ugliest general in the Union Army and almost beyond question the one most despised in the Confederacy. Almost as soon as he took command in Port Royal, he issued a personal emancipation proclamation abolishing slavery in his department—which Lincoln promptly canceled—and that alone branded him an outlaw in the minds of Southerners. Later in the war he would show his willingness to deliver justice to order by presiding at the kangaroo court-martial of one of his fellow officers and at war's end by presiding at the military trial of the Lincoln murder conspirators, two of the most unusual and, in some respects, unjust trials in American judicial history. In 1864 in the Shenandoah Valley he would take particular delight in wantonly destroying private homes and public buildings. He thoroughly enhanced his reputation in his attempt to take Charleston. After the landing, Hunter carefully disassociated himself from the actual operations, leaving it in the hands of General Henry Benham, and when Benham was defeated at Secessionville, halfway across the island toward Charleston, Hunter arrested him and charged him with disobedience of orders.

Perversely, no one gave General Pemberton much credit for the victory over Benham, but then he was not present at the fight. Neither were any other generals, and it is a shame, for Richmond had stationed an interesting group here to defend Charleston. In immediate command on James Island, though he reached Secessionville only after the fighting ended, was Brigadier General Nathan G. Evans, known to friends as "Shanks" Evans. His ability as a fighter stood unquestioned. At Bull Run, or Manassas, the first real battle of the war, his part in the Confederate victory was probably greater even than that of "Stonewall" Jackson, who would get most of the credit. Yet Evans was not without his flaws. He drank prodigiously, detailing a special orderly to follow him constantly carrying a small keg of whisky that he called his "barrelita." He would be court-martialed once for drunkenness in this war and once more for disobedience of orders. Worse, he was the most accomplished braggart in the army. Just after the victory at Bull Run, he told his staff that there was "no use for other Generals to brag about what they did in the battle—that he inaugurated the fight, he . . . fought it through and he . . . whipped the fight before any reinforcements came." Upon mature reflection, he finally decided to share the glory with another, allowing that "the fight was really won by God Almighty and a few private gentlemen."[6]

As for the other generals commanding in Charleston and the vicinity, while they lacked the peculiar antecedents of Pemberton or the eccentric character of Evans, they nevertheless enjoyed their measure of unusual distinction. For pure patriotism, however, the Gists of South Carolina stood above the rest. Their father had been an ardent patriot during the Revolution, in consequence of which he named his first son Independence Gist. Independence without some sort of restraint being close to anarchy, however, the father tempered his zeal by naming the second son Constitution Gist. But in 1831 when his third son arrived, it was already evident that Independence and Constitution were not enough. The liberties for which he fought still stood endangered by radicals in Washington. Consequently, as an admonition to all, he named this youngest boy States Rights Gist. Brigadier General States Rights Gist was here in Charleston ably defending his namesake cause. Two years later he would die for it.

With the victory at Secessionville, Charleston lay secure for months to come. However, back in Washington the decision had finally been made that the Union should undertake a concerted effort to conquer the city. It was largely due to Assistant Secretary of the Navy Gustavus V. Fox, who had tried unsuccessfully to relieve Major Anderson's beleaguered garrison in 1861 and for whom Charleston remained thereafter an obsession. Eventually he pressured Flag Officer DuPont into making an attempt in April 1863. DuPont did not like the look of those powerful and well-placed batteries ringing the harbor. He did not like the fact that Hunter could not be counted on for military assistance. It would have to be purely a naval attack. And most of all he did not like the ships in his own fleet.

Everyone is familiar with the story of the *Monitor* and the *Virginia*. They were not, in fact, the first ironclads or even the first armored ships to engage in battle. But they were the first to do so at a time when technology and the public mind were ready for them. As a result, a virtual mania called "monitor fever" swept the North. The *Monitor* had stopped the *Virginia* almost without a scratch. Surely this new type of vessel was impregnable and could do anything with impunity. This attitude, and the extremely effective lobbying of the industrial interests that stood to gain by building more such ships, resulted in an extensive program of monitor building. It was with a fleet of such ships, aided by a few of more conventional design, that DuPont was to try taking Charleston.

On April 7 the Yankee fleet steamed slowly toward the entrance to the harbor. The Confederates held their fire at first, and at the same time the sailors aboard the leading vessels began to see strange buoys ahead of them in the water. Unknown to them, the Rebels had placed them as markers and carefully sighted their guns on them. As a result, once the Confederates opened fire, it was with telling accuracy. Before long at least seventy-six Southern guns were concentrating their fire on the slender line of nine Union ships, mounting just thirty-two cannons among them. In the two-hour fight that followed, the Confederates fired some 2,209 shots, of which fully one-fourth found their marks. Percy Drayton's new monitor *Passaic* was hit once per minute for thirty-five minutes. The *Passaic* fired only four times in return. Within a few minutes the *Keokuk* took nineteen hits that penetrated its waterline and suffered ninety hits all told. The ship sank the next day. Aboard the *Nahant* enemy shells hitting the exterior of the gun turret knocked loose bolt heads inside and sent them flying through the interior like deadly missiles. Other Federal ships collided with each other, and in the confusion DuPont's fleet managed to fire only 154 shots. By twilight he had ordered a withdrawal, with almost no damage done to the enemy and five of his nine warships disabled, two of them under tow. "These monitors are miserable failures where forts are concerned," he lamented.[7] He had been proved right, but at the expense of a battered fleet. Washington did not learn the lesson so well, and when DuPont opposed any renewal of the fleet attack on Charleston, he was finally relieved of his command.

That made it the army's turn to try again. Even before DuPont's replacement, John Dahlgren, arrived to relieve him, the War Department sent General Quincy Gillmore to try a hand at Charleston. He was one of the foremost engineers in the service, had already used his siege artillery to blast a fort similar to Sumter into submission, and now promised to do the same to Sumter. With it out of the way, Dahlgren would be able to steam right into the harbor. Gillmore landed his 10,000 men south of the city and on July 10 he took the south-

ern portion of Morris Island. His plan was now to advance against and capture Battery Wagner. From that point he could bombard Sumter at will, and
with it out of the way Dahlgren could do his part.

The only problem was that Wagner proved a great deal stronger than Gillmore supposed. On July 18 he bombarded it with 9,000 shells from his own
guns, while Dahlgren fired on it from his offshore fleet. It was a well-executed
combined operation, and the general believed he had silenced the fort entirely.
As a result, he ordered two fresh brigades forward to the presumably easy task
of taking it. The trouble was that he had done almost no damage at all. The
Confederates merely withdrew into dugout bombproofs in the sand when the
shells started raining down and came out again when the bombardment concluded. And well before the commencement of the shelling, they had prudently
buried some of their lighter cannons in the sand, thus protecting them from the
hail of shells. As a result, when the attacking Federals approached Wagner's
parapet, they found not the easy walkover they expected but a ferocious firefight
on their hands.

Leading the assault was the Fifty-fourth Massachusetts, a regiment composed of free black men who, in fact, were not from the Bay State at all but
rather from Pennsylvania, New York, and elsewhere. Their colonel, Robert G.
Shaw, was a Bostonian, and he bravely led a part of his regiment right onto the
parapet of Wagner in a desperate attempt that saw almost all of them killed. The
rest of the attack soon broke up with dreadful losses. With the exception of a
single captain, every commander in the attack was either killed or wounded.
And when the retreat sounded, it could not affect several hundred Federals who
had penetrated inside the parapet. Isolated, they fought on for three more hours
until exterminated or captured. Beauregard himself ordered that special care be
taken of the wounded bluecoats taken inside Wagner. "Men who were brave
enough to go in there," he said, "deserved the respect of their enemy."[8] As for
Shaw and his black regiment, there would be no such respect. The idea of white
officers leading blacks against Southerners incensed the defenders. Shaw was
laid at the bottom of a common trench, his dead blacks piled on top of him, and
the sand pushed in. Months later, after Morris Island fell to the Federals, a suggestion was made to Shaw's father that his son be disinterred and brought home
for burial. His father refused. There could be no greater honor, he said, than for
his son to lie in the South Carolina sand with the men for whose freedom he
and they had died.[9]

Gillmore now decided to lay siege to Wagner since he could not take it by

Quincy Gillmore's handiwork—an almost demolished Fort Sumter, which still managed to hold out.

U.S. Army Military History Institute, Carlisle, Pa.

storm, but even that plan went awry when his siege works got close enough that the enemy guns on Fort Sumter could fire at him. As a result, Gillmore turned his attention to that island of masonry in the harbor. In the first great bombardment of Fort Sumter, Gillmore spent fifteen days hurling tens of tons of iron at it from his long-range siege guns. The result was the near-destruction of the southwest wall. So proud was Gillmore of his work that he had a photographer make an image of Sumter and sent it to Washington to display his handiwork. Two more times in the next six months he would do the same thing after massive bombardments, providing the War Department with a running illustrated account of the gradual destruction of the formidable fortress.

With the fire from Sumter interrupted by this bombardment, Gillmore was able once more to advance inexorably on Battery Wagner, and finally in September 1863 its garrison abandoned the works. The Federals read more into the act than they should have. Dahlgren, now an admiral thanks to heavy politicking, believed that Sumter, too, had been abandoned. At night he sent five-hundred sailors and marines in a landing party. The Confederates were waiting for them. The Federals had barely landed in the darkness when guns on all sides opened on them, and the defenders inside Sumter hurled huge chunks of masonry down on them from the remaining parapets. It was a scene from a medieval nightmare, needing only flaming arrows and boiling oil to be complete. Those Yankees not killed or captured hastily rowed away to safety, and again Fort Sumter survived.

Indeed, Sumter seemed always to survive. Not until Gallipoli in 1915, during World War I, would warfare witness again such a defense against combined military and naval attack. Bombarded by an ironclad fleet, by scores of enormous siege guns, attacked by amphibious parties, battered into a shapeless pile of brick and rubble, at times with every cannon in the place dismounted or out of commission, and sometimes with fevers and disease doing more damage than the enemy, still the place held out. At one time in 1864 the entire functioning defensive armament of Fort Sumter consisted of foul shoulder rifles. The men burrowed inside the rubble, finding that it provided a wonderful defense. The loose mortar and brick absorbed the enemy shells better, more harmlessly, than had the standing walls. Deep within their tunnels, the defenders could sit out the bombardment in comparative safety. Indeed, the greatest loss of life in the fort in any single day came not from the enemy shelling but from, of all things, whiskey. There was a barrel of it stored deep within one of the tunnels, and a candle flame or perhaps a spark came too near. The cask of spirits ignited, perhaps exploded, and soon set off a powder magazine. The resulting blaze turned the underground passages into an inferno, killing or injuring sixty-two men, and as the fire blazed out of control, the interior of the fort had to be all but abandoned. It took ten days before this brick oven cooled sufficiently for the garrison to reenter the catacombs.

While the Rebels were being done in by their own whiskey, the Federals did not remain entirely inactive, and they, too, had a little liquid fire of their own. Gillmore decided to bombard the city of Charleston itself, thinking that this might force the city into submission and its forts with it. He built an island of wooden pilings in the marsh between Morris and James Islands, and there emplaced a huge eight-inch rifled cannon. It could fire a two-hundred-pound shell five miles into Charleston, presumably doing extensive damage. With typical soldiers' gallows humor, its gun crew dubbed the cannon the "Swamp Angel." But the Confederates refused to give up the city on Gillmore's ultimatum, and so he opened fire. The gun burst after thirty-five rounds and did little damage at all to morale in the city. Later in 1863, however, Gillmore resumed the bombardment, this time reaching back into the days of mythology for a weapon, Greek fire. Incendiary shells were designed to carry the highly unstable potion into the city, where they would burst into flames on impact. Fortunately, most of the shells proved defective or burst too soon, filling the sky over the city with spectacular clouds of seething flame.

For the next year and a half Charleston endured a sporadic bombardment. It leveled much of the city, but not the spirit of its citizens. Sumter, too, came in for two more mammoth bombardments, each one flattening the pile of rubble more and more. Admiral Dahlgren made renewed attempts to steam into the harbor, but to no avail, and poor Quincy Gillmore became so disillusioned that he asked for assignment elsewhere. There were no reputations to be made by butting heads with a city that would not give up. A new Federal commander came, Major General John G. Foster, who had been a captain of engineers in Major Anderson's command at Sumter in 1861. Thus, it was something of a homecoming for him, and he announced his arrival with the declaration that "to capture Richmond would be grand, but to capture Charleston would be glorious."[10] That glory eluded poor Foster, for he proved no more successful than Gillmore in taking the city, though he made one effort after another. Though continuously outnumbered, still the Confederates managed to thwart every probe aimed at Charleston and its forts, even after the Yankees learned to read and decode Rebel signals.

During the months that became years, the Confederates put their imaginations to good use in devising new means of evening the disparate odds against them. Thanks in part to funds raised by contributions of silver and gold, jewelry, fine paintings, watches, and more, the ladies of the city financed the construction of two ironclads to help defend the harbor. The *Chicora* and *Palmetto State* were completed and ready for action by the end of 1862 and late in January forayed in the night out into the harbor and beyond, among the Yankee blockading fleet. The two ironclads engaged seven enemy ships and caused considerable consternation for a time, but in the end they failed to seriously interrupt the blockade. It was their first and last sortie. Two years later the Confederates destroyed the gallant little ships themselves to prevent their capture.

Even before the *Chicora* and *Palmetto State* plied the harbor waters, the Confederates had other deadly bits of flotsam awaiting their enemies. The underwater mine, or so-called torpedo, came into its own during this war, and the harbor teemed with them in the main ship channels and off the principal forts. Little more than tin or wooden casks filled with about seventy pounds of powder, they could be detonated either on contact or by electrical wire from ashore. A mine narrowly missed destroying the USS *Weehawken* during

DuPont's 1863 attack, and in the same day's fight the mammoth ironclad *New Ironsides* hovered unknowingly for fifteen minutes or more directly over a mine that refused to explode when its contact wires were touched to the batteries. If it had, the blast would have blown the ship out of the water.

The *New Ironsides* suffered another narrow miss from disaster with another less passive Confederate innovation. Since the Yankees would not brave the channels too often and come to the waiting mines, the Southerners determined to take the mines out to them. They designed a "torpedo steamer," an odd little vessel fifty-four feet long and five and a half feet wide, powered by a converted locomotive engine. When launched, the steamer floated deeply in the water, with only its smokestack and a few inches of the upper hull visible. In the hope that a biblical allusion would bring good fortune, the builders named the vessel the *David*. From the *David*'s bow they extended a long spar and at its end attached a contact torpedo. On the night of October 5, 1863, the *David* crept out from its moorings and steamed toward the blockading fleet, choosing as its target the *New Ironsides*. The little vessel rammed its torpedo into the enemy ironclad's hull with a deafening roar. The *David* itself almost became a casualty. The explosion sent a wave of water back toward it that rushed in the stack and doused the boiler fire. Some Confederates began to abandon ship before the *David* became operational again, but by then two of the crew had been picked out of the water by the Yankees and would later be imprisoned and charged with using an engine of warfare not recognized by civilized nations. As for the *New Ironsides*, it lived to fight again. So did the *David*, though never successfully.

Not so the CSS *Hunley*. It fought with complete success, but like the bee, it stung once and then died. Horace Hunley had built two previous submarines for the South, neither used successfully. For this third ship he took a twenty-five-foot-long boiler cylinder and converted it into a cigar shaped vessel just four feet wide and five feet tall. The screw propeller that drove it was operated by hand, by seven crewmen. At its bow there was a twenty-two-foot yellow pine spar mounting a torpedo. In every respect the little ship resembled a floating— and sometimes not floating so well—coffin. It could submerge completely, steering blindly and by compass. It could stay down as long as two and a half hours before the air became so depleted of oxygen that the men could not breathe. Sometimes it stayed down longer.

About August 23, 1863, the submarine, dubbed the *Hunley*, was ready to try its own foray against the *New Ironsides*. It was just leaving dock when a swell of water from a passing steamer poured in the open hatch and swamped the vessel. Only its commander, standing in the hatchway, survived. The Confederates raised the ship, and six days later it was practicing diving and surfacing in the harbor when again it sank, taking another crew with it. Only two men, one of them the officer who had survived the first sinking, escaped. He prudently transferred out of the submarine service forthwith. Again the submarine was raised, and, incredibly, another crew was recruited, this time including Hunley himself. On October 15 the submarine made more practice runs, but the number of dives was greater than the number of surfacings by one. A week later divers found the vessel on the bottom. By now some thirty-three men had died in the *Hunley,* yet another crew came forward, and finally on February 17, 1864, it bravely made its way out toward the blockading fleet. Just after 9:00 P.M. an explosion ripped the stern away from the USS *Housatonic,* and it sank where it stood. And with the ship went the fourth and last crew of the *Hunley.* From causes not yet fully known, it went to the bottom a few hundred yards from its victim, the first submarine in history to sink an enemy vessel. Ironically, the *Hunley*'s officers and crew were drawn almost entirely from the Confederate States Army.[11]

And so the siege continued, the Confederates unable to stop it and the Federals unable to complete it. General Foster and his subordinates became increasingly frustrated and desperate. He even proposed that he build giant rowing galleys like the Romans of old, equipping them with tall platforms from which he could storm Sumter's walls. The War Department prudently told him to put the notion from his mind. The frustration showed on his subordinates, most notably on Brigadier General Alexander Schimmelfennig. A Prussian by birth, Schimmelfennig was no stranger to frustration. He began the war by having his horse fall on him, and that was followed hard by a dose of smallpox. Then at Gettysburg on the first day of the fight, his corps was routed and fled the town, leaving him behind in the midst of thousands of Confederates. He took refuge in a handy pigshed, and there he had to sit out the battle, being brought food and water hidden beneath the pig slops by local civilians. In after years the lowly pigsty became "Schimmelfennig's headquarters." Unwilling to serve any more with the corps that had abandoned him, he got a transfer to South Carolina and promptly contracted malaria.

So he should have been ready for his experiences in Charleston, but obviously his patience was exhausted. The mosquitoes bothered him, so he smeared kerosene on his face. The insects kept their distance thereafter, but so did his officers, and even more so when he revealed his attitude toward their duty to their country. Schimmelfennig conceived a plan for taking Sumter by storm and called the colonel of the Third Rhode Island Artillery to explain it to him. Volunteers were to row out to the fort undetected, he said. Then, in the heavy dialect that made him sometimes even harder to understand, the general said that "ze Rhode Island Artillery will bore ze hole in ze wall of Sumter about ze size of ze barrel, then you will take ze keg of powder in ze boat, place it in ze hole made by ze artillery, then ze fort and yourself will be blown to hell; and your whole duty as a soldier will be done."[12] There were no volunteers.

By this time Schimmelfennig had had enough. When he prepared his own map of the roads and streams on nearby John's Island and sent a party out with the map, along with orders to halt where a certain road turned right, he simply could not accept a bewildered report that the road turned left there instead. "The map is all right," he shouted. "But this country is all wrong."[13] Suffering his trials with something less than Jobbish patience, Schimmelfennig must have been secretly relieved when, just as the war was ending, he contracted tuberculosis and died.

The Confederates, too, had their frustrations, not helped much by the Richmond government's penchant for using the South Carolina command as a place for shelving inadequate or out-of-favor generals from other fields of the war. Beauregard actually called the command the "Department of Refuge," a quip given proof in 1864 when he was relieved in command by Major General Samuel Jones, a man who had failed in almost every assignment but who had the distinction of being the most photographed general of the Confederacy next to Lee and Beauregard himself.

He could hold a smile, but he could not Charleston. Pluck and spirit and ingenuity cannot last indefinitely against overwhelming might and a resolve to win. Nevertheless, the people of Charleston maintained their morale with a remarkable dedication. Perhaps they felt it incumbent upon them as citizens of the first city of secession. "No Charlestonian has any right to be absent," wrote one woman. "Every son of Carolina should be at his post in the day of trial."[14] The women and civilian men of the city looked to their sons and brothers and husbands to protect them from the Yankee horde. The men in the forts and earthworks looked to their women to encourage and maintain their own resolve. The result was a seemingly unified determination not to surrender no matter the cost. Through four years of attack and threat, Charlestonians lived by the declaration of one of their own: "We intend to die hard."[15]

The price Charleston paid for being the cradle of secession. The view up Meeting Street after the disastrous fires.

U.S. Army Military History Institute, Carlisle, Pa.

With the increasing scarcity caused by the blockade, the men and women of the city found challenge in making do. They maintained the semblance of an active social life. Balls and parties were given as of old; only now the coffee came from burnt corn and the whiskey from fermented pine boughs. There were even dances and dinners amid the rubble of Fort Sumter. The city survived an epidemic of yellow fever in 1864 and a disastrous fire in 1861, and despite all the attempts of the good generals and the bad, Gillmore and Hunter and Foster and the intrepid Schimmelfennig, in the end it took the coming of William T. Sherman to bring the city's fall. Late in December 1864, after completing his fabled March to the Sea, Sherman captured Savannah, Georgia. Then he advanced north into South Carolina. With the Federals on Morris and the other islands, backed by their fleet, and with Sherman now approaching from the rear, the Confederates had no choice but to evacuate the city to avoid being surrounded. On February 17, 1865, after every major Confederate city but Richmond had fallen to the enemy, the Southerners spiked their guns, destroyed their ships, burned their papers, and fired the cotton on their wharves and in the warehouses. In the confusion, fires soon broke out all over the city, and accidental explosions began taking lives. From the Ashley to the Cooper, Charleston was in flames.

Once the Federals occupied the city, though the fire went out, the fires of their hatred for the cradle of secession were only fanned. Despite genuine efforts by officers to contain Union soldiers, many of them looted and vandalized homes and public buildings at will. By April the city was nearly dead. Even Sherman, who could make war hell, was appalled. He visited in May 1865. "Any one who is not satisfied with war should go and see Charleston," he said, "and he will pray louder and deeper than ever that the country may in the long future be spared any more war."[16] Happily, Charleston would be spared from anymore war. It ended within weeks of the city's evacuation, and on April 14, 1865, broken in health and spirit, Robert Anderson, now a major general, came back to Fort Sumter. There, four years to the day since his surrender, he raised once more the Stars and Stripes over the now unrecognizable mound of debris.

It flies there still, symbolic not only of the spirit and heroism of the people and soldiers of the city that would not give up but also of the determination of its would-be conquerors, who, though never successful, still never gave up. It was, after all, the spirit of the times.

5

A Different Kind of War: Fighting in the West

IT WAS "WAR TO THE KNIFE, and the knife to the hilt." That was how many in the Trans-Mississippi west described the conflict they fought in the vast reaches beyond the great river. It was a war of brutality and savagery and outrage unparalleled in the American experience—all fought side by side with innovation and daring and pathbreaking in all the best traditions of American ingenuity. Perhaps nowhere else in the troubled continent in the 1860s were all the extremes of war so intermingled. Of course, it would be greatly misleading to maintain that the Civil War in the west was unique and apart from that in the east in the way it was fought. Men battled with the same weapons, for the same causes, with the same valor and desperation. Their pain was the same. On either bank of the Mississippi, blood was just as red.

Yet there were significant differences in the ways men made war, certain features that were distinctly western, features that led to a very individual kind of war, and nothing cast a greater influence over it than the nature of the men who were to fight that conflict. Men west of the river *were* different—of that no one had a doubt. They were still a new people, many of them immigrants and more of them no more than first-generation natives of the region. Their lean bodies spoke of the generations of rugged Southern hill people who had spawned most of them. In some the bronze in their faces recalled the Indian women their fathers had taken, just as the scars on their bodies told of the Indian men they had battled. Missouri was well settled by now, even urbane in areas, with an international flavor thanks to thousands of recent European immigrants, but for many of the other hard westerners, of Arkansas and Texas especially, Fort Sumter brought nothing very new. For them, life itself had been an intermittent warfare. Now only the enemy was different; the unending struggle to survive remained the same.

The differences showed most readily when these men—whichever side they espoused—found themselves thrown together with regiments from the more refined east. Happily for all, this did not happen often. Not infrequently,

the men of high-toned outfits from the better parts of the east might find themselves encamped next to a regiment of hardscrabble Missourians. Inevitably
complaints ensued. The unkempt westerners were dirty, they drank and
whored, and they paid little enough attention to drill and almost none to the
Sabbath. They smelled peculiar. It offended the sensibilities to be quartered beside such ruffians. Usually unsaid was the fact that the rakehells were also besting the easterners at cards, stealing their campsites blind, whipping them at
marksmanship, and frequently scaring the hell out of them for the mere fun of
it. It tended to be a little difficult to hold a teacup with the little finger elevated
at the proper stylish angle when there was a half-crazed frontiersman practicing marksmanship on the teapot.

Indeed, while these westerners engaged in every manner of fun, shooting
and riding appealed to them the most, and better yet in combination. After the
Battle of Elkhorn Tavern, or Pea Ridge, in March 1862, as the Confederates made
their withdrawal, the dejected lieutenant colonel of the Third Texas Cavalry
heard firing in his rear. Fearing that he was being pursued by the Federals, he
formed the regiment for battle, put a battery in position, and waited, expecting to see his rear guard come thundering up the road with the Yankees in hot
pursuit. Instead just one man came leisurely riding up to him. "Is the enemy
coming?" asked the officer. "No, colonel," came the reply, "it's just the boys
shooting chickens out of the trees."[1]

The informality of the Trans-Mississippian was evident in everything he
did as well as in the way the people of the region behaved toward him. As with
the armies of the east, a command moving toward a battle often lost a lot of
stragglers and deserters along the way. But out here, nevertheless, as often as not
an army also grew as it moved toward the sound of the guns. Out of the hills
and towns sometimes scores of citizens, old men and young boys, simply appeared and attached themselves to the column, carrying their old squirrel rifles
or, more often, double-barreled shotguns. Unorganized, untrained, they simply came along for the fight. The battle done, they would melt away again into
the countryside from whence they had come. Confederate general Walter P.
Lane recalled that just after the Battle of Mansfield in the Red River campaign
of 1864 he met "two superannuated old gentlemen, with vengeance in their eyes
and old double-barreled shot-guns in their hands, going down to participate in
the battle." He told them that the battle was done and that they should go back
home rather than join the army and consume its already meager rations. But
the old warriors would not be dissuaded. As a result, one was nearly shot when

he took an armful of corn for his horse from the commissary, and the other was put on picket with orders not to fire and promptly started a small stampede when he got bored and blazed away at a squirrel in a tree. The old men "enjoyed themselves hugely for about two weeks," recalled Lane, "when, seeing no prospect of murdering any of the enemy, they returned quietly home."[2]

Indeed, Lane was also evidence of the peculiar sense of equality out here. Being a general did not necessarily win a man any great degree of deference from soldier or civilian. One evening, riding alone in Texas, he could not find a house where someone would let him stay the night. At last one kind husband and wife let him sleep in the same room with them in their modest dwelling. Apparently, it did not occur to the general to tell them that occasionally he had been known to walk in his sleep. The next morning when he awoke, he came near his hostess, and she promptly screamed. Then at breakfast both his hosts behaved in a strange manner whenever he spoke. Finally realizing what must have happened, Lane asked if he had disturbed them during the night. "I should think you did, sir," came the reply. "Yelling and whooping like a wild Indian; upsetting the table and throwing the chairs, and raising Cain generally." In fact, for nearly two hours during the night the man had stood with an ax poised, intending to strike Lane down if the somnambulist came near enough. Three times the general had approached, but his host, "wanting to make a sure blow," waited for him to come one step nearer. Happily, Lane did not and finally lay back down and slept soundly the rest of the night, his host all the while standing vigil over his terrified wife, ax in hand. Lane was mortified at the story, apologized profusely, and soon thereafter left. In parting, his host said, "I want you to do me a favor." Of course, the embarrassed Lane agreed. "If you ever happen to travel through this country again," said the man, "please don't make it convenient to stay all night with me, for there is not a wild 'varmint' in the woods but I would rather sleep in the same room with than you." The men parted company mutually disgusted with each other, said Lane, "he for my nearly frightening the life out of himself and wife" and the general "for his trying to murder me."[3] It seems hardly conceivable that any household in Virginia would deny lodging to Robert E. Lee, even if he rose in his sleep and danced about the bed singing, "Hallelujah," but out here a general was just another nuisance.

Perhaps it was because of all the other hardship and deprivation faced by men in the Trans-Mississippi that they had little time or patience for the privileges of rank and station. For one thing, existence could be simply miserable in the region at times. In winter there was no protection from the bitter cold, and in summer the winds blew sand and dust in the eyes. Even for those raised here life was a trial, and how much more so for those not native to the region. One Louisiana Confederate found the weather almost intolerable. "The heat here is suffocating," he wrote of North Fork, Arkansas; "the thermometer stands at 110°, and the prairie breezes are as refreshing as steam from an escape-pipe." The nights were not bad, "but the days perfectly awful with their suffocating atmosphere." "If you wish to imagine yourself in this country," he complained, "just get into a hot oven, and if there be any difference, it will be in favor of the oven."[4]

Equally taxing were the handicaps of shortage faced by the Trans-Mississippi Confederates and even those in blue. Pay was infrequent or nonexistent, weapons and equipment often badly worn with replacements scarce, and rations sometimes invisible. General John B. Magruder, commanding Confederates in Texas and the territories west, estimated his arms shortage at 40,000 weapons in 1863—meaning virtually every man in his command lacked a proper weapon. A year later he confessed that he could not campaign at all in the coming spring if not resupplied.[5] Throughout the department generally, supply would never meet demand. And when sufficient arms and supplies were available, the vast distances they had to be transported to reach commands usually defeated the generals' attempts at distribution. And so the soldiers did without, lived off the land, and took their weapons, when they could, from fallen comrades and enemies. One Confederate leader actually armed his command, in a fashion, by sending them out to confiscate squirrel rifles and old shotguns from local citizens.[6]

Thus it was that these men of the west lived a war rather different from that of their comrades east of the river, and thus it was that they fought it in some ways uniquely their own. Many of these men, of Missouri especially, had considerable experience in a certain kind of fighting, for they had been involved in a shooting war of sorts since 1856, the days of John Brown and "Bleeding Kansas." Some 2,000 or 3,000 of them who lived in the counties bordering Kansas, and especially the hemp-growing areas along the Missouri River, had been active in the border warfare. It had been a time of bushwhacking and ambuscade, of swift raids and swift withdrawals, of innovative use of whatever materials came to hand. Old Brown himself, in his barbaric attack at Pottawatomie Creek in May 1856, used ceremonial broadswords taken from an Eagles lodge to murder and mutilate his victims.

That sense of innovation showed itself on nearly every battlefield in the region, and it appeared early in the war. In September 1861 when General Sterling Price's Confederates laid siege to Lexington, Missouri, neither side was well equipped for the major conflict that followed. Price gladly accepted the services of the odd local who came out of his parlor for the fight. One sixty-year-old farmer came from his house every morning to join Price's men, bringing his antiquated flintlock and a basket of fried chicken to tide him through the day. At dusk he simply went back to his fireside.[7]

A few days before the fighting began in earnest, a captain had suggested to Price that several score bales of hemp piled in a warehouse along the Missouri River might be useful in the coming battle. Price had well over one hundred of them hauled out and brought to his headquarters, but he did not use them until September 19, when—apparently without actual orders—a couple of his regiments began using them as breastworks. The next day General Thomas Harris took 132 of the bales and started to soak them in the river so they would not catch fire if struck by hot shot. But the water made the bales so heavy that the men could not haul them out of the river. Instead Harris had dry bales placed in a long line, perhaps as much as 250 yards in length, and then the men poured water over them.

Then began the advance. Some of the bales were pushed with poles from behind; others apparently were dragged by brave souls out in front. Mostly, however, three or four soldiers simply set their weapons aside and started butting the bales with their heads. As the long line of weed breastworks slowly advanced by fits and starts, other Confederates maintained a continuous fire from behind their protection, offering the Yankees nothing to shoot at in return. Even when a cannonball struck a bale, it would not penetrate; the cannonball merely rocked the bale back a bit before the headstrong attackers resumed ramming the bales forward. The Yankees even tried firing red-hot heated shot at the wall of hemp, hoping to set it ablaze, but the soaked bales refused to take fire. If they had, the resulting cloud from scores of bales of the mildly narcotic weed might have led to a battle unique not only to the Civil War in the west but also unparalleled in the annals of humankind! As it was, Colonel James Mulligan, commanding the Federal defenders, lamented that "all our efforts could not retard the advance of these bales." Within a few hours he surrendered, the victim of the ingenuity—and iron skulls—of Price's Missourians.[8]

Such examples of inventiveness, however effective, could seem almost comical by comparison with a far more frequently used—and infinitely more effective—technique: ambush. Though surprise was and is certainly a fair and desirable stratagem in warfare, it was always difficult to achieve with large numbers. In the eastern theater such devices were tried on occasion, but rarely with great effect. Widespread were the rumors early in the war that the Confederates had the routes of approach to Manassas protected by a series of deadly "masked batteries" ready to spit fire and death upon unsuspecting Yankees as they approached. As with so much else that was expected of war in the innocent summer of 1861, the masked batteries were mostly imagination, and not one of them materialized when the Federals marched on Bull Run.

But out in the west it was another matter. Perhaps as a result of experience in the days of Bleeding Kansas, and certainly of decades of experience at Indian fighting, the men of the Trans-Mississippi knew how to do more than talk about ambush, and the regular enlisted forces of both sides made excellent use of it. At Pea Ridge that same Walter Lane—who himself bore the scars of an Indian ambush in Texas years earlier—led his Third Texas in a charge up a hill, only to see suddenly two hundred Federals rise from the brow, and perfect concealment, to deliver a deadly fire. Shifting his position, he charged again, and this time—by his own estimate—he ran into yet another concealed force, this time numbering nearly one thousand. At the same time he saw the camouflaging brush pulled away from a battery of six guns not sixty yards away. He gazed in astonishment as they all blazed away, then called on his men to "fall back, or you will all be murdered!" Lane later recalled that neither he nor his men "stood . . . on the order of their going."[9] It was a scene repeated time after time out here by both sides, though raised to the level of perfection by a particular species of soldier whose exploits follow presently.

When going into battle, the soldier of the Trans-Mississippi was not expected to perform any differently from his eastern counterpart. Generals wanted the same things from their men, and their battle orders—when they issued any—were quite similar. Aim for enemy officers. Kill artillery horses. Wait until within range before firing. Aim at the knees. Stay quiet except in the charge. Leave the wounded where they fall. Yet there were a few things directed specifically at these westerners that might not have appeared in any one of Robert E. Lee's battle orders. Prior to the fight at Prairie Grove, Arkansas, in December 1862, General Thomas C. Hindman admonished his men: "Do not break ranks to plunder. If we whip the enemy all he has will be ours." As a result, he issued specific orders to his file closers on either side of companies to shoot plunderers on the spot. It did not help much, for even the closers were happy to loot when they could. All of these men were born scavengers.

And a battle order could reveal one thing more about war out here: why it was different from elsewhere. For here hatred of the enemy became almost institutionalized as an element of military doctrine. In Virginia the armies fought, and certainly there were men who hated, but nowhere on a scale such as in Arkansas and Missouri. In so many cases it was but the continuation of animosities already years old when the war began. "Remember that the enemy has no feeling of mercy or kindness toward you," Hindman told his army. "His ranks are made up of Pin Indians, free negroes, Southern tories, Kansas jayhawkers and hired dutch cutthroats. These bloody ruffians have invaded your country, stolen and destroyed your property, murdered your neighbors, outraged your women, driven your children from their homes and defiled the graves of your kindred."[10] Such rhetoric was hardly calculated to keep warfare on a refined level.

Hindman's Prairie Grove order hinted at something else that was different about the war out here, at least in 1862. Most of the service arms performed much as they did east of the Mississippi. Both artillery and infantry served primarily their same functions, though the sheer vastness of the Trans-Mississippi required of them a degree of mobility unthought of in Maryland and Tennessee. But there was something unusual about the makeup of some of these western outfits. Hindman spoke of Indians and free Negroes coming against him. Of the Indians, more anon. But of the blacks, it can be said that here in the west a genuinely new chapter of the Civil War had its introduction.

Talk of raising black regiments commenced on both sides immediately after the conflict began. Surprisingly, even President Jefferson Davis had to turn down a host of requests from Southern blacks, free and slave, to become soldiers for the Confederacy. Little was done in the matter during the first two years of fighting. Senator James Lane of Kansas, however, did not wait. In summer 1862 he began pressuring Lincoln for permission to enlist blacks into the service and on January 31, 1863, mustered the First Kansas Colored Volunteers into the army. However, individual companies of blacks had been informally organized several months before, and on October 28, 1862, at Butler, Missouri, a detachment of Lane's blacks battled with a force of Confederate guerrillas in the first action of the war in which blacks fought. The next year in battles at Cabin Creek, in the Indian Territory later to become Oklahoma, and at Honey Springs, the new regiment distinguished itself. The Confederates at Honey Springs, knowing that they would be fighting blacks, had brought slave manacles with them to the battlefield but were never able to use them. Though the issue of the black man's usefulness as a warrior would remain a point of controversy for some time yet, in the Trans-Mississippi it was first demonstrated that, given the chance, the black man would fight and fight well.[11]

In only one branch of the service did the conduct of the war differ radically from that east of the Mississippi, and once again it was a difference that sprang from the nature of the people and the country. The plains and prairies were a nation on horseback. More than that, they were a people used to handling firearms as well and to using them from the saddle. As a result, the region was a natural spawning ground for hordes of cavalrymen, North and South, but particularly on the Confederate side. Furthermore, the Trans-Mississippi service put to the test all the latest developments in cavalry tactics to a degree unheard of in the east. Indeed, the mounted arm rose to the greatest extent of its potential out here. Of course, it served all the normal functions—engaging in reconnaissance, raiding, escorting supply trains, and fighting as auxiliary to infantry. But quickly the nature of the region, and of the people fighting, pushed the horsemen beyond their traditional roles.[12]

Just how pervasive the cavalry was to become is evident in the figures for General E. Kirby Smith's command. At the end of 1864 he reported 39,700 effective troops in his Confederate Trans-Mississippi Department. Of that number, 22,800 were cavalrymen, more than 57 percent.[13] By contrast, in the department commanded by Robert E. Lee, horsemen rarely constituted more than 10 percent of the total. Indeed, so numerous were the horsemen that their numbers became onerous to both sides. Late in 1862 a Federal officer in Arkansas could complain that "cavalry are plenty among us, and go in any direction you may for miles you will find their horses hitched near every dwelling. They scour the country in every direction and generally help themselves to anything they wish." And if weary foot soldiers asked at a house for something to eat, the answer all too often was "The cavalry has been here and there is nothing left." No wonder that many Yankee soldiers regarded their own horsemen as "mere vampyres hanging on the infantry—doing but little fighting but first in for the spoils."[14] It was an unfair assessment—typical of infantrymen's attitudes everywhere—but the excessive numbers of cavalry were a very real problem. The natural outgrowth of the need for high mobility in a region so vast, and of the inhabitants' preference for mounted service, the cavalry grew to such size that Kirby Smith had to commence a conscious program of reducing the cavalry's numbers that cut his mounted arm in half by war's end.[15]

In the regular pitched battles in the region, the cavalry played a role of considerably greater importance than in the eastern battles. At Pea Ridge, for instance, Southern horsemen went into battle alongside their comrades in the infantry and yet remained mounted and actually charged against a Federal battery. "So impetuous, so sudden was the charge," wrote a witness, "that no time was given the foe to meet the rushing host of horsemen. In less than five minutes the battery was captured, the infantry force supporting it shot down, ridden over and scattered like chaff before a whirlwind."[16]

Perhaps the most significant battle for Southern cavalrymen was Prairie Grove. Though cavalry, particularly Confederate, played a large role in the battle and in the achievement of what few gains were to be had for Hindman, the

General Edmund Kirby Smith, who complained that the Trans-Mississippi was no "bed of roses."
Author's collection

Forgotten Wars

fight's real relation to the mounted arm lay in the future. With Confederate infantry driven out of Missouri and now Arkansas virtually for good and denied
the interior bases needed for active campaigning, the situation virtually dictated that any future attempts to regain territory would rest with lightning swift
and highly mobile raids by Southern horse. Thus, Prairie Grove became a moment that turned Confederate cavalry from an army auxiliary into a body of
raiders unparalleled elsewhere in the warring continent.[17]

Surely the premier example of cavalry, a virtual army of it, on a great raid

General Sterling Price of Missouri, one of the troublesome,
often bumbling, officers who helped lose the perhaps
untenable Trans-Mississippi for the Confederacy.
Author's collection

is Sterling Price's 1864 Missouri expedition. Already the South had sent three major mounted raids into Missouri. In January 1863 cavalryman John S. Marmaduke led 2,400 troopers north out of Arkansas in an attack on Springfield. Driven out of the state, Marmaduke returned again in April and May to attack supply and communications and to assault the Yankee base at Cape Girardeau, not to mention looting indiscriminately from friend and foe alike, a trait in western Confederates that alienated much of the support they desperately needed. This raid, too, failed, but that fall yet another, deeper thrust into Missouri came when General Joseph O. Shelby led 1,200 raiders on a 1,500-mile ride that penetrated as far as the Missouri River, did nearly $1 million worth of damage, and captured 6,000 horses and mules and 1,200 weapons, as well as more loot taken from friends.[18]

Then came 1864 and Price's raid. It, like both of Marmaduke's efforts, ended in failure. Yet in numbers involved on both sides, it would prove to be the major cavalry action of the entire war. Price left Arkansas with 12,000 cavalry, 1,000 of them unmounted and 4,000 without arms, to be sure, but still the greatest assemblage of cavalry in the history of the Trans-Mississippi. To meet him Federal generals Samuel Curtis and William S. Rosecrans assembled an army that totaled perhaps 20,000, more than 8,500 of them cavalry led by General Alfred Pleasonton. By the time the two armies met in the decisive battle at Westport, Missouri, on October 23, Price's numbers had dwindled through desertion and straggling to about 9,000. In what was to be the largest battle of the war west of the Mississippi, cavalry played from first to last a decisive role, though distinctive to this kind of fighting, Price's cavalry fought almost exclusively dismounted. Armed with muzzle-loading rifles that could not be reloaded easily on horseback, this Confederate cavalry acted chiefly as mounted infantry, riding to the battlefield, then fighting on foot. Numbers are very incomplete for the campaign and battle, but perhaps as many as 17,000 cavalrymen, mounted and unmounted, participated in the actions making up Westport, ranking it second only to Brandy Station among the great cavalry battles of the war.[19]

Thus it was that the Confederacy in particular had to rely upon virtual armies of horsemen for its offensive operations in most of the Trans-Mississippi, while its opponents as well looked chiefly to mounted men to counter the constant threat posed by Southern cavalry. Much as this differed from the nature of the war to the east, so, too, did some of the tactics used by horsemen out here stand out. In particular, while in the east cavalrymen were generally expected to ride to the battlefield and then fight on foot, in the west they preferred fighting from the saddle when weapons and circumstances allowed. It was the mode of combat learned from the Indians, and the frontiersmen had been obliged to become adept at it in self-defense. Further, these fights in Arkansas and Missouri were not to take ground but to strike quickly, capture or destroy, and then swiftly return to friendly lines. Indeed, as the war progressed, it was with first surprise, then glee, that some defenders on either side, especially guerrillas who fought almost exclusively from horseback, saw opposing cavalrymen dismount to attack or fight afoot. It was that unusual. In one of the innumerable fights in Arkansas, when General James M. McIntosh's command prepared to attack a body of Federal Pin Indians, the defenders looked with delight as the Confederate cavalrymen got off their mounts. "The Indians on the hill raised a yell," wrote a Southerner, "thinking we were going to attack them on foot, and they, behind the rocks and trees on the eminence, could 'have cleaned us all up' before we could have reached them." But the Rebels were only tightening their saddle girths. Remounting, they charged up a hill so steep that some horses could not make the climb, and the Rebels routed the foe.[20] Much later in the war, outside Centralia, Missouri, men of William "Bloody Bill" Anderson's guerrilla command were approached by 147 Union mounted infantrymen. As the Yankees came near, their commander ordered them off their horses into a skirmish line. It was the only way they could use their long muzzle-loaders, besides which they were new recruits with no fighting experience. So surprised were Anderson's men that one of them cried out, "My God, the Lord have mercy on them, they're dismounting to fight!" When the mounted Confederates charged, they rode right over their opponents. Out here only a very brave man or a fool allowed himself to be separated from his horse in a fight. Friendly lines could be too far to the rear and a merciless foe too near.[21]

For the cavalry roving in smaller detachments, the favorite targets were supply trains, small garrisons, quartermaster warehouses, and telegraph lines. Yet now and then cavalrymen, particularly Confederates, singled out a particularly unusual quarry: Yankee boats. The same was done occasionally east of the Mississippi, most notably by Nathan Bedford Forrest in Tennessee and Alabama, but nowhere with the frequency exhibited here. In June 1864 the noted Confederate Indian general Stand Watie led his cavalry and three pieces of artillery to attack the supply steamer *J. R. Williams* on the Arkansas River. In fact, it had become common practice for Yankee boats on these rivers to travel with a cavalry screen in front of them on either side of the stream, but the *Williams*

The one near-great victory for the Confederates came when low water on the Red River almost stranded Porter's ironclad fleet, shown here above Alexandria, Louisiana, waiting for the water to rise.

U.S. Naval Historical Center, Washington, D.C.

had no such protection and was taken completely by surprise. In this one capture, Watie took 150 barrels of flour and 16,000 pounds of badly needed bacon.[22]

Other Rebel horsemen tried even more ambitious enterprises. General Walter P. Lane led his Texas riders and four pieces of artillery in an attack on the formidable Union ironclad *Essex* as it steamed up the Mississippi. It was a case of biting off more than he could chew. Lane stood directing his command's fire when the ironclad opened up. "I was on the levee," Lane wrote, "when a hundred and forty-pound shell struck the bank below me and exploded, turning over the planks I was lying on and piling about eight wagon-loads of earth on me. I thought I was murdered," he said, and he would not believe to the contrary until his men pulled him out from under the earth. For some time thereafter he continued to maintain that he was, in fact, really dead.[23]

Perhaps the most ambitious such undertaking came during the Red River campaign when General Thomas Green and 750 Confederate cavalry on April 12, 1864, attacked Admiral David D. Porter's fleet of thirteen ironclads and seven gunboats on the Red at Blair's Landing. Though the cavalrymen inflicted only minor damage, they hastened the precipitate withdrawal of the fleet, but the success cost them the life of Green, killed in the action.

The attack by Watie's men reflected yet another unique feature of the Trans-Mississippi fighting. Nowhere else in the Confederacy was there such a mixture of ethnic and racial soldiery. In addition to the black regiments in the Yankee service, there were two Colorado regiments composed chiefly of men of

Forgotten Wars

Mexican descent. On the other side, the Thirty-third Texas was led in part by Refugio Benevides and manned mostly by Mexican Confederates. And both sides employed several regiments of Indians, mostly members of the Five Civilized Tribes who had been removed to Indian Territory. Most notably of all, of course, was the Cherokee Stand Watie, the only Indian on either side in the war to rise to the full rank of brigadier general.[24]

Naturally, the Indians were chosen as the most ideal cavalry, even if undisciplined. At the same time, they were also seen as an effective deterrent to one another. Federal Indian troopers would know best how to fight and neutralize Confederate Indians and vice versa. Because there were old intertribal rivalries dating back generations before the war, Union and Confederate authorities could play on them in enlisting young warriors to their banners. Indeed, even Watie, who was not only the foremost Indian leader of the war but also one of the finest cavalry leaders in the Trans-Mississippi, was not above mixing personal revenge with his military duties. He went some little distance out of his way in December 1863 to ride through Park Hill in Indian Territory to destroy the property of archrival John Ross.[25]

In all the Confederates raised three regiments and two battalions of Cherokee cavalrymen, two battalions and a regiment of Chickasaws, three regiments and a battalion of Choctaws, two mixed regiments of Choctaws and Chickasaws, two regiments of Creeks, and one battalion each of Osages and Seminoles. All told, it appears that over 12,000 Indians served the Confederacy alone. Figures for the Federals are sketchy, but perhaps as many as 6,000 took arms for the Union.[26] That military authorities consciously attempted to arouse old tribal hatreds is evident throughout the course of the Indians' participation. Colonel William A. Phillips, commanding Federals in Indian Territory for a time, admonished his command as they were about to face Confederate Indians that "those who are still in arms are rebels and ought to die. Do not kill a prisoner after he has surrendered. But I do not ask you to take prisoners. I ask you to make your footsteps severe and terrible."[27]

Impelled by invective such as this, even the best cavalrymen in the department, Indian or white, were all too often prone to pillage and plunder, or worse, and to a degree that would have shocked their eastern counterparts. Wherever Watie's command passed, Union citizens and Indians were robbed of whatever could be carried, and what could not be removed was destroyed. When William C. Quantrill, an infamous guerrilla, arrived in Lawrence, Kansas, on a raid that left the town in ruins, he announced matter-of-factly that his goal was "plunder." He, like the Indians, was doing more than fighting a war; he was settling old scores. And all too many on either side out here used the conflict as an excuse to legitimize personal vengeance.[28]

Alas, among the regular cavalry plunder all too often was not enough. In a regular battle, of course, aroused passions and bloodlust could make even well-reasoned men act out of character. In the fight at Westport, part of Shelby's command attacked 300 militia on the Mockbee farm. The militiamen had made the fatal mistake of dismounting, and when the Confederates charged, they scattered the horseless militia everywhere. Left behind were 30 men manning an antiquated cannon. They surrendered, but by the account of one of the militia, 24 of them were shot down.[29] At Prairie Springs, in Indian Territory, on September 14, 1864, Watie's command attacked a detachment of the First Kansas

General Albert Pike, chiefly responsible for maintaining Confederate-Indian relations and enlisting the disparate tribes—and their often brutal ways of war—to the Southern cause.
Author's collection

Colored Infantry, routed it, and killed every black who fell into the command's hands. The Federals could be just as guilty of such excesses. In March 1863 when an Iowa regiment turned some Confederate prisoners over to the Thirteenth Kansas for delivery to Springfield, Missouri, the guards were barely on their way before they simply killed their charges and left them. Any regiment North or South might be capable of such acts, but some made it more of a habit than others, most notably Charles Jennison's Seventh Kansas "Jayhawkers" and Watie's Cherokees.[30]

Somehow more remembered were the individual acts by which men wreaked their vengeance, isolated events of terror and mayhem. A Louisiana Confederate recalled meeting one Indian who boasted that "one of my brothers is a murderer," then later in the Battle of Pea Ridge saw the proof of it when some of the Confederate Indians indiscriminately killed whomever came in their way, scalping Union and Confederate dead alike. Watie's own son Saladin murdered a Federal prisoner, impelling his mother to urge him "to always show mercy." Watie himself constantly tried to control his men, condemning the brutality of many of the Rebel guerrilla bands with whom he found himself compared. He had, he said, "always been opposed to killing women and children although our enemies have done it," and he tried to restrain the passions of his men. "I am not a murderer," he protested. Alas, others could not say the same, and the institutionalized brutality that appeared early in the war in the Trans-Mississippi escalated throughout the conflict. Among regular troops, such acts reached their nadir for the Federals when Major John M. Chivington, on November 29, 1864, attacked Cheyennes and Arapahoes encamped at Sand Creek, in Colorado Territory. Several hundred women, children, and peaceful warriors were butchered. The Confederate counterparts were many. Witness the attack at Dove Creek, Texas, on January 8, 1865, when Texas troopers killed and scalped twenty-three unarmed Kickapoo men and women.[31]

Of course, it was among the irregular mounted men in the west that the real savagery appeared. For men who had been Jayhawkers long before the firing on Fort Sumter, the fighting out here began in the mid-1850s. Savagery, indiscriminate bloodletting, acts of revenge and barbarism, were commonplace for many of the men enlisting, or just attaching themselves to, the roving bands of guerrillas led by men of the stripe of Quantrill, Anderson, George Todd, and more.

It cannot be denied that these mounted terrorists did some genuine good service in the interest of their causes, particularly the Confederates. They sev-

ered enemy communications, captured couriers, cut off or more likely murdered small patrols, sabotaged a host of buildings and bridges and telegraph
wires, wrecked railroad lines, and destroyed towns. General Hindman observed
that they also compelled "the enemy to keep there a large force that might have
been employed elsewhere," though most of the Federal troops assigned to
counter the guerrillas were local state militia that would not have been sent out
of the state in any case.[32] More than that, the guerrillas often succeeded in turning the local population against the enemy. Confederate raiders struck not only
Yankee soldiers but also those civilians who might sympathize with them, offer
them assistance in campaign, or give aid in adversity. Indeed, the irregular often
made no distinction between a Federal in uniform or out. An enemy was an
enemy, soldier or civilian, to be dealt with in like manner. It is no wonder that
such an attitude quickly led to the most gross sort of excess under the legit-
imizing banner of the "cause." At least a few of the guerrillas were straightforward about it. One of Quantrill's officers was forced to state frankly that "guerrilla warfare claims no kinship to a pink tea." The partisans, knowing that they
would themselves be killed if taken, resolved to kill first.[33]

Understandably, the measures taken to combat guerrillas were of the most
summary kind and in the end succeeded only in urging them on to greater excess, seeing that they had no hope of mercy if captured. Early in the war in Missouri Federal authorities published an order stating that any man serving in a
partisan band for the South "forfeits his life." If captured, they were not to be
treated as prisoners of war but to be shot or hanged at once. Thereafter, several
department commanders issued directives of their own, all of which resulted
in numerous summary "drum-head" courts-martial and even swifter execu-
tions. It became a matter of almost casual interest in the region. "Five rebels
have been picked up in the brush . . . who cannot give a good account of themselves," wrote a Yankee lieutenant, "& they were taken care of." "I pity them, for
Provost Marshall shows no mercy to such men."[34] Another Federal officer wrote
to his commander of the capture of several enemy partisans, apologizing that
he had been unable to bring them in as prisoners because, along the way, they
had accidentally fallen off a log with nooses around their necks. In fact, a few
Federals sensed that this draconian policy would only make matters worse. An
Iowa officer, learning of the shooting of seven Rebel partisans, confessed that
"I hope this may prove incorrect for it is establishing a precedent which must
end in rapine & murder." He could not have been more right.[35]

The individual acts of barbarism were too many to number. In October

1862 in Cross Hollows, Arkansas, a purported Union man enlisted the aid of two Iowa soldiers in moving his family. He led them into an ambush in which they were killed. When a bushwhacker was taken and accused of being responsible for setting fire to woods at Pea Ridge where Union wounded from the battle were trapped, he was shot at once. In February 1863 near Forsyth, Missouri, guerrilla Alfred Boland was killed when a man posing as a friend caved in his skull with a broken plowshare as Boland stooped over a fire.[36] Ironically, the guerrillas did not entirely condemn their slayers, recognizing that each operated by the same simple, brutal code. Kit Dalton, supposedly one of Quantrill's gang, left a highly exaggerated account of his wartime service, which nevertheless spoke most accurately and eloquently on this subject:

> The purpose of war is to kill and the object of its votaries is murder, sanctioned by Christian and pagan nations alike.... Civilized, barbarous, savage, guerilla, bushwhacking, jayhawking, and all methods of modern and ancient warfare have the same aim in view—death, devastation, pillage, and plunder.... Leaden death from a high power rifle in the hands of a regular is just about as permanent as death from a blunderbuss in the hands of a jayhawker. The "regulars" who answer to taps and reveille have no higher aim in view than to kill those who oppose them.... There is no more moral wrong in a small body of men seeking to take advantage of another small body than there is in a vast army seeking to out-manoeuver another army of equal importance. They are both after the enemy's throat.[37]

As individuals or in groups, the irregulars in the Trans-Mississippi went for their foes' throats with a gusto, even delight, that turned their grisly work of war into something macabre. The more flamboyant even publicized their work. Bloody Bill Anderson, after repeatedly besting the patrols in Missouri sent to take him, actually wrote a letter to the Union commander in the area, complaining about the poor quality of the men being sent after him. "They are such poor shots it is strange you don't have them practice more," taunted the guerrilla. "Send them out and I will train them for you." And Anderson's trusted little lieutenant, psychopath Arch Clement, became perhaps the first man of the war actually to sign his handiwork. After two Federal cavalrymen were killed in an ambush, Clement scalped them both, then mutilated their foreheads. He pinned a note to one of the dead men. "You come to hunt bush whackers," it read. "Now you are skelpt. Clemyent Skelpt you."[38]

A few days later Anderson would kill twelve Yankees, scalping five and slitting the throats of three others. In time, the depredations of the irregulars on both sides became an embarrassment even to their own people. One Confederate general complained of Quantrill's men that they valued "the life of a man less than that of a sheep-killing dog."[39] North and South would each attempt to control, and later to disband, their western guerrillas or else transfer them into the regular volunteer service, where restraints of law and discipline might be imposed.

However repulsive the individual acts of butchery were, there is no question that the most dramatic, the most savage depredations of these men came when they fought together, the bloodlust of each serving to stimulate the other. The raids on Centralia, Missouri, and Lawrence, Kansas, and the fight at Baxter Springs, Kansas, would all become synonymous with the worst features of warfare and would also characterize the most unique feature of the war out here—the utter savagery to which it could suddenly and frighteningly descend.

The Lawrence raid is well enough known. In August 1863 Quantrill led about four hundred of his men and other loosely affiliated bushwhackers on what was ostensibly a raid into Kansas for plunder. It was also a blow of personal vengeance against a town that had not treated Quantrill well before the war, and it was as well the home of Senator and General James Lane, archenemy of all Rebel guerrillas and a man guilty of some ghastly depredations of his own.

At 5 A.M. on August 21, the raiders rode into town. Soon their pistols were blazing. As their marks they took any male who happened to be on the street; then they rode over a company of 22 recruits camped in town, killing all but 5. As the looting and burning began, the raiders rode through the streets dragging men from their homes to kill them, setting ablaze other buildings that housed fugitives from their deadly accurate revolvers. In a four-hour orgy of bloodletting, about 150 men were killed and several more wounded without anyone fighting back. The only guerrilla casualty was one who was too drunk to ride out with his companions. Lagging back, he was shot by a townsman, then dragged by the neck around town as citizens took out their wrath by stoning him to death.[40]

Equally savage was the Baxter Springs massacre six weeks later. On October 6, 1863, after unsuccessfully attacking a small Union fort, Quantrill turned his attention to a wagon train seen approaching. It was the personal escort and baggage train of General James C. Blunt, commanding Federals in Kansas. Incredibly, Blunt halted the train barely a quarter mile from the fort without hearing any of the firing from Quantrill's attack, and then when some of the guerrillas approached—dressed largely in captured Yankee jackets—he at first mistook them for friends. The raiders' first volley revealed who they were, and their terrifying charge, reins in their teeth, pistols firing from either hand, so unsettled the few armed soldiers with Blunt that they barely made a resistance before fleeing in terror. One at a time and in little groups, the guerrillas rode down the panicked Federals, shot them, took their clothing and valuables, and then often mutilated the bodies. Of the 100 men with Blunt, only the general and a score of others escaped to safety.[41] Then making his way toward Texas for the winter, Quantrill continued his path of blood. Proudly he would report to General Sterling Price that he "caught about 150 Federal Indians and negroes in the [Indian] Nation gathering ponies. We brought none of them through."[42]

But Centralia paled all else, if not in numbers, then in sheer savagery. This time it was not Quantrill but his onetime lieutenant, Anderson, who led. On September 27, 1864, Anderson, George Todd, and 80 or more of their followers rode into Centralia and without any resistance pillaged stores and homes, got roaring drunk, and then saw in the distance that a train was coming. They blocked the tracks, and as the train came to a halt, out poured an odd lot of civilians and furloughed Federals from Sherman's army in Georgia. The civilians were sent aside and robbed, and the 24 Yankees were told to line up on the station platform. Anderson drew his revolvers and faced the doomed men, then yelled, "You are all to be killed and sent to hell!" The soldiers glumly stripped their uniforms, and then despite their entreaties, Anderson and his men put pistols to their heads and one by one murdered all but one. To make sure of the work, every man was shot three times. Those who did not die instantly were clubbed to death, and at least two were scalped.[43]

That was not to be all. Later that day after the raiders left Centralia, a detachment of 147 mounted Union infantry set out in pursuit of Anderson and Todd, and the guerrillas, riding high on their earlier success, made so bold as to lure the Yankees toward them. Then the raiders charged on horseback just as the Federals ill advisedly dismounted. The raiders rode right over them. The Federals fired but a single volley, then fled in panic, on foot. Gleefully Anderson's men rode after them, shooting at will as the now unarmed soldiers begged for their lives. Of the 147 who began the skirmish, 124 were killed. And the butchery had only begun. One man playfully hopped across the field on the backs of the Yankee dead, saying, "This is the best way to count 'em." The major commanding the Federals was scalped, along with 12 others. Ears and noses and genitals were chopped from the dead. Bayonets were jammed into the corpses for the fun of it. Guerrillas cut the heads from several of the slain and then had a high time rearranging them on different bodies. Some heads were mounted on the muzzles of guerrilla rifles and tied to saddles as souvenirs, and a few wound up unceremoniously perched atop nearby fence posts, facing each other with obscene phrases cut into their foreheads. It had been Bloody Bill's greatest day.[44]

Sadly, this is the most distinctive single feature of the Civil War in the Trans-Mississippi: the unmitigated ruthlessness and senseless brutality to which it could sink at times and the unbridled passions that led to such deeds. The men of the west were not any more or less evil than were those in Virginia. They simply had more reason to fight from hatred than for a cause, while the vastness of the region and the rugged frontier edge clinging to it encouraged a relaxing of the restraint that in war separates the soldier from the savage.

Yet for all that set the war out here apart from the rest of the conflict, the most lasting impact of those differences remained to be seen after the conflict, not during it. For here, just as Fort Sumter had not begun the fighting, neither did surrender end it. Some Confederates, most notably General Joseph O. Shelby and his brigade, refused to accept defeat and instead rode south into Mexico, preferring to involve themselves in another internecine conflict rather than submit to Yankee rule. Thousands, including Price and Hindman, exiled themselves from their Arkansas and Missouri homes. Hundreds of others, having tasted blood and plunder, could not return to farming and clerking. A direct outgrowth of the Civil War in the Trans-Mississippi would be the so-called Wild West. A host of the desperadoes of the 1870s and 1880s learned their trade in the 1860s with Quantrill and Anderson. Frank and Jesse James, the Younger brothers, and many more found the war a proving ground for outlawry.

More than plunder, perhaps, these men were impelled by hatred. They began the war knowing how to hate, and the years that followed only nurtured that obsession. It was something that extended beyond just the bloodthirsty guerrillas. Shelby and his men hated and would not live again with the objects of their enmity. And the civilians hated just as much as the soldiers, perhaps more, which explains the sympathy the civilians later showed when Confederate raiders turned outlaw.

It is all illustrated so forcefully in the story of an unknown woman who roamed over the battlefield at Prairie Grove after the fight. A Yankee officer watched her as she walked among the dead, looking in their faces. Finally he heard her utter a smothered groan. She had found her Confederate brother,

Forgotten Wars

dead. "Her emotion seemed gone," said the Federal. Then a few yards on she found yet another brother, one she had not even known to be in the battle. After a brief release of grief, she passed on, her children clinging to her skirts. Then she found her husband lifeless on the ground, staring sightlessly into the sky. Soldiers about the field heard her utter a "wild unearthly shriek," then saw her fall over her husband's body. In an instant she arose once more, without tears, with no display of emotion from a heart that must have been shattered. The Federals watching could not but be moved. "The suffering of that woman none but God can know," wrote one. She walked from the field after leaving instructions for the care of her fallen men but paused to look back upon the field of dead. Within the hearing of scores of Yankee soldiers, in a voice that rang clearly over much of the bloody ground, she exclaimed, "The death of thousands of your number cannot revenge my wrongs."[45] In the mangled bodies of her husband and brothers, she had learned hatred. She and tens of thousands more would never forget it. In the Trans-Mississippi, that was to be the most lasting legacy of a war that had begun long before 1861 and did not end until long after 1865.

6

Forgotten Wars: The Confederate
Trans-Mississippi

FOR MUCH OF THE WAR General Edmund Kirby Smith felt as if he commanded an island, one isolated even from its own capital in faraway Richmond, especially after the loss of the Mississippi to Confederate traffic. He felt
genuinely neglected and even complained of how "the country west of the Mississippi has been exhausted of its fighting population to swell up the ranks of
our armies in Virginia, Tennessee, and Mississippi." He had few men left to fill
his ranks and replace his losses but "the aged, the infirm, and," as he put it, "the
lukewarm." Everything ran in short supply, and what his department could
produce was often as not siphoned away for the benefit of Robert E. Lee in Virginia or Braxton Bragg in Tennessee. Well might Kirby Smith complain, and
he was not the first in western territory to fear that no one heard him.[1]

By the time he uttered his complaint in September 1863, Kirby Smith commanded a department that, in theory, contained more real territory than all of
the Confederacy east of the Mississippi River combined: Missouri, Arkansas,
western Louisiana, Texas, Indian Territory, and Arizona Territory, which
stretched all the way to the California border. This was a virtual empire, con-
taining perhaps 600,000 square miles. It was also a wild and often turbulent region. Only months before the outbreak of war, the frontier U.S. Army was still
battling Comanches, Kiowas, Apaches, and others. A combination of Federal
troops and local regulators, such as the Texas Rangers and militia groups, pre-
served what peace there was on the border. Men in Missouri still sat bitterly divided over the issue of slavery, with the memory of the days of Bleeding Kansas
still fresh. Far to the south issues were completely different in the territory along
the border with Mexico, the largely Spanish-speaking population uninterested
in this Anglo war and many still carrying resentments over the last war, when
the United States had forcibly taken this land from their native country. A variety of motives and impulses coursed through this enormous territory, just as

in a major nation, and anyone trying to cope with it administratively invited a nightmare. Anyone trying to cope with it militarily asked the near-impossible.

It was a territorial command that evolved considerably, both for the Yankees and the Rebels, with no little confusion and overlapping of authority. Even before the outbreak of actual fighting in 1861, the Davis government assumed immediately that an attempt would have to be made to hold as much of the west as possible. Arkansas and Texas as well as Louisiana had seceded to make common cause with the Confederacy. That was fine. They also entertained high expectations that a pro-Southern majority in Missouri would bring that state within the pale as well. Some sort of formal organization of all this territory would be necessary, and in April 1861 Jefferson Davis created the District of Texas, with General Earl Van Dorn in command. On July 22 the District of Arkansas, including most of western Louisiana, came into being, with Major General William J. Hardee commanding. The Indian Territory would not be formally organized into a department until November, and no formal department organization ever included the New Mexico and Arizona lands. Unfortunately, when Davis created all these separate commands, he failed to authorize one central governing authority to coordinate all of them, just as he failed to do so east of the Mississippi until the final months of the war.

As a result, any gains in these far-flung commands had to depend upon cooperation and mutual understanding, the one quality that most Confederate department commanders everywhere in this war lacked. Indeed, much of the time the several commanders of these districts seemed not to be entirely certain themselves of just who commanded what. And as a final impediment to efficient and—more to the point—speedy cooperation, all department commands ended on the east at the Mississippi. Commanders in Tennessee, Mississippi, and eastern Louisiana held sway on the other side. This meant that communications, the shipment of men and supplies from one side to the other, and any operation for defense of the Mississippi could not be directed by a single leader. Instead, the general in charge on the one bank always had to count on the timely and willing cooperation of the general on the other. It rarely happened. And the only overall power that could direct such coordinated efforts was in Richmond, so far away as to be out of the picture, especially later in the war when the disruption of communications was such that any directive from the capital might take weeks to get out here, if at all.

Difficulties set in almost at once. In the beginning, 1861 looked like a good year for the Confederates in the west. They enjoyed repeated success in Missouri. Nathaniel Lyon and his Federal forces gained a minor victory at Boonville in June, but the next month a reverse at Carthage evened the score, and then at Wilson's Creek in August Lyon was killed and his small army defeated. The next month the Confederate advance reached Lexington on the Missouri River, besieged the Federal garrison, and forced its surrender. It looked as though the state was fairly won, and on August 19 the Confederate Congress "admitted" Missouri into the new nation. Unfortunately, the state's legislature itself never voted for secession. Instead it split, with two legislatures and two governors. Even at this early date, however, General Sterling Price was already complaining to Richmond of the apparent neglect of the west. President Davis tried to assure him that "the welfare of Missouri is as dear to me as that of other states of the Confederacy," but to most who commanded out here these and future words of comfort from Richmond sounded hollow when not accompanied by more men and guns.[2]

Yet the interest of Davis in the far west could not be entirely denied. Indeed, one of the first Confederate offensive campaigns of the war came to play on this stage, its principal actor being himself a native of the area, Henry Hopkins Sibley of Louisiana. With Davis' authorization, Sibley mounted a campaign in July and August 1861 to "liberate" the future Arizona and New Mexico. But the campaign started late, moved slowly, and saw a few small skirmishes. Finally, Sibley withdrew his little army, with nothing to show for his campaign and a command that was shattered. Sibley himself, already reputed to be a heavy drinker, would not be heard from again in this war. His career, like the Confederate hopes for Arizona and New Mexico and a southwestern empire stretching to the Pacific, ended in the heat and mesquite and cactus.[3] An early 1862 repeat invasion of New Mexico fared no better.

By the time Sibley returned to Texas, there was at last a new center of command in the region, which showed that Richmond had begun to realize the importance of coordinated control of the vastness. In January 1861 the War Department created the Trans-Mississippi District, to combine the two commands of Sterling Price and his Missouri state troops with the Arkansas and Louisiana regiments of General Ben McCulloch. The two generals had been feuding over just who should command whom; now Richmond sent General Earl Van Dorn to command both of them. Van Dorn seemed to get around a lot in these early days of the war. Indeed, given his assassination by an outraged husband a year later, he did not limit his circulation to the military.

Yet before Van Dorn could assume his new command, another campaign

A typical fighter of the west, Brigadier General
Ben McCulloch eschewed uniform trappings and
used his years of experience as an Indian fighter
and Texas Ranger to aid the Confederate struggle.
Author's collection

was already under way that, combined with Sibley's loss, would lose the Confederacy more territory in a single season than any other until the end of the war. The ensuing battle of Pea Ridge proved to be one of the hardest fights this side of the Mississippi. Van Dorn's attack was stopped, McCulloch was killed, and orders had to be given to retreat out of northern Arkansas. The Confederates withdrew some one hundred miles south, to the Arkansas River, leaving Missouri indisputably secure to the Union for the present and perhaps for good.

Then came more changes. With the fall of Forts Henry and Donelson in February 1862, and the preparations to attack Ulysses S. Grant's Yankee army at Pittsburg Landing, Van Dorn and his army were ordered across the Mississippi. Arkansas protested loudly and immediately, for Van Dorn thus virtually abandoned the state to the Federals. There may have been no choice for Richmond, but the gesture also demonstrated the way in which Davis viewed the Trans-Mississippi. Clearly it was a backwater of the war, not important enough to hold when its troops could be used elsewhere. That the same did not, and would not, hold true of other departments was demonstrated by the failure in future campaigns to weaken the army in, say, Virginia, for the benefit of other theaters of the war. That would happen only twice. To the Trans-Mississippi it happened repeatedly.

Despite temporarily removing its principal army, Richmond now actually extended the limits of the command and redesignated it the Department of the Trans-Mississippi. On May 26, 1862, the War Department redefined its borders to include Texas, Arkansas, Missouri, Louisiana, and Indian Territory. That looked fine on paper, when in fact Missouri and most of northern Arkansas were already behind enemy lines, and Indian Territory was too thinly manned by both sides for either to claim real hegemony. The following week, with Van Dorn now in command in Mississippi, a new general arrived, determined to, as he put it, "drive out the enemy or to perish in the attempt."[4] He was, of course, the prominent Arkansan Major General Thomas C. Hindman.

What he found on his arrival was not encouraging. There were barely 1,000 soldiers in all of Arkansas and only scattered and inadequately supplied commands in the rest of the department. Hindman set out ruthlessly to remedy the shortage, and though his highhanded methods outraged many—and got a few of them shot—within a few weeks he had over 18,000 men under arms and more awaiting organization. Despite this miraculous reversal of his weakness, Hindman held command for only two months before Richmond, in its wisdom, replaced him with yet another commander, Major General Theophilus Holmes.

Here was a perfect example of a phenomenon that P. G. T. Beauregard observed when he referred to the Confederacy's South Carolina command as a "department of refuge." Richmond had the unfortunate habit of detailing failed or incompetent officers who were too influential or high-ranking for dismissal to backwater areas like the Trans-Mississippi. Holmes had failed at everything thus far in the war, but he was close to Davis, a senior general, and one of the higher-ranking officers of the Old U.S. Army to come over to the South. He could not be dismissed. Instead Richmond simply banished him to Arkansas. If the people out in the Trans-Mississippi had resented Hindman for being something of a tyrant, they quickly came to feel even less enthusiasm for this new general, whom they quickly dubbed "Granny Holmes." At least one of his associates declared that in addition to being incompetent, he was also "a man suffering from softening of the brain."[5] Ill, almost deaf, unable to make a decision, he was a kindly man who wanted nothing more than to be left alone. Almost as bad, Richmond sent him subordinate commanders who were little better. General Gustavus W. Smith had fallen prey to complete nervous paralysis when command of the Army of Northern Virginia briefly fell to him after General Joseph E. Johnston was wounded at Seven Pines in June 1862. Davis never liked him anyhow, thanks to a prewar squabble between them. General John B. Magruder left the same eastern army under a cloud because of his performance during the peninsular campaign. Now both, along with the imperious Hindman, were assigned to Holmes as his senior generals. Thus, to manage the Confederacy's largest territorial command, and one of its most vital given its long border on the Mississippi, Richmond sent leftovers, invalids, and rejects, the flotsam of the war in the east.

Hindman, to his credit, at least felt an instinct to fight. He raised yet another 10,000 men in Arkansas and that fall set out to clear the state of the Yankees. Ignoring an order from Richmond that would have withdrawn another 10,000 men from the state to Mississippi, virtually all of the men he had just enlisted, Hindman advanced north to confront the Federals in the cliff-hanging battle at Prairie Grove. Defeated in the end, Hindman saw his army disintegrate on its retreat so that only a shadow was left when he came to a halt in Little Rock. Still undaunted, Hindman sent a small cavalry raid led by John S. Marmaduke north into Missouri, and so successful was Marmaduke that the Federals pulled almost entirely out of northern Arkansas to protect Missouri. For the rest of the winter almost all of that part of the state lay unoccupied by either side, and for the Confederates that was at least something of a victory.

But Arkansas was always the key to Missouri, especially for the Confederates. If they could not hold it, then all hope of regaining Missouri was gone, and Missouri was the key to the Trans-Mississippi. At the same time, the loss of Arkansas made Indian Territory to the west hard to hold and left western Louisiana virtually untenable. By holding the state, the Rebels posed a constant threat to Union security in Missouri and Yankee control of the Mississippi. As evidenced even by Marmaduke's small raid, a Confederate base in Arkansas could cause extraordinary consternation in the Union's western command by using only moderate resources.

The story was much different along the southern border of the department. There was action here, too, and this sector of the department could also bemoan its full share of third-rate generals. The Yankee blockade touched the department here, for Texas measured seven hundred miles of coastline from the mouth of the Rio Grande to the Louisiana line. The Confederates had to make attempts to fortify their more important harbors and early installed works at Galveston, Sabine Pass, and other river outlets, but no one could defend the entire line. Indeed, at one time Galveston's entire defense consisted of a battalion of city militia and several wooden tree trunks mounted on wheels and painted black to look like cannons in the hope of deceiving distant blockade ships into thinking these were formidable seacoast artillery. When the Federals prepared to attack the city in fall 1862, its garrison evacuated first. Hints of real action only came that winter when Magruder arrived, reorganized the forces in the District of Texas, turned two river steamers into gunboats, and attacked on New Year's Day 1863. He took Galveston back, and three weeks later, at Sabine Pass, more Rebel steamers helped capture Sabine City from the Yankees. These twin triumphs, small as they were, kept a steady stream of blockade runners coming into the ports thus opened for the South. After the fall of Vicksburg and the loss of the Mississippi in 1863, these ports would be the only routes of stead supply and communications for the department.

Then came Kirby Smith. He had been an unlucky general so far in the war. Just as his brigade reached Manassas for the first battle, a bullet wounded him before he ever got into the fight. In Braxton Bragg's invasion of Kentucky in late 1862, Smith feuded with Bragg, and their falling out contributed to the eventual doom of the campaign. But Kirby Smith remained a favorite of the president, gained a promotion, and was sent west to command western Louisiana in January 1863. A month later Richmond gave him the entire Trans-Mississippi. "It requires some energetic genius to restore affairs in that quarter," wrote a War Department bureau chief, and in Smith Davis thought he had the man.[6] Kirby Smith himself was not entirely easy about it. "My troubles will soon commence," he confided. He knew that everyone would find fault with him, that no commander could successfully administer the largest department of the Confederacy with its smallest army. With resignation, he said, "I shall be happy and cheerfully and manfully discharge my duty."[7]

When he assumed the new command on March 7, 1863, Kirby Smith began an inspection tour, his first destination Little Rock, where Holmes made his headquarters. As Smith made his way there, the new commander saw evidences all along the path of the mismanagement of the department. Deserters were everywhere along the roads. When he reached the state capital, he found Holmes positively delighted at being relieved. He told Kirby Smith that he gave up "charge of the elephant," as he called it, with enormous satisfaction.[8] In no time at all Smith would come to know the weight of that elephant.

Actually the new general found Arkansas, desertions to the contrary, to be not as bad as he had heard, but he saw immediately the cause of the disaffection and confusion in the department. "There was no general system, no common head," he reported to Davis. "Each district was acting independently." Attention seemed to be focused only on the point most immediately threatened at any one moment or else the point of most interest to the local commander. Thus, while Holmes and Hindman both wanted Smith to make his headquarters at Little Rock, close to the action, such as it was, Smith chose instead Shreveport, a more central location. Once there, he began to make other changes. Magruder, though difficult, had done well in Texas. He would retain that command. Major General Richard Taylor would command in western Louisiana. Hindman was sent off to Mississippi, where he could be troublesome to someone else for a change, and Holmes succeeded him in command in Arkansas for the time being.

Then there were the numbers Smith had to contend with. Officially on paper the department totaled 40,000 men, half in Arkansas, 11,000 with Magruder, and the rest with Taylor. In fact, sickness, lethargy, and incompetence had pared those numbers down by half or less, and the quality of many of the men in the ranks was not up to the standard of the early war regiments from these states. The cream of western soldiery had been drained away to the east, and Kirby Smith soon complained to Richmond that "the male population remaining are old men, or have furnished substitutes, are lukewarm, or are wrapped up in speculations and money-making."[9]

Nevertheless, Davis and the War Department expected that Kirby Smith would use this paper army, such as it was, in the great task not of defending its own territory but of supporting the struggle to save Vicksburg and preserve the Mississippi. This was sound policy for the moment, though it reflected the continuing attitude that the Trans-Mississippi was a secondary theater of the war and also failed to provide any uniform command for the struggle to save Vicksburg. Smith was told to ignore his own threatened northern border in Arkansas and throw troops across the Mississippi whenever and wherever possible to harass Grant, relegating Smith's command to the role of diversionary raiders. As for the Trans-Mississippi Department itself, Secretary of War James Seddon himself put into eloquent words the absolute lack of understanding of its problems in Richmond. "From the nature of the country," Seddon wrote (and Seddon had never *seen* that country), "I am satisfied that the whole country is among the most defensible in the world, and that comparatively few resolute, experienced men could repel hosts of invaders."[10]

Kirby Smith got the chance to see how his department could so easily repel hosts of invaders sooner than he expected. All through March and April he found himself unable to move in support of the Vicksburg garrison. He simply had too few men under arms to cover too much territory. Then the Yankees took the initiative. Ordered to take Port Hudson, Louisiana, on the Mississippi, Federal general Nathaniel P. Banks decided first to move west from his base in New Orleans to clear out some of the western side of the river and incidentally confiscate some cotton for speculation. Banks moved in April, and Taylor was ready to meet him at Fort Bisland, near Brashear City. Taylor stopped Banks at first, then had to begin a fifty-mile withdrawal north to Opelousas, and then moved on to Alexandria on the Red River. Smith, fearing a threat to the entire department, ordered all his forces to concentrate to Taylor's assistance. But Banks forced Taylor back even farther and threatened Shreveport itself. Banks took Alexandria, while Smith began to organize a counteroffensive. The Yankees finally left of their own accord to move at last on Port Hudson. Kirby Smith, left behind, was frustrated. Thinking that the fate of his own department depended largely on the struggle for Vicksburg, he felt, even while retreating, that he was at least contributing to the cause by keeping Banks away from cooperating with Grant. Alas, this action was not enough.

Kirby Smith endured mixed feelings of relief and anger at the result of the campaign. His department lay territorially as intact as before, though now destitute of cotton, crops, even thousands of slaves who had flocked to Banks' army. Worse, many citizens of Louisiana actually gave assistance to the enemy, even taking oaths of allegiance to the Union. Clearly, disloyalty ran rife within the Trans-Mississippi, yet another of the plague of problems that beset this entirely unhomogeneous command. And with Banks gone, Smith now had to move at once to give what assistance he could to Vicksburg. He ordered Taylor north to hit Grant's communications, but the movement came too late. Holmes fared no better when allowed to take his Arkansas command to threaten Grant on the west bank of the Mississippi. On July 4, even as the Vicksburg garrison was surrendering, Holmes made a bungled attack at Helena that was easily repulsed. Indeed, the only success of the season, and a small one, came when Taylor marched back south and captured the Yankee garrison at Brashear City.

In sum, Smith could take little pleasure from his first season of campaigning in the department. He could not help Vicksburg or Port Hudson; he could hardly defend Louisiana; the enemy still held much of northern Arkansas, into which it would advance again that spring; and now with the Mississippi lost the department sat utterly isolated from Richmond and the eastern Confederacy, except through the uncertain fortunes of blockade runners and an occasional mail runner stealing across the great river. Smith faced an enormous problem now, one not offered to other department commanders in the Confederacy. President Davis managed to state it very nicely on July 14 when he wrote to Smith, "You now have not merely a military, but also a political problem involved in your command."[11] The Confederate civil government could no longer maintain control over the region (to the extent that it had ever done so). Kirby Smith would have to exercise that control now.

In tandem with the governors of the states in his command, he would have to be general in chief and "exercise powers of civil administration." Kirby Smith would be war department and legislative and executive branches all in one. In all-encompassing powers, he would be the closest thing to a dictator ever seen on this continent. Davis did not actually specify this, but it was a natural effect of the loss of the Mississippi. There had to be a central authority, with the authority to maintain itself, and that could only be the general. He recognized this without being told. The day before Davis wrote to Smith, he had already convened his first meeting with the governors and the state supreme court justices. When they met in August, it seemed clear that the general regarded his authority as superior to theirs. Soon thereafter he turned to affairs of foreign policy, flagrantly outside a military commander's normal area of authority.

On September 1 Smith wrote to Confederate commissioner John Slidell in Paris about the intertwined affairs of France and Mexico and the Confederacy; all centered in his department, he felt. Declaring that the recent French intervention and occupation of Mexico made the establishment of the Confederacy a matter of profound importance to the French since it would provide a buffer between Mexico and the United States, Kirby Smith urged Slidell to talk with the emperor Napoleon about the preparations being made by the Yankees to subjugate the department. Should the Yankees overrun it, said the general, then

Napoleon would find "a grasping, haughty, and imperious neighbor" on its northern border. If the emperor wanted to avoid the threat of a Yankee invasion of Mexico itself, he would first have to aid the Confederacy in establishing its own primacy in the region and in gaining its independence. "This succor must come speedily," he added, "or it will be too late." Without foreign assistance, "or an extraordinary interposition of providence, less than twelve months will see this fair country irretrievably lost, and the French protectorate in Mexico will find a hostile power on their frontier of exhaustless resources and great military strength impelled by revenge and the traditional policy of its government to overthrow all foreign influence on the American continent."[12] Kirby Smith was declaring, in effect, that the Monroe Doctrine was a Yankee policy, not a Confederate one.

But if Napoleon decided to act, he would have to do it at once. "If the policy of the emperor looks to an intervention," said Smith, "he should take immediate military possession of the east bank of the Rio Grande." That would give Kirby Smith his only route of supply since the loss of Vicksburg and the Mississippi. Then, dangling the old carrot of cotton, he assured Napoleon that the staple trade west of the great river "will thus be secured to the French market." "I have not written for diplomatic effect," said Smith disingenuously, "but have stated truths which should have weight."[13] Yet in one brief letter he had invoked diplomacy, economics, foreign trade, military intervention, the foreign policy of his enemy, and a neat summation of the change in the military situation since Grant's conquest of the Mississippi. It was a letter such as none other written by any Confederate general in this war and showed clearly the all-encompassing scope of his powers in the Trans-Mississippi as the general experienced them. Indeed, by the end of 1863 people were already beginning to refer to the Trans-Mississippi as "Kirby Smithdom." The man and the region were to become inseparable in the minds of its inhabitants.

In addition to his other worries, the general found himself, thanks to the peculiar needs and resources of his command, forced to rely heavily upon a type of soldiery little seen in the war to the east: guerrillas. It was a mode of warfare he did not like. "It only entails additional persecution and distress upon our friends," he lamented, "without advancing our cause."[14] Yet the guerrillas were undeniably skilled fighters—as well as being magnificent plunderers and scoundrels. Their mode of warfare did at least allow for maximum disruption of enemy affairs over the widest possible area with a minimum of manpower.

Hindman had encouraged them, and Smith had to confess their occasional utility, but after the Lawrence, Baxter Springs, and Centralia massacres, they were an embarrassment and soon proved to be uncontrollable.

Yet by the end of 1863 Kirby Smith could point to few other "victories" except those of the bushwhackers. That left him little choice but to defend the likes of Quantrill when other regular Confederate officers assailed them. The guerrillas, he declared, were "bold, fearless men . . . composed, I understand, in a measure of the very best class of Missourians."[15] If this was the *best* class of Missourian, then it spoke for a sorry state of affairs in Missouri manhood. Generals such as Henry McCulloch characterized the guerrillas as "but little if at all removed from the wildest savage. I regard them as but one shade better than highwaymen."[16]

Such, then, was the pitiful state of the Trans-Mississippi at the end of 1863, and it did not get any better during the balance of the war. Often forgotten and sometimes scorned by Davis and Richmond, used as a graveyard for incompetents and a recruiting place for the eastern armies, stripped of its produce, and now cut off from the rest of the Confederacy, the department and its semidictator could look with embarrassment only to murderers and cutthroats for its successes. There would be other small triumphs to be proud of in time, armies fighting honorably once more, but in 1863, as before, nearly one-half of the Confederacy was left to fight a singular, solitary war, largely on its own.

No wonder that in September Kirby Smith revealingly appealed to Paris and not to Richmond. No wonder that as 1864 dawned, he felt in a mood to complain. "The Government must not send me any more cast off material," he said. "I shall protest against the sending of any more supernumerary brigadier generals to this department." He already had too many officers who had been exiled here from the east, men without commands who stayed "shelved away somewhere in the interior of Texas, comfortably drawing their pay in retirement." Given his preference, he would hand them all muskets and put them in the ranks. "The means and resources of the Government will be centered with the armies of Tennessee and Virginia," he lamented. "We here will be left to struggle against immense odds, as best we may, with the feeble resources at our command." "The commander of this department," he declared sadly, "has no bed of roses."[17]

As 1864 dawned, Kirby Smith could number some 38,356 men present for duty in his far-flung empire, and that was a dramatic improvement over earlier days. Just a year before Hindman had had in all of Arkansas a mere 5,600. But there was still little that the general could do with such a force when it was spread out over tens of thousands of miles. For the rest of the war, with one exception, the initiative in the department lay with the enemy. Indeed, the impact of Grant's great 1864 overland campaign in Virginia was to be felt here first when in March, fully two months before the campaign opened, Banks set forth once more from his headquarters, bound on a campaign up the Red River toward Texas, its intent largely to establish Federal military power near the border with Mexico and the French interventionists there who had Lincoln a bit worried.

Banks bungled the campaign from the start. He moved slowly, failed to secure cooperation from the widely scattered wings of his army, and encountered low water on the Red that encumbered the passage of the gunboats cooperating with him. Kirby Smith's subordinates, chiefly Taylor, did a good job in delaying and harassing the enemy. Finally, at Sabine Crossroads Taylor won a victory, and though suffering a defeat the next day at Pleasant Hill, he had discouraged Banks from going any farther. Banks retreated to Alexandria, and there the Rebels sniped at him sufficiently to drive him back out of the department for good, almost losing his fleet in the process. Banks would be relieved of command, something of a blow to the Confederates because his incompetence had always been a boon to them, and Smith and Taylor had a falling out. Soon Taylor was relieved, too.

At the same time, another expedition had been launched in Arkansas, its object to invade the southwestern part of the state to divert troops from resisting Banks. In the end the Federals got as far as Camden. But then, with Banks turned back, Kirby Smith moved his command north to strike, forcing the Yankees out of Camden and pushing them to Jenkins' Ferry, where he narrowly failed to cut off the Federals' retreat to Little Rock with nothing to show for their efforts.

There matters rested until the fall, when out of the Trans-Mississippi shot not only the last offensive of the Confederates in this department but also the Confederacy's final invasion of Union soil. In September Sterling Price led all of the cavalry of the department on a raid north through Arkansas and into Missouri, its objective the Missouri River. It was an ill-conceived and ultimately ill-fated effort to retake Missouri for the South, a case of attempting far too much with far too little. Many of Price's troopers were not even armed. But he made excellent progress, penetrating deep into Missouri before being stopped finally and decisively in the Battle of Westport, the largest engagement west of the Mississippi. Retreating constantly thereafter, Price suffered several more rearguard defeats and did not finally arrive back in friendly lines in Arkansas until early December, having lost the majority of his army in casualties, stragglers, and desertions along the way. It was a sad end to a bold campaign and was the final organized military operation in the Trans-Mississippi. Thereafter, for the balance of what little remained of the war, Kirby Smithdom saw only guerrilla activity.

Unwilling to accept the verdict of defeat when it finally came, many of the men and officers of the department declined to surrender and instead went off to adventure in Mexico or into other exile at war's end. In time, most returned to the reunited states, confused, uncertain, wondering what lay ahead.

A number of questions beg to be asked when one considers the Confederate Trans-Mississippi experience. It is in the nature of history that few can be answered definitively. Was it worth trying to hold the department? Could it have been held? What did the South gain from the Trans-Mississippi? What was the soundest grand strategic use of the region? Did Davis and Richmond have any choice but to follow the course they pursued? The answers depend largely on hindsight, which all too easily ignores the political and emotional pressures of the time that could not then be ignored. Thus, Davis and his government are entitled at least to caution on the part of those who would judge them. The answers that may be illuminating to us today can hardly be taken as truths that should necessarily have been obvious 130 years ago.

In the end, the attempts to hold onto the Trans-Mississippi were probably not worth the effort and expenditure. For all of the complaints of Smith and others, the material and manpower resources withdrawn from the region were not that significant, and even though the Trans-Mississippi received fleeting attention from Richmond, that was probably more than should have been diverted from the truly decisive operations in Tennessee and Virginia. And especially after the loss of the Mississippi in 1863, the Confederacy ceased to derive any military benefit at all from the department, unless it was the convenience of having a "Russian front," as it were, into which incompetent officers could be banished.

Even the oft-quoted justification that Kirby Smith kept significantly larger numbers of Federals occupied out west, away from Grant and Sherman, does not really stand under scrutiny. At the end of 1863 the Federals directly arrayed against Smith totaled just over 40,000 men and 163 cannons. At this same time, his forces numbered 38,356, a difference of less than 1,700. In fall 1864 Smith's army counted 45,927 and 120 guns, while the Federals in the Departments of Missouri and Arkansas and Kansas totaled 41,018 and 148 guns, a difference of almost 5,000 in Smith's favor. And at war's end Smith himself would boast that he had an army of 60,000 men, a boast corroborated by Yankee intelligence, while Union forces contesting the territory came to 63,700.[18]

Thus, far from holding significantly larger numbers of Yankees from joining the armies east of the Mississippi, Kirby Smith's forces rather consistently held down almost exactly their own equivalent numbers of the enemy and sometimes even fewer. It would be more accurate to say that Yankee forces in the region successfully tied down vital *Confederate* manpower that might have achieved much more elsewhere (if Davis could have overcome the political consequences of abandoning the department or even had the ability to move those regiments east of the Mississippi). That accomplished nothing at all, of course. The 60,000 Confederates out there in 1865 were proportionately a lot more important to Richmond than the 60,000 Federals were to Washington. How much more might those 60,000 have accomplished if used to reinforce Lee in Virginia or Johnston or Hood in Georgia?

Furthermore, despite Secretary of War Seddon's ill-informed opinion, those 60,000 faced a task that may have been impossible, for in the context of Civil War military operations, the region possessed relatively few defensive advantages. To be sure, the Gulf Coast was tough to penetrate, and the border with Mexico was secure, but the entire western and northwestern territories were open to easy invasion, the rivers ran in the wrong direction to provide defensive barriers, and the northern border in Arkansas and Missouri was little better. In short, whereas the geography of, say, Virginia, was almost all in favor of its defenders, the terrain of the Trans-Mississippi, especially south of the Arkansas, favored the enemy invaders.

So given all the problems inherent in what the South tried to do out here, what—in the light of hindsight—*should* Davis have done with the Trans-Mississippi? Arguably, his best course would have been the one that, above all, he could never have pursued—give it all up at the war's outset in the greater interest of the rest of the Confederacy, which was so much more defensible. The Trans-Mississippi was a border full of vulnerabilities. The Mississippi made a natural barrier, formidable and easily defended with sufficient manpower. Writing off Missouri, Arkansas, Texas, and western Louisiana might well have denied troops from those states to Confederate armies east of the river, yet the fact is that the overwhelming majority of soldiers from the Trans-Mississippi never left the department anyhow, Smith's complaints to the contrary.

The withdrawal of such troops as he could raise and the abandonment of the region without a fight would not necessarily have been such a boon to the enemy, either. Tens of thousands of pro-Confederate men in the region would still have practiced the guerrilla and bushwhacking trade, one mode of warfare that always occupied large numbers of Yankees. More significant by far, however, the abandonment of Texas to the Federals would have put Lincoln face to face with the French interlopers in Mexico, with diplomatic and even military possibilities that could hardly have failed to benefit the Confederacy. In the end, by the theory that half a loaf is better than none, Richmond might have greatly enhanced the chances of independence for the Confederacy east of the river by abandoning the west. And then, independence achieved, Texas, Arkansas, and the rest might have been able to negotiate a peaceable transfer from the United States to the Confederate.

Of course, it would have been political suicide for Davis and his government to give up such ground without a fight, and he certainly never considered it an option. These states had seceded along with the rest and were making common cause. Southern nationalism and honor required that he try to hold *all* of the South, even those portions that had relatively little to contribute. But in the end he tried to accomplish simply too much with too few resources. Valor alone was not enough.

Part Three

Excuses, Turning Points, and Defeats

Lost Will, Lost Causes

O N CHRISTMAS DAY 1862 an unknown soldier of Company C, Fourth Kentucky Infantry, serving with Braxton Bragg's Confederate Army of Tennessee camped at Murfreesboro, repeated a custom he had commenced the
Yule season before. Opening his company's clothing account book, he wrote a
distinctly nonmilitary entry for the holiday. "December the 25th, 1862," he
penned. "Another Christmas has come and still we are engaged in the Bloody
Struggle to be free. . . . For more than two years we have been combating with
the Vandal horde—to Day our army is stronger and more thoughroly equipped
than ever before." He confidently hoped for eventual victory.[1]

That nameless Kentuckian was hardly alone in this, the continent's second
dark war winter. Following the almost leisurely pace of the conflict in 1861, succeeded by months of relative inactivity, 1862 erupted upon North and South
with a ferocity that many had not imagined, and on the surface most of the
laurels went to the Confederacy. Five months of campaigning on Virginia's
York-James Peninsula saw Lincoln's armies beaten, outfoxed, stymied again and
again, climaxed by George McClellan's defeat in the Seven Days and his final
withdrawal from the Old Dominion. In the Shenandoah Valley "Stonewall"
Jackson played nemesis to three separate Yankee armies, driving back each in
turn, then joining Lee in the summer to visit yet another disaster on the enemy
on the fields of the old Bull Run battlefield. Only at Antietam in September did
Lee finally suffer defeat, yet militarily it was rather a hollow victory for Mc-
Clellan because it did not change the status quo in the eastern theater of the
war. Then in December Lee revenged himself when he handed McClellan's successor, Ambrose Burnside, a crushing and humiliating disaster at Fredericksburg.

From the Yankee point of view things looked a great deal better in the west,
yet the bluecoat Christmas out there was not that much more encouraging than
for Burnside's battered veterans on the Rappahannock. Ulysses S. Grant's cap-
tures of Forts Henry and Donelson in February opened the rivers that flowed

Excuses, Turning Points, and Defeats

into the Confederate heartland. David G. Farragut's fleet took New Orleans in April, leaving Lincoln in control of both ends of the Mississippi. And an initially successful invasion of Kentucky by Bragg had been turned back in October, leaving that vital state more or less secure for the Union. But then Grant was surprised by the enemy at Shiloh in April, a battle that narrowly missed ending in disaster for his army. Efforts that summer to take Vicksburg failed spectacularly, Baton Rouge was lost to the Rebels for a time, a major new river fortress at Port Hudson seemed to close the Mississippi to the Federals' further attempts to move north, and Grant's overland drive on Vicksburg from the north was stopped dramatically in December by the destruction of his supply base at Holly Springs, Mississippi, while William T. Sherman's waterborne move against Vicksburg ended in frustration at Chickasaw Bayou.

As if unable to let 1862 end without one final blow to the already oppressed Union effort, the very last day of the year saw Bragg having it all his own way in yet another battle just commencing at Murfreesboro, along Stones River. Meanwhile behind the lines, while the blockade interfered with Southern commerce, it did not stop it; Union command in Virginia lay in chaos, while Lee led the finest and most experienced command system of the war to date; and even the moral uplift of the Emancipation Proclamation met with scorn and skepticism from the Federal soldiers who were to fight for it. "Old Abe has got to whip the south first," smirked an Indiana soldier in the wake of Fredericksburg, "and that is a thing that he will not do very soon."[2] As the old year died and a new one loomed, Union morale fell to its lowest ebb yet, while Confederate optimism reached its highest level since the euphoric days after Fort Sumter and First Manassas. If those emotions could have been weighed each against the other, then the balance of will between North and South—the will to continue, whatever the cost, the will to win—would not have shown a promising measure on the scale for the old Union.

But then came 1863, the year that changed everything irrevocably. In the east, where all before had been a tale of defeat, came crushing Union success. Despite handing Lee one of the most brilliant victories of the war at Chancellorsville in May, the Army of the Potomac, under its newest and last commander of the war, George G. Meade, inflicted on the Army of Northern Virginia a beating at Gettysburg from which it never entirely recovered, in the process virtually shattering the command system Lee had so ably assembled. At Brandy Station Federal cavalry finally showed itself the equal of Rebel horse, and the whole Southern cause suffered an enormous emotional blow with the death of its paladin Stonewall Jackson.

Out west matters were even worse for the South. Grant resumed his relentless advance on Vicksburg and took it in July, with the fall of Port Hudson following in a few days, thereby leaving the Union in control of the full length of the Mississippi for the rest of the war. The Confederacy was now divided, its vast Trans-Mississippi Department permanently cut off from the rest of the country. The battle at Stones River that Bragg began so auspiciously on December 31, 1862, had turned to defeat by January 2, 1863. For the rest of the year, when not fighting the enemy, Bragg battled with his own generals, in the process crippling his own command system. He won only one great victory in this theater in 1863, at Chickamauga in September, and then lost all its gains, along with Chattanooga and east Tennessee, with his crushing defeat at Lookout Mountain and Missionary Ridge, followed hard by James Longstreet's repulse at Knoxville in December. It was, in short, a year of unparalleled disaster for the Confederacy, easily the equivalent of what 1862 had been for the North in its emotional impact and arguably much worse. And for those fighting for the Union, the year turned night into day. "The dawn has broken," a Yankee officer wrote as victory followed victory, "and the collapsed confederacy has no place where it can hide its head."[3] And somewhere in that frantic year a will to win was born, and across the lines there grew a willingness to accept defeat.

A human experience like the Civil War in which millions of men and women participated, and from whom innumerable letters, diaries, and memoirs have survived, naturally offers the selective student the opportunity to find somewhere all of the statements and citations necessary to assert just about any theory, whether right or wrong, no matter how profound or absurd (and some get pretty absurd). But a random sampling of a dozen or so such expressions, out of a pool of millions of participants, hardly offers a base for meaningful broad conclusions. Much greater numbers of sources are required, and while the subject of numbers of any kind is always a problem in Civil War historiography, some are available that may provide telling clues to the changing states of mind and will on either side of Mason and Dixon's line.

Obviously there are few, if any, indicators of sentiment in an armed conflict more telling than the numbers of men willing to risk their lives for their cause by enlisting. At the same time, it is almost axiomatic that volunteer enlistments always run the highest in the initial months of a conflict, when pa-

Excuses, Turning Points, and Defeats

triotism and martial spirit are at their peak. Certainly that was the case in 1861, when both sides experienced the greatest enlistment turnout of any year of the war. But then came 1862. In that year of victory upon victory, 100,000 or more Southern men volunteered for Confederate service, or about 30 percent of the number who had volunteered in 1861.[4] Comparable figures for the North are elusive and are complicated by the wholesale reenlistment of many of the nine- and twelve-month regiments raised in 1861. Nevertheless, the total number of men present for duty in 1862 rose by 170,000, and at least 90,000 of them were new enlistees in new regiments.[5] Yet that was only about 20 percent of the enlistment volume of the year before and barely 5 percent of all wartime enrollments. By comparison, the South enlisted 12 percent of its total wartime manpower in 1862, more than doubling the enemy performance.

But then a year later, with the battlefield turning against the Rebels, how much different were these evidences of patriotism and commitments. In the Union another 90,000 men volunteered in 1863, most of them for terms of three years or the duration of the war, essentially the same performance as the year before, even though the available pool of manpower was static or increasing slightly by the extension of enlistments to black men.[6] Across the lines, however, Confederate enlistments fell by 25 percent to 75,000.[7] Of course, the available manpower pool was always smaller in the South, and the proportion of military-age men below Mason and Dixon's line who enlisted was always higher than among those above. On both sides the enactment of conscription laws had the effect of boosting the impetus to volunteer instead. Yet all factors considered, it seems evident that something was at work in 1863 that was not there in 1862, and that something was staying the natural fall-off of enlistments in the North while failing to stop it in the South.

This is even more evident in an equally significant barometer of moral and emotional will and commitment—desertion. In 1862 in the Union Army it was epidemic. When the year began for the Army of the Potomac, for instance, not more than 10,000 were absent without leave. By year's end, however, that number had risen to 100,000 for just this army alone. Since those present for duty numbered just over 100,000 in December 1862 following Fredericksburg, it requires only a small command of math to see that fully 50 percent of the officially enrolled Army of the Potomac was absent without leave and subject to being regarded as having deserted. From some states as many as 25 percent of their 1862 recruits deserted.[8] But after a year of success in the field, the desertion rate for the entire Union Army in 1863 was down to 4,647 a month, or about 56,000 for the year.[9] Of course, that is still a dramatically high figure, as desertion rates always were for Civil War armies, but when compared to the 18 percent increase in the Confederate desertion rate between 1862 and 1863, it suggests a stiffening of resolve and willpower—or self-respect—on the one hand and a decrease on the other. Toward the end of the latter year the Richmond government estimated that from 33 to 50 percent of all soldiers officially in service were absent from their commands.[10] Federal troops captured Confederate mailbags in which the commanding sentiments expressed by private soldiers were weariness of the war and a growing conviction that the North was too powerful to beat. In August 1863 an enrolling officer in South Carolina lamented to Richmond that "it is no longer a reproach to be known as a deserter," and more and more once-committed Rebels were beginning to agree with the Georgia boy who wrote in dejection after the loss of Chattanooga, "There is no use fighting any longer no how, for we are done gon up the Spout."[11]

It did not help that thousands of Confederate soldiers were held in service beyond the expiration of their enlistments when Richmond automatically extended the service of many twelve-month regiments to three years or the war. Discontent over such arbitrary treatment led to small-scale mutinies in some regiments and to long-lasting resentment in more. Thus, voluntary reenlistments in the Confederacy dwindled, and the resort to military conscription proved a substantial failure thanks to defective laws, inadequate machinery for the execution of those laws, and what one historian has called "the failure of the spirit of the people."[12] By November 1863 Major Samuel Melton of the Adjutant and Inspector General's Office in Richmond was warning the secretary of war that "the crisis is a fearful one, and men must be found to constitute our armies, else all is lost."[13]

But those men came forward only in ever-decreasing numbers in the years following 1863, while the Yankees' strength remained overwhelming despite the heavy losses that attended their offensives. The South began 1862 with 210,000 men present for duty, and at the end of that banner year those numbers had grown to 253,000. A year later, at the end of 1863, that strength had declined by 10 percent. Federals present for duty also diminished in 1863, but Lincoln's armies still ended their great year with 611,000, 16 percent more than they had had at the dawn of 1862.[14]

Of course, any change or shift in the balance of willpower in a conflict can-

Excuses, Turning Points, and Defeats

not be measured solely by the men in the field. Virtually every single soldier had been a civilian when the war began, and many remained such through several months or even years of its progress. Equally important for almost every man in uniform on either side, there was a family back home whose attitudes, morale, and willpower played an integral role in sustaining his fighting spirit. Any war, and most especially a conflict fought on home territory, is decided as much on the hearth as on the battlefield.

There is an oft-stated political axiom heard with annoying regularity every four years that elections are decided far less by grand issues than by the price of bread and milk. Certainly the same can be said in large degree of the commitment of any people at war. However much they may be buoyed by the success of their armies, if they cannot eat, if they cannot earn a living, if they cannot afford to buy or cannot produce the goods they need, then disillusion, dissent, and demoralization are the almost inevitable result. Give people those things, and their support for men in arms soars. Deny these things, and concern and commitment for the war effort disappear in the overriding concern for individual survival.

During the Civil War neither government had a department of commerce to calculate and release annual figures for gross national product, and such numbers do not in any case necessarily indicate the personal, individual consequences of an economy upon the men and women called on to support a war effort. Yet even without such numbers, we know full well of the enormous industrial, manufacturing, and agricultural superiority of the North both at the outset of the war and throughout its course. So healthy was Yankee manufacturing that industrial job opportunities were the chief deterrent to volunteer enlistments. Why would an ambitious young man enroll in the army for $13 a month when he could make four times that as a sign maker or a clerk in a dry goods store?[15] No wonder the governments, state and federal, paid bounties to attract men to the military.

The salient point is that there was plenty of work for everyone, including unskilled immigrants and increasing numbers of women. To be sure, agriculture had a bad year in 1863, thanks to a terrible drought that left overall yield down 78 million bushels in grains alone over the year before. Yet crops such as tobacco soared, and livestock production—at least as evidenced in rising exports—went up some 10 percent.[16] As for industrial output, despite the conversion of much of manufacturing to military necessities, there was no shortage of consumer goods evident to the great bulk of Union citizens. In short,

Yankees had enough to eat, employment for those who wanted it, stores well stocked with the things they needed, and sufficient money to buy at least some of them.

Of course, the war put strains on the individual. Inflation was inevitable. A survey of fifty-five basic consumer goods and manufacturers' raw materials showed an overall average price increase of 29 percent in 1863. The coffee that was $2.80 a pound in 1862 was $33.00 by the end of 1863. Corn went up 60 percent thanks to the drought.[17] And despite the increase in wages, the accompanying growth of inflation canceled any gains for most people. By the end of 1863 the rise in prices had resulted in about a 20 percent decline in real buying power for most Northerners.[18] Certainly there were protests and strikes over such a situation, but many proved successful as new unions formed and employment remained high and with it the workers' sense of national morale.

How much different the situation was in the Confederacy by the end of 1863. Production of almost everything lagged or suffered diversion to the military. The same drought that hurt Northern harvests took its toll on the South. With a much higher proportion of military-age men in uniform, the struggling nation had far fewer able-bodied men to remain at home to earn a living or get in a crop to feed a family, and in any case there was little available employment. The rampant inflation of Confederate currency produced price increases at the start of 1863 of 300 percent, while workers earned only 55 percent more than the year before.[19] And the inflation continued at an ever-worsening pace. In the four months after Gettysburg, prices went up 70 percent. The price of gold escalated by 700 percent of its December 1862 rate, whereas in the North it inflated by only 17 percent. To put these figures in the kind of terms so beloved of economists, with a base point of 100 in February 1861, by the time 1863 dawned, overall the price index in the Union had risen only to 114. In the Confederacy it had hit 686.[20]

It needs little grasp of national psychology to anticipate what such devastating economic woes do to people at war, especially when they know themselves to be military, industrial, and economic runners-up from the start. Little work, less hard money, inflated currency, scarcity of consumer goods, equally scarce foodstuffs thanks to drought and military impressment, all combine to produce on the hearthside an impulse for self-preservation that takes easy precedence over national survival, especially when the armies defending that hearthside are meeting defeat.

Active demonstrations of the loss of will are less directly obvious in a civil-

Excuses, Turning Points, and Defeats

ian population than among soldiers, who simply desert. For the most part, this loss is revealed in expressions of defeatism, dissent, civil unrest such as riots, and, in the extreme, overt disloyalty or treason. There were examples of each of these in both the North and South in 1863, but overwhelmingly so in the latter. Indeed, with the exception of some labor strikes, most settled amicably, the only serious outbreak of civil disturbance in the Union during the entire war was the New York Draft Riots of July 12–15, 1863. More than one hundred people were killed, most of them rioters, yet the impulse behind the outbreak proved to be more class and racial frictions than any opposition to the war or conscription.[21] Dissent in the Union chiefly took the constitutional form of political opposition, with even the much-overrated Copperhead movement op-

Destruction like this, rather than loss of will, defeated the South.
U.S. Army Military History Institute, Carlisle, Pa.

erating chiefly within the system. In comparatively few cases, most notably that of Clement L. Vallandigham of Ohio, did Federal authorities feel the threat to be sufficient to justify overstepping the constitutional right of free speech. Though opposition to the Lincoln administration, and even to the war itself, was widespread, the civil population was never sufficiently dissatisfied with its own personal circumstances to shift the balance of will in the Union against prosecuting the war to victory.

Meanwhile those same individual and economic woes that left so many in the Confederacy hungry, cynical, disillusioned, and, most of all, fearful for their individual personal and family welfare contributed enormously to the widespread outbreak of dissent and disloyalty. Bread riots, essentially spontaneous uprisings of wives and widows of soldiers who took violent action against high prices and short supplies, broke out from Richmond to the Gulf Coast in spring 1863. "We are starving," cried one woman. She demanded bread. "That is little enough for the government to give us after it has taken all our men."[22] These riots, too, grew in part from class resentments. "Our children are starving while the rich roll in wealth," some cried, but far more did the series of outbreaks stem from want, scarcity, and the overcrowding of cities caused by tens of thousands of refugees uprooted from their homes by the advancing Yankee armies. The war, even the independence of the South, no longer mattered to these people. They needed to eat. These are the same women who in 1863 begin writing to their husbands in the army, actually encouraging desertion. "Before God," one wife wrote to her man in uniform, "if you do not come home I think we shall die." Such appeals were hard to resist. "We are poor men and are willing to defend our country," one Mississippian had written earlier in the war, "but our families [come] first."[23] National defeat, in other words, was preferable to personal ruin.

From such civilian travail and disillusionment with Confederate authorities it was but a small step, first to the formation of peace societies throughout the less affluent parts of the South, and then to the active disloyalty of organizations formed specifically to injure the Rebel war effort. The disaffection took many forms. By 1863 Southern men were enlisting in Union blue, and before the war was done, every Confederate state but South Carolina would send organized white regiments into the Union Army.[24] In the less settled areas where Confederate civil authority was difficult to enforce, bands of deserters and Unionists held virtual dominion. In North Carolina a clandestine group styled the Order of the Heroes of America was formed, with counterparts in most

Excuses, Turning Points, and Defeats

other states and reportedly even within the Army of Northern Virginia. One woman in North Carolina echoed the loss of will of tens of thousands during 1863 when she wrote her husband that "the people is all turning to Union here since the Yankees has got Vicksburg. I want you to come home as soon as you can after you git this letter."[25]

In time whole regions, such as the southwestern counties of Virginia, seethed with disloyalty. By the end of 1863 plans were already being laid by the Heroes of America to form its own "Free State of Southwest Virginia," with a full slate of elected officials, many openly known to Confederate authorities and brazenly parading their sympathies.[26] Not only had these and thousands like them lost the will to win the war—if indeed they ever had it in these largely Unionist rural counties—but also now they were actively committed to seeing the South lose. Not only did they form proportionately a larger bloc of disaffected citizens than did the peace and pro-Confederate elements in the North, but they also did work in sabotage, providing intelligence and encouraging desertions, that did much to disrupt Confederate authority and was measurably more effective and harmful.

For those not willing to make such a strident expression of dissent, the only other avenue of lawful protest was the ballot box. Not surprisingly, their votes cast the same shadow as their deeds. It is, of course, almost traditional that the ruling party suffers some losses in nonpresidential election years, and in 1862, after a year of near-constant reverses, Lincoln's administration took a heavy beating. Two governorships, three state legislatures, and thirty-four congressional seats went to the opposition. While not as bad as many have interpreted these losses, they might well have been the beginning of a landslide repudiation of the war effort if 1863 had not offered victories. But when off-year elections took place in late summer 1863, Lincoln regained majorities in the New York, Ohio, and Pennsylvania legislatures by substantial margins.[27] Gettysburg and Vicksburg had stiffened the resolve of the wavering. At almost the same time, the Confederacy's second general congressional election took place. Of course, there were no parties as such, only pro- or antiadministration candidates, and Jefferson Davis nearly lost his Congress. Thirty-eight percent of the representatives and 46 percent of the senators elected proved to be open opponents of his administration. Governorships were lost, and the Confederate national government, which two years before had been supported by a solid majority, would have to depend largely upon coalitions from now on to function at all.[28]

Thus, by every measurable indicator available, the sentiment of the people at home and of the men in the field shows the dramatic shift from a depressed and faltering North against an invigorated and confident South at the end of 1862 to a near-exact reversal a year later. Yet this is still just the skeleton of the changing balance of will and resolve. This shift needs human expression to give it flesh and form, to remove it from the domain of mere numbers and place it in the realm of the humanity that produced it.

Such expressions, especially those of the Confederate civilians behind the lines, reveal the depths to which their spirits sagged after the euphoric days of 1862. A year later, as New Year's Day 1864 dawned, the oft-quoted Richmond diarist Mary Boykin Chesnut heard tablemates declare, "I think we are more like the sailors who break into the spirits closet when they find out the ship must sink. There seems to be for the first time a resolute feeling to enjoy the brief hour and never look beyond the day"; another was even more glum, saying, "I have no hope."[29] Even before the end of this pivotal year, in late July 1863 a prominent North Carolinian surveyed the loss of heart of his fellow Tarheels and wrote, "The one great demand of the people of this part of the state is peace—peace upon any terms. . . . They may perhaps prefer that the independence of the South should be acknowledged, but this they believe cannot now be obtained."[30] Late that November a man in Richmond observed, "We are a shabby looking people now—gaunt, and many in rags. . . . Everywhere the people are clamorous against the sweeping impressments of crops."[31] One lonely wife had a solution. "I have made up my mind that the only way to end the war is to have the soldiers all rise & kill off the officers & then I do think the[re] would be something done towards ending it."[32] Defeatism and discouragement spread rapidly behind the lines, spurred on by the disasters of 1863. At year's end a Confederate War Department official privately confessed, "I have never actually despaired of the cause, priceless, holy as it is, but my faith . . . is yielding to a sense of hopelessness."[33]

These sentiments were echoed in the armies these citizens were supposed to support, though there the transformation wrought during that twelve-month period loomed more frighteningly. "One cannot imagine the degree of confidence and high spirits displayed by our men," one of Lee's officers wrote a week before Fredericksburg. A lieutenant with Bragg could boast that "by heroic endurance, hard fighting & the favor of a just God, we have successfully resisted their every attempt at subjugation."[34] A year's passing revealed the spread of significantly different sentiments. "Upon the hole I dont think there is much to be made by fiting, " wrote a North Carolinian. "I wish this war was over and we all could come home to stay." "The men in the army generally are heartily sick of the war," declared an Alabamian. Thus, they deserted, as one Reb promised his family he would during the winter of 1863–1864, "so you may depend upon it," he wrote them, "for I intend to get out of this war in some way."[35] At that same time, the Federals noticed the sharp increase in the number of Confederates deserting to Union lines, declaring, as one put it, that "their cause is hopeless, and there is no farther use of fighting."[36] By those last days of 1863 and the first weeks of 1864, rapidly growing numbers of Southerners were facing squarely a shift of balance within themselves—the balance between their commitment to the stakes of the war, their patriotism, and their Confederate ideology, on the one hand, and their commitment to their own and their families' welfare, eating, and living on the other. In the parlance of the cold war of a century later, more and more some of them decided "better blue than dead."

It looked little better among their leaders. At the end of 1862 President Jefferson Davis prepared to tell his Congress that the course of the war to date "affords ample excuse for congratulation and demands the most fervent expression of our thankfulness to the Almighty Father, who has blessed our cause." Their cause, he declared, "afforded another example of the impossibility of subjugating a people determined to be free." A year later he publicly admitted that they had suffered "grave reverses," while privately he owned up to being "in the depths of gloom." "We are," he said, "in the darkest hour of our political existence."[37]

Across the lines a metamorphosis took place. In December 1862, after a year of defeat capped by the Fredericksburg debacle, the soldiers in blue were wallowing in depression. "Patriotism *played out* with me some time ago," asserted one, "the more so after the battle over the River." Weeks later that Fredericksburg veteran deserted. Another confessed that "if it were not treason to tell the truth I would say that the whole army would run home if they had the chance." "We are all tired of the war the whole army," said another; "we never shall whip them I believe." "Why not confess we are worsted and come to an agreement?" asserted another Yank that December. On all sides the bluecoat soldiers wished for peace, at almost any cost.[38] But in twelve more months those who had despaired increasingly saw the matter in a different cast. "There is not now the inthusiasm in the army that we had," a bluecoat wrote in January 1863, but a year later he predicted confidently that for the Confederates 1864 "will be their last hope. With them it is do or die. One more year and the Rebellion

In a ruined economy and in shattered prospects represented by scenes like this of the Gallego Mills in Richmond may be found the doom of the Confederacy. *U.S. Army Military History Institute, Carlisle, Pa.*

must come to an end." The passage of a year had wrought quite a change, with expressions behind the lines and in Washington to match.[39]

The proposition that it was a loss of willpower—which can also read morale, élan, spirit, and more—that doomed the Confederacy is certainly not a new one. As early as 1865 Confederate senator Williamson Oldham of Texas argued that the North had beaten the South not by superior numbers but by superior commitment, for, he said, the Confederacy had everything it needed to continue the war, "morale alone excepted." Many others later agreed, and every generation or so a new exponent of the "loss of will" theory steps forward. It is a notion, however, that simply does not stand up to scrutiny or logic.[40]

Some assert boldly that as late as 1865 "the South could still have won, save only for the rapid diminution and ultimate death of morale, the will to win, during the last year or two of the war." Citing Oldham, they point out that however well the Confederacy managed its military organization—a point that is itself arguable—the South failed to "control and command its moral resources." Echoing the senator's sentiments, exponents suggest that Frank Owsley's old notion that the epitaph on the Confederacy's tombstone should read, "Died of States Rights," ought to read instead, "Died of Guilt and Failure of Will."[41]

Proponents argue, even after recognizing that the disasters of Gettysburg and Vicksburg were pivotal morale moments, that the South could have changed its destiny through willpower. "From July 1863 onward internal will became an ever more important indicator of declining Confederate strength," they say; "at the very moment that the South needed to stiffen its will to compensate for an overall decline in military fortunes, that will became less reliable." Deficient Southern nationalism accounts for this, we are told, the want of an overriding sense of Confederate nationality as opposed to American identity.[42] Had Southerners felt that deep commitment, then Confederates could have continued their war in spite of all handicaps and to a very possible successful conclusion.

How were they to do so? Essentially by scattering their armies in 1865, continuing as partisans and guerrillas, and wearing down their enemy much as the North Vietnamese wore down American resolve a century later. The aptness of any such comparison is debatable, but the important point being made is that victory could derive from will, even over compellingly important matters such as odds and resources. The Confederacy failed because its willpower failed, proponents say; the Union succeeded because it had a stronger sense of national identity and therefore a superior will. How, then, was the South to combat this strength? By improving its willpower, say such proponents. How was the South to do that? By *willing* it to happen. In short, the South was to use its willpower to increase its willpower. Like Peter Pan trying to revive Tinkerbell, Southerners were to close their eyes, clap their hands, and "wish real hard" for something to happen.

Of course, the whole notion of dispersal of forces and continuation of the conflict as partisans ignores the unquestionable facts of the case in the Confederacy in 1865. All of the South's ports were closed to blockade runners. There would be no more supply from abroad. Where, then, were the Confederates to continue getting the weapons and matériel needed to keep fighting? Their own manufactories were virtually all destroyed or behind Yankee lines. With all of the breadbasket areas of the South occupied by the enemy by the beginning of 1865, where were these partisans to get food? How could they communicate and coordinate with each other once they took to the hills? The Federals controlled all main roads and all rail and telegraph communications. Most important of all, throughout history partisans have depended heavily, sometimes exclusively, upon the aid and support of the civilian population where they operate. Francis Marion could not have been successful but for the help of locals during the Revolution. John S. Mosby and other Confederate partisans would have failed utterly without the wonderful support of the civilians in the counties where they hid out, wintered, and mounted their raids. With Yankees in control firmly of all of the tidewater South and all of the urban areas, Confederate armies disbanding to become partisan would inevitably have been forced to take refuge in the hill and mountain country. Yet that is exactly the region where Union support in the South was so strong that Confederate authorities sometimes did not even try to maintain control. To suppose that these "tories" would feed, clothe, supply, and protect armies of partisans competing for scarce foodstuffs and offering nothing in return is preposterous. If anything, the Confederate soldiers would have found themselves fighting on two fronts, Yankees before them and Unionist Southerners behind them.

Beyond this, to suggest that in a conflict of armies and peoples at war willpower *leads* events is to view the scene from the wrong side of the lens. Willpower *follows* events. Wars like the Civil War have discrete, definite beginnings in which a very traditional pattern unfolds. Morale soars on both sides at first, enthusiasm for a glorious adventure, the certainty of speedy victory in a righteous cause, and all the other self-delusions. It is a spontaneous public sentiment that both produces, and is produced by, events. But once the first guns are fired, national attention on all sides is immediately, unremovably linked to the armies, and thereafter public morale is inextricably keyed to the battlefield in a sequence of events that begins with the first victory and defeat and thereafter seesaws up and down in direct reaction to the course of the war. It is much like a political campaign. The polls go up for a candidate only after he or she scores some good point on the opposition, never before. Willpower is the *creature* of events and only secondarily—and subsequently—their creator.

Of course, at the end of 1863 the outcome of the war between the states was still very much unsettled. It was not yet won, and it was not yet lost. Much yet unforeseen could happen to influence that shifting balance of will before the

Excuses, Turning Points, and Defeats

time came when the soldiers in the field and the civilians at home on one side or the other reached the point where their commitment to persevere succumbed to an unwillingness to accept the cost. But it was here in that pivotal year of 1863 that for the first time, and for both sides, the seemingly impossible of 1861 and 1862 became the possible. The Union looked at last upon a solid foundation of victories on which to base a confident belief in ultimate triumph; the Confederacy reflected upon a past year of almost unbroken disaster on the hearthside and the battlefield, forcing millions to question or abandon the notion of the *inevitability* of their success and to contemplate or even accept the *possibility* of their defeat. When these realizations emerged north and south of the Potomac and the Ohio, then the progressively more rapid stiffening and erosion of will commenced.

All of which leads to another Christmas, a year from that December at Murfreesboro in 1862. In camp now at Dalton, Georgia, after the disaster at Missionary Ridge and the loss of eastern Tennessee, that same unnamed Kentuckian sat down once more with his company's clothing book. Gone were the enthusiasm and optimism of his earlier Yuletide entries. "Dec. 25th 1863," he began. "Yes, old Brick, and *another* Christmas has come and gone, and we are still combatting with the Vandal horde; Are likely to be doing that same this time next Christmas. What a pity." It was the last holiday entry he would make, for at Christmas in 1864, with his brigade in retreat before Sherman near Savannah, the account book is silent on December 25. The conclusion is inescapable that this unknown scribe, like so many of his fellow Southerners, had already left either the last of his blood or the last of his will to continue in the soil of the dying Confederacy.[43]

The Turning Point That Wasn't:
The Confederates and the Election of 1864

EVERY CONFLICT HAS ITS SHARE of so-called turning points, some real, some only perceived, and some purely illusory. Our Civil War offers a host of claimants, some of them events on the battlefield, like the qualified Union victory at Antietam, and some battles fought in other arenas. Of the latter, none has enjoyed more popularity, especially recently, than the presidential election of 1864 in the North. Simply stated, the strong belief exists that had Lincoln been defeated and his Democratic opponent George B. McClellan been elected instead, Confederate independence would naturally and quickly have followed, making the 1864 political contest truly the turning point of all time for Americans.

Months beforehand, on March 18, 1864, Georgia congressman Ben Hill declared that "the presidential election in the United States, in 1864, then, is the event which must determine the issue of peace or war, and with it, the destinies of both countries."[1] Vice President Alexander H. Stephens agreed and in May 1864 predicted that "if they gain no victory before mid-summer there will be with them a tremendous collapse—a fearful and disastrous crash—from the stunning effects of which they can not rally soon." That happening, he predicted, Lincoln's bid for reelection would be defeated, and that "will effect results which without doubt will end after a while in peace without any further effusion of blood on great fields of battle."[2]

Given such expectations on the part of a portion of Southern leadership, it was inevitable that they would bring to bear pressure on the president, the cabinet, Congress, and the armies to make every effort to influence events in the North. Sensing that the Union populace was war-weary, disillusioned with casualties and costs, and dispirited by the military stalemate that had existed in Virginia, at least, since the beginning of the conflict, such men could hope that a combination of events would lead to Lincoln's rejection at the polls.

Excuses, Turning Points, and Defeats

Their efforts and hopes focused in four areas. First, obviously, the Confederates needed to win victories in the field or at least prevent the enemy from achieving any substantial successes. As a practical military matter, this meant turning back William T. Sherman's invasion of Georgia and saving Atlanta and repulsing Ulysses S. Grant's drive toward Richmond. Where possible, the Con-

The Kesler photograph of Lincoln, taken in Chicago before his election, shows some of the reserves of determination that would see him through the war and reelection.
U.S. Army Military History Institute, Carlisle, Pa.

federates might even attempt some limited offensives, even if only temporary raids, to further embarrass Yankee commanders. Second, the Confederates needed to provide every encouragement possible to the peace party in the North, chiefly Democrats, and made up of onetime war supporters grown weary and disillusioned, and the Copperheads who had always opposed Lincoln and the war. Third, the Confederates had to offer encouragement and assistance to the active Southern sympathizers in the North, reputed to be in the hundreds of thousands and willing to take militant action, groups such as the Knights of the Golden Circle and the Sons of Liberty. And fourth, and most daring, the Confederates needed to become active agents themselves by directly subverting the election and stirring disaffection, even panic, among the Northern populace. Acts of espionage, subversion, destabilization, even what later generations would call terrorism, could and should be employed. The cumulative effect of all this, if vigorously and effectively prosecuted and, more important, if carefully orchestrated and coordinated by Richmond, could well cast deciding ballots against Lincoln. It could, in short, be the most comprehensive and sinister campaign to subvert an election in the history of American politics. Beside it, Watergate would appear about as threatening to democracy as a Tupperware party.

Military efforts by the Confederates to influence the election are almost impossible to separate from movements they would have made in any case. After all, with Sherman invading Georgia, naturally the Rebels would try to turn him back, regardless of the forthcoming election. So, too, would Lee try at the very least to prevent Grant from getting any closer to Richmond, let alone hoping to send him, too, retreating to the North. Even the South's own few offensives and raids were movements entirely consistent with President Jefferson Davis' policy of the offensive defensive, of taking advantage of occasional opportunities to capitalize on a Yankee weak point to make the enemy feel the hard hand of war. Moreover, with his two main armies heavily beset, Davis would naturally look to such diversionary actions in the hope of relieving the pressure on Lee and Atlanta.

Thus, Jubal Early's summer raid down the Shenandoah and into Maryland, threatening even Washington for a few hours, was almost exclusively an attempt to divert Grant's growing stranglehold on Lee at Petersburg. While Lee expressed some hope that if Early could take Washington, it might influence foreign powers again to consider recognition, neither he nor Davis nor Early ever mentioned any potential impact the raid might have on the election.[3] Similarly, Sterling Price's fall raid into Missouri was planned by department commander General E. Kirby Smith exclusively as a means of clearing the Trans-Mississippi of the Yankees and of helping take the pressure off Johnston in Georgia and Lee in Virginia. From beginning to end of the operation neither Smith nor Price ever spoke of any hoped-for political effects beyond the conquest of Missouri and the installation of a Confederate governor. The campaign, in the end, was a botched affair that failed in every objective and may actually have added votes to the Republican column in the fall.[4] Meanwhile, John Hunt Morgan's summer raid into Kentucky certainly hurt the cause. Not only did Richmond not authorize it in advance, but also Morgan undertook the raid on his own initiative knowing that his superiors wanted and needed him elsewhere. He presented them with a fait accompli by leaving first and notifying them later. Thereafter, he bumbled and plundered, even from Southern sympathizers in Kentucky. Far from injuring Lincoln's support in the state and the North, Morgan's raid damaged Democratic hopes.

Similarly, the Confederates scarcely made an effective effort to hold Mobile Bay. The fall of New Orleans in April 1862 and the Yankee conquest of the Mississippi as well as the capture of Port Royal on the Atlantic coast had long since demonstrated that stationary masonry forts could not stop the passage of a steam-powered armored fleet.[5] Nevertheless, in Mobile Bay Richmond placed its faith chiefly in the powerful but unreliable ironclad *Tennessee* and the guns of Forts Morgan and Gaines. As a result, though the city of Mobile and its forts held out until 1865, the much more important harbor was lost and with it control of the Tensas, Alabama, and Tombigbee Rivers.

In none of these major actions did concern for impact on the fall election play a role, or even elicit a mention, in the planning of Davis and his government. Indeed, the only political implications that authorities expected from them were internal, in the case of the recovery of Missouri, and international, in the case of Early's raid. Moreover, many Confederate leaders, including Vice President Stephens and some prominent editors, believed that these invasions and raids actually hurt the cause by inflaming Northern sentiment against them. The Confederacy had always portrayed itself as the weak defender. It had no dreams of conquest. The Confederates only wanted, as Davis had said, "to be let alone." But here they were acting as invaders, looting and burning in some cases, and thus only stiffening Yankee resolve and perhaps driving some who favored peace over to Lincoln's war policy and his reelection. "The Maryland campaign is the climax of a long series of blunders," complained Stephens' friend Henry Cleveland. "Lincoln's election is now beyond all doubt, and the Northern armies will get a flood of reinforcements."[6]

Only from Lee and Johnston did Richmond expect results that might influence the Union's fall elections, and there it was only Johnston who had the option of open movement, for after June Lee was pinned to Richmond and Petersburg, from which he could not venture. Perhaps building on an idea suggested by General James Longstreet in March 1864, President Davis suggested to Johnston in mid-April, just two weeks before the opening of the Atlanta campaign, that the general lead the Army of Tennessee north on an invasion of its namesake state. It would, said Davis, "depress the enemy, involving greatest consequences."[7] But of course, Joseph E. Johnston would never in his life lead an offensive on anyone or anything other than Jefferson Davis, and that occurred years after the war. In 1864 "Little Joe" was interested only in retreat, mostly without resisting. Even when Congressman Hill called on Johnston and implored that failure to repulse Sherman would make "Lincoln's power at the North . . . absolute, his re-election certain," the general only nodded and replied that he needed more cavalry.[8] That nod is as close as Johnston got to taking any active part in attempting to affect the outcome of the election in November. His successor, John Bell Hood, at least tried, but only when Johnston's retreats had already made Atlanta's fall practically a forgone conclusion.

While the military option to encourage Lincoln's defeat came to nothing, those other arenas simultaneously seemed to offer some hope. The peace party at the North, made up as it was of a disorganized and uncoordinated assemblage of Southern sympathizers, so-called Copperheads who simply opposed waging war to restore the Union, and other disaffected elements, *seemed* growing and powerful. In fact, its numbers were considerably exaggerated both by the peace factions themselves and by men in the Confederacy who allowed wishful thinking to influence their hopes for support in the North. A few Confederates suggested that the South should funnel money to the Peace Democrats to aid them in organizing themselves and funding their campaign to defeat Lincoln. Others, revealing the basic conviction that Yankees were soulless men devoid of any ideology but greed, proposed using Confederate cotton as bribes to buy anti-Lincoln votes. "I say we can control that election," claimed one Rebel congressman.[9] Twenty years later Jefferson Davis, writing his memoirs, averred that "the aspect of the peace party was quite encouraging, and it seemed that the real issue to be decided in the Presidential election of that year was the continuance or cessation of the war."[10]

Excuses, Turning Points, and Defeats

Davis' much more temperate estimate of the potential for influencing the election revealed what was, in him, a welcome change. Despite being a man of unusual intelligence, he was never particularly perceptive in judging men, either friends or enemies. However, his political instincts could at time prove keen. Now, in approaching some way to capitalize on the disaffection in the North, he all but ignored suggestions such as bribery and vote buying and instead looked to some more active—and honorable—means of costing Lincoln votes. One thing was certain. He could do little from Richmond, with Yankee armies separating him from the North. Consequently, he determined upon establishing an unofficial diplomatic mission in Canada. There, just across the border from the North, his agents could maintain easy and intimate contact with peace elements, providing assistance with money, propaganda, and organizational counsel.

The idea itself was sound. Unfortunately, though foredoomed in any case, it foundered on Davis' woeful lack of judgment in men. He appointed to the commission Jacob Thompson, an old Democratic Party hack from Mississippi, a man around whom often swirled rumors of corruption, and to work with him, Clement C. Clay of Alabama, a weak-willed sycophant whose chief claim to favor was that he never said "no" to Jefferson Davis. The two commissioners, assisted by others, quickly fell out over the handling of the funds provided them, and Clay soon moved away from Thompson's headquarters in Toronto. Thereafter they rarely cooperated.

But also thereafter the bulk of the Confederacy's efforts to influence the election emanated from Canada and chiefly from the slippery Thompson. Both he and Clay made contact with Clement L. Vallandigham, the most notorious Copperhead and advocate of peace, even at the price of separation. Beyond that, they attempted to secure communication with numerous secret societies in the North. For some time exaggerated reports of the numbers and intentions of such groups as the Knights of the Golden Circle, the Sons of Liberty, and the Order of American Knights had tantalized Confederate hopes. Some of these groups had their origins even before the war, but by 1864 their strength was reported at almost 1 million, many of them armed men anxious to rise up, awaiting only the signal from their leaders to seize arsenals and overturn Republican institutions.

Unfortunately, such bellicose promises had their origins exclusively in the land of myth. Some groups were run by charlatans who hoped to lure money from the Confederacy, ostensibly to arm their "knights." Others were run by deluded men like George Bickley of the Knights of the Golden Circle, crackpots who saw themselves as saviors and simply believed their own fantasies. The fact was that none of these societies posed any real threat. Their actual numbers were small, barely more than a few thousand genuine members, with no organization, no fixed plans, and more secret handshakes and passwords than weapons. They represented, at least on the part of Vallandigham, Bickley, and other presumed leaders, one of the most stupendous self-delusions in history. Thompson, Clay, and the Confederates would only find out the hard way just how little substance there was to the myth and that only after paying out large portions of their secret service funds to buy supposedly friendly newspaper editors, support the campaigns of some peace candidates, and help organize and equip various so-called castles of the supposedly innumerable knights of this or that. Scarcely a dollar of it rebounded to the benefit of their mission. Worse, as summer and fall 1864 wore on, these peace groups became heavily infiltrated by U.S. civil and military agents, and the subsequent exposure of their schemes —not to mention their megalomaniacal delusions—severely embarrassed not only the peace Democrats in the North but also the Confederacy.

Thompson and Clay also attempted to destabilize Union finance by buying up gold in New York and shipping it to Canada, expecting that a resultant shortage of hard currency could lead to economic panic, but the scheme was woefully underfunded and had no significant impact. In the end the Canadian venture's only real success came, ironically, in the failure of its involvement in actual peace overtures and negotiations. Through Clay, New York editor Horace Greeley inaugurated what he hoped would be peace talks. The problem was that he did not understand that Clay and Thompson were not empowered by Davis to negotiate. Nevertheless, Greeley secured from Lincoln a statement of his requirements for peace. They were an end to hostilities, a return to the Union, and Southern acknowledgment of abolition of slavery. This last outraged conservative and peace elements in the North, which protested being made to fight a war that appeared to have as its irrevocable objective an end to slavery. They were fighting for reunion, not emancipation.

Unfortunately, even the little publicity benefit the Confederates gained from widely publishing and capitalizing on Lincoln's declaration was nullified when Davis issued his own emphatic statement that he would accept no terms short of full independence for the Confederacy. Of course, Clay and Thompson and most Confederate leaders understood and shared Davis' position, but in the publicizing of it they feared that the president's seeming intractability

Excuses, Turning Points, and Defeats

would work against them. Better, said Stephens, the Canadian commissioners, and others, to fudge the question—to appear ready to sit down to peace talks on general terms calling for an immediate armistice and then trust to ensuing negotiations to draw out the process so long that the Yankees in the end would tire and, unwilling to resume hostilities, finally bid the Southern states farewell. But that sort of equivocation—not to mention diplomatic subtlety—was not in Jefferson Davis' makeup.[11] And in any case it depended on half a million or more Northern fathers, brothers, and sons, almost all of them voters, being at some point willing to write off their sacrifices, say that a man they loved had died for nothing, and stand behind McClellan as he gave away the victory. Undiplomatic Davis may have been, but he was not naive.

Finally, the Confederates, partly on orders from Richmond and partly on coordination out of Canada, made efforts that went beyond passive things like propaganda. They attempted to take direct, sometimes terrifying action; to disrupt the peace of the Yankee homefront; to "take the war into Egypt" and hope that Northern fear or even panic might translate to repudiation of Lincoln at the polls. Most of the schemes were in some measure fantastical, many were just harebrained, and all of them failed, frequently even before they started.

Thompson believed that disaffection in the northwest—Illinois, Indiana, Ohio, Kentucky, and Missouri—was so great that with his encouragement the Democrats of those states would rise up in the fall and declare their own northwest confederacy, forming a defensive alliance with the Confederate states. Thompson believed this solely on the assurances of a succession of crackpots, most notably Clement Vallandigham, many of whom wanted money from him. In the end several promised dates for the uprising came and passed without a single man taking arms.[12]

A small band of agents, most of them Kentuckians who had once ridden with Morgan, hatched a scheme to set fire to New York City, thinking the panic would do irreparable damage to Lincoln. Unfortunately, they planned their sabotage to coincide with one of several expected uprising dates in the northwest, this one on election day itself. When nothing happened, the incendiaries waited until the end of November before they lit their matches. Not only were their fires quickly extinguished and some of the saboteurs caught, but they seemed also to have missed the rather elemental point that, even if successful, their act could have no impact on the outcome since they set their fires three weeks after the election.[13]

Jacob Thompson also developed a plan for seizing a warship on the Great

Lakes and using it to take control of the waterways and launch raids out of Canada onto Northern border cities. His special targets were the prisoner-of-war camps on Johnson's Island off Sandusky, Ohio, and at Camp Douglas in Chicago. Free the tens of thousands of Confederate prisoners there, he reasoned, miraculously arm them somehow, and he would have a virtual army perched at Lincoln's back door. Thompson seems not to have thought through the diplomatic implications of this. Any such "army" would have to have been supplied and armed through Canada and probably even refitted and based in that British possession. Any such action, far from endearing the Confederacy to Whitehall, would inevitably have provoked the sternest response from Britain.

Nevertheless, on September 19 a small party of Confederates boarded and took the steamer *Philo Parsons* shortly after it left Detroit. They steamed directly for Johnson's Island, where they expected to board and capture the USS *Michigan* after nightfall. Only they found it waiting for them, their plot having been infiltrated and exposed, as indeed almost every Confederate scheme was compromised. Thompson soon purchased another steamer and tried to outfit it as a warship, but the election came and passed before it was ready, and even then all of Thompson's acts were anticipated by Federal authorities. "The bane and curse of carrying out anything in this country is the surveillance under which we work," Thompson complained to Richmond in December. "Detectives and those ready to give information stand on every street corner. Two or three cannot exchange ideas without a reporter."[14]

This notion of launching hostile operations against the Yankees from Canada also infected Clement Clay, and it was he who helped facilitate Bennett Young's famed October 19, 1864, raid on St. Albans, Vermont. It was a modest affair to begin a supposed wave of terror. Young had only twenty raiders but managed to capture the undefended town. Unfortunately, Confederate aims were made to appear at best equivocal when the only damage Young did was to empty the town's banks of about $220,000, steal a number of horses, and liberate one citizen's hat. All that Young's men actually destroyed in this raid that was supposed to bring the war to the enemy was a lone woodshed. Hotly pursued, they raced back to Canada, where eventually most were captured by Canadian authorities. The only influence, if any, upon the coming election was a wave of indignation that hurt the Democrats by showing the Confederates to be low plunderers rather than high-toned champions of constitutional rights as they proclaimed.[15]

Excuses, Turning Points, and Defeats

Best known of all these schemes, of course, was the so-called Northwest Conspiracy, and in this one, at least, Davis himself took something of a hand, for it was he who originally sent Captain Thomas H. Hines, yet another one-time cavalryman with Morgan, on a mission. Hines had come to Davis with a plan to lead a band of followers to Chicago, there to attack Camp Douglas and release its inmates that they might foment a revolution in the northwest. The president, however, only authorized him to free prisoners and help them get south to return to regular service in the Confederate armies. Davis did, however, empower Hines to discuss affairs with any prominent or influential peace men he encountered in the North. Thereafter Hines communicated directly with Thompson in Canada and between them carried their scheme some distance beyond Davis' original intent. They also completely bought into the exaggerated claims of Southern sympathy upon the part of a supposed army of Democrats in the northwest. As a result, when Hines actually found out in August how pitiful were the organization and support behind the Sons of Liberty and the Knights of the Golden Circle, he called off an attack on Camp Douglas planned to coincide with the Democratic convention in Chicago. Later Hines planned a similar attack and uprising for Chicago on election day itself, by which time, of course, it would have been too late to influence the balloting in any case. But as so often occurred, Federal agents had completely penetrated the conspirators' counsels and knew their every planned move. Most of the conspirators were arrested.

In short, everything planned by the Canadian connection came to nothing. They had been impractical schemes doomed by credulous dependence on nonexistent sympathy in the North, compromised by intentions that seemed to confuse plunder and indiscriminate vandalism with legitimate war aims, mismanaged by an ineffectual Clay and an often imperious Thompson, and none of them well coordinated with or by Richmond. Not one scheme achieved anything, and perhaps the only Confederate to derive any benefit at all from the whole operation was the wily Thompson, who escaped to England at the end of the war with $200,000 or more of the Confederate gold remaining in his hands, which he refused to turn over to Confederate executors afterward. In his later years, always a risk taker, Thompson invested some of it in a venture that he hoped might yield reward. Sometime around 1880 he bought $100,000 worth of shares in an untried new enterprise called the Bell Telephone Company.[16]

Thus, we see in the end that by November 1864 not only had Confederate attempts to influence the Northern election been uncoordinated, disorganized, and ineffectual, but also the public exposure of schemes like the so-called Northwest Conspiracy and the revelations of the Sons of Liberty and the Knights of the Golden Circle actually excited public outrage against the South anew, if anything *adding* votes to the Lincoln column. Moreover, in retrospect it is easy to see that thanks to that same lack of coordination, scarcity of funds, bumbling managers like Thompson and Clay, and lack of sure expectations or commitment on the part of the Confederate president, these attempts to sway Yankee voters were foredoomed to failure. Davis, especially, bears responsibility, for ultimately it was up to him either to formulate a coordinated policy to influence the election or else to ensure that someone else did. Part of the problem, however, was that the legalistic Davis, even though in the midst of a war for the existence of his infant nation, simply did not believe that it was proper for one nation to interfere with the constitutionally mandated democratic process of another. It was fair to attempt to influence public opinion but not actively to subvert. Davis wavered back and forth throughout the campaign, always placing his hopes and attention in the arena where he thought they would accomplish the most—on the battlefield—and where he achieved the least.[17]

In the end the only Confederate acts that could have—not necessarily would have—affected the outcome were those in that one theater in which the war was being decided from the outset: the battlefield. *If* Jubal Early had captured Washington and held it for some appreciable time. *If* Sterling Price had wrested Missouri from the Union and been able to hold it. *If* the forts at Mobile had been able to repulse Farragut and his fleet. *If* Lee had been able to take some action against Grant, however small, to embarrass him in the trenches at Petersburg. And most important of all, *if* Joseph E. Johnston or John Bell Hood had been able to turn Sherman decisively, not just away from Atlanta, but back on his base at Chattanooga. If all these "if's" had come to pass, they would have constituted a series of body blows to Union morale and Lincoln's prestige, at the rate of one every few weeks during the last four months of the election campaign. Then quite possibly, even probably, sagging Northern spirits would have translated into Democratic votes.

But what if they had? Any discussion of Confederate hopes in the election of 1864 begs us to ask the questions "What if Lincoln had lost?" "What would have ensued?" "Would the Confederacy have achieved at last its independence?" "Was the election, in fact, the 'last best hope' for Southern nationhood?"

Antietam, we are told, was the moment when the South came closest to achieving its independence. Why? Because at the moment the battle was raging, the prime minister and his cabinet in Britain had scheduled a meeting to consider granting formal diplomatic recognition of the independence of the Confederacy. If Lee had won at Antietam, his renewed demonstration of Rebel strength would have resulted in that recognition, and the inevitable result of recognition would have been an alliance and with it massive infusions of money, weapons, ships, and perhaps even armies from England. Moreover, once Britain had moved, France and perhaps Spain would have followed. With such an array of might against it, with the reinforced Confederates to the south and British regulars threatening an invasion from Canada, the Union would have had no option but to sue for peace and itself recognize the Confederacy. Fortuitously, McClellan's victory at Antietam instead persuaded the British to stay out of the conflict, to wait and see. For the moment there would be no recognition.

It makes for a great story, with plenty of drama and a hair's-breadth salvation of the Union, and has been repeated again and again, by buffs and scholars and by distinguished historians, until it is now part of the canon of the Civil War. Most recently Stephen Sears in his *Landscape Turned Red: The Battle of Antietam* declares that British foreign secretary John Russell had written to the prime minister, Lord Palmerston, "suggesting an October cabinet to debate the matter of recognition of the Confederacy" and that if they decided for recognition, "the next step should be a proposal for concerted action by Britain, France, Russia, and the other powers."[18]

Unfortunately, the whole interpretation is nonsense, a fiction based upon carelessness with the facts, false logic, and a willingness to which all too many of us are prone simply to accept what we have always heard without examining it further. The facts in this case are that Russell did propose a meeting and Palmerston agreed, stipulating only that the cabinet wait until after there had been one more battle. Then if the Confederacy prevailed, the cabinet would meet.[19] But what they were to discuss was not recognition but only the possibility of making an offer to each side to act as a mediator in settling their differences. Britain was offering not to talk about guns and ships and armies but to talk about "talking."

Antietam put an end even to that. But what if Lee had won and the cabinet had met and offered to mediate? Transatlantic communications took at least five days one way. Merely getting all of the details of the first mediation meetings taken care of would have occupied weeks, if not months, especially since each president would have realized that playing for time worked to his benefit, that more victories might lend advantage to his side. A century later it took months for the parties to the Paris peace talks on the Vietnam War merely to agree on the shape of their conference table. A masterful diplomat like Lincoln could have easily delayed any such talks long enough for hoped-for victories to dissuade foreign powers from meddling any further. And look at what happened in the three months following Antietam. Lee did inflict another humiliating defeat on the Union at Fredericksburg. Yet it lacked any strategic military significance. He gained nothing, merely preserving the status quo in Virginia exactly where it had been for the previous eighteen months. Meanwhile in the western theater a Confederate invasion of Kentucky was turned back decisively in October, and then the Confederates were forced to abandon middle Tennessee after Stones River. At Iuka and Corinth the Confederates were forced out of northern Mississippi. And in the November elections Lincoln held his Republican majority in the House and won five new Republican seats in the Senate. Though divided, clearly the people of the Union backed the Lincoln administration, while their armies had gained thousands of square miles of Rebel territory. Though there was no speedy end to the war yet in sight, from an international point of view by January 1863 all of the momentum and all the advantage clearly lay with the Union. In the face of that, it is inconceivable that Britain and the rest would have moved toward recognition when any mediation inevitably broke down on Lincoln's refusal to negotiate on any basis other than the South laying down its arms and coming back into the Union. In short, the notion of foreign recognition and Confederate victory being narrowly averted by McClellan's equivocal win at Antietam is purely a myth. They were never even a remote possibility.

If this seems a pointless digression, it is only to provide an example of how unquestioning acceptance of old and shopworn clichés about the Civil War can cloud the realities behind the facade. And when we take the same careful look at the operative events and the driving men involved in the aftermath of the election of 1864, we see that here, too, the notion of Lincoln's loss leading directly to Confederate independence is but a fable. This is not to say that the course of the months ensuing after Lincoln's defeat might not have been substantially different from the actual events of November 8, 1864, to March 4, 1865, and beyond. But when we look at the men with the power to make decisions and affect events during Lincoln's speculated lame-duck incumbency, and at the attitudes and dynamics driving those who would have succeeded him, the conclusion that Confederate independence would or even might have been the result becomes at best inconceivable, if not ridiculous.

The key lies in five men and what we know of their emphatically stated war aims and policies. The first, naturally, is Lincoln himself. If we are to believe him, he feared that he could lose the election. And his attitude, as expressed in his confidential cabinet memo of August 23, 1864, was not to give up. Rather, he committed himself and asked his cabinet to commit itself, as he put it, "to save the Union between the election and the inauguration."[20] There can be only one meaning to that. Lincoln would call on Grant not to rest during the cold months but to employ all possible Union forces in a full winter campaign on every front.

It would be fruitless to speculate on just how Lincoln and Grant would have gone about that specifically, but in broad outline we can infer from their previous statements the ends they would have sought to achieve. Both agreed on the symbolic importance of Richmond and the Army of Northern Virginia, not just militarily but also in the minds of the peoples of the North and South. "Lee, with the capital of the Confederacy, was the main end to which all were working," said Grant.[21] We also know from his earlier planning for the 1864 campaigns that Grant foresaw more than one potential role for William T. Sherman's armies. Atlanta was not even a stated objective in Grant's campaign orders to Sherman on April 10. Rather, Sherman was to "knock Jos. Johnston and do as much damage to the resources of the enemy as possible."[22] Atlanta, as Grant later put it, was "of less importance" than were Richmond and Lee. In short, and in Grant's wording, Atlanta was only "an important obstacle" on the road to capturing Richmond.[23] But whether Atlanta fell or not—and if Lincoln had been defeated, we must assume it would have been in part at least because Sherman had failed to take Atlanta by early November—it was always in the back of Grant's mind that Sherman, when able, would march at least a major portion of his mammoth force northeast to Virginia. Then Grant and Sherman could pinch Lee between them.

There are really only three logical explanations for Sherman failing to hold Atlanta by November. One is that he was vigorously attacked and pushed back in late spring or early summer by Joseph E. Johnston before he penetrated deep into Georgia—which anyone who studies Johnston knows to be an absurd speculation on the face of it. Another is that the Yankees invested Johnston or his successor Hood in Atlanta and had the Confederate commander virtually surrounded and under siege but had not taken the city. The third is that Sherman was driven back from Atlanta's outskirts by desperate and costly assaults in the summer by Hood.

Even with the first alternative out of the question, either of the latter two still leaves Sherman with the upper hand in Georgia. Even if Hood had pushed Sherman away from Atlanta, it could only have been at the cost of crippling casualties to the Army of Tennessee, as evidenced by the offensives Hood did launch during the battles for Atlanta and his subsequent Tennessee campaign. Thus, Sherman, with his considerable numerical and logistical superiority, could have divided his command, left part of it to hold a weakened and depleted Hood in Georgia, and sent the rest to Virginia. If, however, Hood had been besieged, Sherman would have had more than sufficient force to man his own trenches while detaching up to 40,000 men to Grant in what would now have been a frantic push to achieve victory.

Whether Sherman sent them by rail through Chattanooga and the North or overland, where there were no Confederate forces to impede their progress, in any case Grant could have had a reinforcement of fresh troops in numbers equal to Lee's entire army available before the end of the year. Grant would have opted for the overland route, which, though slower, would still have had Sherman approach Lee from the southwest, thus cutting off Lee's only route of retreat from Petersburg. Contrary to popular misconception, Atlanta was always an expendable objective for Grant, and from what we know of Sherman's character and attitudes, his actions would have been in perfect accord with Grant's wish to abandon the Georgia campaign and concentrate against Lee. Sherman wanted to make the South "howl," as he put it. Faced with the prospect of seeing the war lost when Lincoln left office, Sherman would have bent every sinew to hearing that howl first.

What we have then are Lincoln's determination to win before March 4, Grant's determination that Richmond and Lee were psychologically the decisive targets, and Sherman's ruthless dedication to punishing the Confederacy, along with the availability of his large army, relatively fresh, seasoned at hard marches, and not worn down and exhausted like the Army of the Potomac. Whether surrounded and overwhelmed in the trenches, or cut off on an attempt to break out and retreat, Lee, his army, and Richmond as a result would inevitably have fallen before March 4. The only imaginable alternative to this scenario is the inconceivable notion that Lincoln, Grant, and Sherman would all suddenly have run against type, turned their backs on the convictions and plans they had expressed repeatedly in 1864, and sat back and left the initiative to the Confederates.

But the fall of Lee and Richmond by March 4 does not necessarily mean the war would have been over. What it does mean, however, is that when McClellan took office, he would have found the Confederacy on its knees, its major army and its commander out of action, its capital fallen, its government in flight, and its only other substantial army east of the Mississippi virtually cast adrift somewhere in Georgia, battered, undersupplied, and perhaps still under siege in Atlanta or else trying to make some headway against the holding force left by Sherman. In any case, from the moment of Richmond's fall, if not before, major portions of every Federal army from Virginia, Tennessee, Mobile, Louisiana, and even the south Atlantic coast would have been marching to converge on poor Hood.

Faced with this, what would McClellan have done? Consider "Little Mac," the fourth of our decisive characters. He was an egomaniac. He still fancied himself the greatest general of the age. Now he would have been commander in chief, and in front of him he would have had complete and total victory served on a plate. All he would have had to do was take it. The war could have been over in weeks, and much of the credit his because it would have happened on his watch. Are we really to suppose that this man, of all men, given the opportunity to claim the ultimate triumph in a war in which to date his own victories had been few to nonexistent, would have chosen to snatch defeat from the jaws of victory, recall his armies, evacuate Richmond and New Orleans and Nashville and Chattanooga and Mobile and Pensacola, free Confederate prisoners, hand back tens of thousands of square miles of conquered territory, and send Jefferson Davis a basket of roses and a note saying, "You win"? The very thought ignores everything we know about McClellan and represents a light-speed flight from reality.

And yet this is substantially what a long-standing and unquestioning assumption has told us would have happened. Why? Because, we are told, McClellan would have been elected on a "peace" platform. Indeed, that is true, but peace has many definitions and methods of achievement. The fact is that when it came to the subject of reunion, McClellan and Lincoln held almost identical views, and the differences between their party platforms were not wide enough to insert a blade of grass. The Democratic platform explicitly called in no fewer than three places for "a restoration of the Union" and a return of peace "on the

Major General George B. McClellan. Even had he defeated Lincoln in November 1864, only a bent for self-destruction would have impelled him to oversee Confederate independence.

International Museum of Photography, Rochester, N.Y.

Excuses, Turning Points, and Defeats

basis of the Federal Union."[24] For McClellan to have granted Confederate in-dependence—assuming he even had had the power to do so—would have vi-olated his pledge with his party and the Democrats' pledge with the electorate. Moreover, Little Mac himself, in accepting his nomination, issued a statement that went beyond the platform. The only way to peace, he said, was reunion. If the Confederates refused to negotiate on the basis of a return to the Union, then, he said, "the responsibility for ulterior consequences will fall upon those who remain in arms against the Union." That, of course, was political double-speak. His original draft bluntly said, "We must continue the resort to the dreadful arbitrament of war."[25]

In short, there would be no Confederate independence for President Mc-Clellan. He made his reasons clear. "I could not look in the face of my gallant comrades of the Army and Navy, who have survived so many bloody battles, and tell them that their labors, and the sacrifice of so many of our slain and wounded brethren had been in vain."[26] And even had he been willing to betray his platform and his own conscience, McClellan's Democratic backers would not have let him. With Lincoln's defeat the Democratic Party would have re-covered the White House and possibly Congress as well. But the Republicans were still a powerfully large bloc of voters in the North. The only way to ce-ment overwhelming Democratic power for the long term was to bring the South and its 1 million and more Democratic voters back into the system. Not only would granting Confederate independence have failed to do that, but also the wave of outrage that would have touched every household that had lost a father or brother or husband or son, the indignation that would have inflamed every veteran with an empty sleeve, a disfigured face, a mangled body, and a blighted future, would have been disastrous at the midterm elections a year later. The Republicans could have been counted on to wave the bloody shirt and make full capital of the Democrats' betrayal of the sacrifice of millions, a betrayal that would certainly have cost them their hold on Congress in 1866 and on the White House itself two years later. It would, quite possibly, have meant the virtual destruction of the Democratic Party for a generation. In the very thought of granting Confederate independence, the Democrats would have had absolutely nothing to gain and absolutely everything to lose.

And at the risk of belaboring a discussion that has already gone on too long, there is one more pivotal figure whose character and intentions must be taken into account in any speculation on the outcome of a Lincoln defeat. In-terestingly, in all the generations of uncritical repetition of this reckless notion about Confederate independence, he is the one who is never considered, and yet he, of them all, is the one who would have had the final word, the one whose decision could have negated the efforts of Lincoln, Grant, Sherman, and, most of all, McClellan. He is Jefferson Davis.

As far back as his inaugural as provisional president on February 18, 1861, Davis made his position on reconstruction emphatically clear. "We have entered upon the career of independence," he said, "and it must be inflexibly pursued. . . . A reunification with the states from which we have separated is neither practical nor desirable."[27] Thereafter, regardless of the shifting fortunes of the war, Davis' commitment to independence or defeat only grew. Never during the ensuing four years did he once countenance the *possibility* of a peaceful return to the Union. Occasionally from 1862 onward third parties made peace overtures to the two antagonists, but invariably they broke down short of actual peace talks because Lincoln's and Davis' bedrock positions were mutually exclusive. Lincoln would negotiate anything but disunion; Davis would negotiate only on the basis of independence.

As recently as February 1865 a final attempt at negotiations was made in the so-called Hampton Roads Peace Conference, but the whole affair was a waste of time from the outset, as Secretary of State Judah Benjamin and Vice President Alexander H. Stephens, one of the negotiators, recognized beforehand. For they were bound by Davis' intractable demand that any peace settlement would have to include Confederate independence. Yet consider that this was in February 1865. By then Atlanta had truly fallen, Hood had been all but eliminated in his Tennessee campaign, and Sherman had marched to the sea, taken Savannah, and was even now marching north. Fort Fisher and Wilmington, North Carolina, had fallen, and Columbia, South Carolina, was about to go up in flames. Even now Charleston was preparing for inevitable evacuation. In short, the Confederacy was crumbling to dust, the pace of its disintegration accelerating daily. A cabal in the Confederate Senate was meeting secretly to press for negotiations that could include reunion, and the new secretary of war, John C. Breckinridge, was already meeting in private with prominent leaders in Richmond who shared his view that the situation was hopeless and that they should start preparing for an honorable surrender. Yet in the face of all this, Jefferson Davis refused to consider anything but independence or utter defeat.

Given this, how are we to suppose that his attitude would have been any more flexible in the wake of a Lincoln defeat in 1864? If McClellan had won, we have to assume that it could only have been because the Union military situation in November was not as good as in reality it had been. Assume that Sherman did not take Atlanta. Moreover, assume even that Lincoln, Grant, and Sherman all sat on their hands for the next four months and did nothing; assume that the suggested scenario of a concerted move against Lee and Richmond would not have come to pass. In such a dramatically improved outlook for the beleaguered Confederacy at the moment of a McClellan inauguration, can we conclude that Davis would have been any more willing to negotiate for a return to the Union than in fact he was at Hampton Roads in the midst of utter ruin? Of course not. If anything, his inflexibility on the reunion issue would have been even greater.

Given the position of Jefferson Davis, and given both the Democratic platform and McClellan's own attitude, which was, if anything, a bit more militant than his platform, the new president would have had no choice but to continue prosecuting the war to inevitable victory. To do less violated his pledge with the voters and risked virtual ruin for his party. And he had nothing else to offer Davis to change his mind, excepting perhaps a repudiation of the Emancipation Proclamation and possibly the promise of an attempt to insert guarantees of the right to hold slaves into the Constitution by amendment. But several problems make that an unlikely lure to Davis. For one thing, there was no certainty that enough Northern legislatures would join with the reunited Southern legislatures in ratifying any such amendment. After all, to do so would be to admit defeat for the Northern people, yet another way of saying that their men had suffered maiming wounds and painful deaths, only in the end to see the Southern slaveholders—who from the Yankee viewpoint started the war to protect slavery—get their way after all.

Quite probably, a McClellan administration would have withdrawn the proclamation in any case since it also threatened property rights in Union slave states such as Kentucky, Missouri, and Maryland. But that does not mean that such an act really represented much of a lure to the Confederates by March 1865. After all, following years of sporadic debate, the Confederacy itself was now officially experimenting with emancipation as a policy in order to raise black troops to wear the gray. And in December 1864 President Davis sent Duncan Kenner to London and Paris armed with an offer to abolish slavery in return for their diplomatic recognition and military aid. It is immaterial that Davis did not have the unilateral power to end slavery. The important fact is that months before March 1865 Davis had crossed a Rubicon. He would sacrifice slavery itself to achieve Confederate independence. Given that, any offer from McClellan to withdraw the Emancipation Proclamation in return for reunion becomes meaningless to Davis. Parenthetically, it also offers an interesting irony, that being that if the Kenner mission had succeeded, and if McClellan had won the election, then the Confederacy would have been abolishing slavery at the same time that the Union was protecting it by withdrawing the proclamation!

In the end there is only one way that a Lincoln defeat in November would have led to McClellan's preference of peace discussions based on reunion, and that is if Jefferson Davis were no longer Confederate president. Strong as was his opposition, it never enjoyed a fraction of the muscle needed to impeach him. Numerous though the occasional calls from his enemies were for his forcible overthrow, even assassination, no one ever showed either the courage or the ability at organization to mount a coup. Since he lived on until 1889, we can hardly suggest that he might have died in office. That being the case, the only other means of his removal would have been constitutional, in February 1868, when his term of office expired. While all of this speculation of the "what if" kind is ultimately pointless, surely the notion that the Confederacy, whether on the battlefield or at the negotiating table, might have lasted three more years strains credulity much too far.

Jefferson Davis himself never had illusions about a Lincoln defeat benefiting the Confederacy. Indeed, Stephens believed that Davis preferred that Lincoln be reelected, since Davis felt that such an unequivocal restatement of a war to unconditional victory and reunion policy from the North would renew the resolve of the South not to be conquered. "We are fighting for existence," Davis told a Georgia audience less than a month before the election, "and by fighting alone can independence be gained."[28] Because he knew himself and his own mind, and because he believed that he knew his people, Jefferson Davis knew that a Lincoln defeat and a McClellan victory offered the Confederacy not a prospect for peace and independence but only a promise of more war. Bullets, not ballots, would decide the fate of the Confederacy.[29]

John C. Breckinridge and Confederate Defeat

IN ALL OF THE SPECULATION on why the South lost its bid for independence, a finger is often pointed at a class of forgotten men, the several secretaries of war who filled that hapless office. No other individuals of comparable station in this war have been as ignored by historians while at the same time receiving so much blame for their weaknesses. And in fact, with one exception, no men of such exalted status exerted so little real influence. The one exception is John C. Breckinridge of Kentucky. The least studied of all of them, he proved to be the most capable of the lot. Chronologically the last of them, he was in fact the first and only functioning secretary of war the Confederacy ever had, the only one to leave the stamp of his personal influence on the course of the life of the Confederacy.[1]

The reasons for the failure of Breckinridge's predecessors have been oft repeated and at length. In sum they reduce to a name, Jefferson Davis. Convinced of his own military omniscience, yet placed in a high civil position rather than a field command, Davis appointed as secretary of war a succession of men of mediocre talents and, more important, of totally domitable will. All of these men had been, in the words of one historian, "alternating ghosts [who] might flutter through the executive building in Richmond, but it was Jefferson Davis who organized armies, appointed officers, supervised military campaigns, and attended even to the details of the office."[2] In light of this, the appointment of Breckinridge on February 6, 1865, represented a major shift in Davis' attitude toward that office, a redefinition of the role it would play in Confederate leadership, and a tacit recognition that Davis himself was losing his iron hold on power in Richmond.

Of all of the statesmen who joined the Southern ranks, Breckinridge was at once the most popular and illustrious. Davis himself was believed by some to be jealous of the man's popularity. Envious or not, Davis did esteem and respect the Kentuckian. He had been vice president of the United States, and in

Major General John C. Breckinridge, the only secretary of war
who stood up to President Davis and the man who, in effect,
ran the Confederate government in its last weeks.
Author's collection

Excuses, Turning Points, and Defeats

1860 his presidential candidacy carried all but two of the now Confederate states. Nearly half a million men who were now Confederates had voted for him, and the trust this expressed was only enhanced by Breckinridge's three years as one of the more capable major generals in the army. Furthermore, the irascible Confederate Congress liked him, voted him its official thanks once, and on another occasion allowed him a special seat on its floor. Expressions were abroad that if the cause lasted long enough for Davis' term as president to expire, Breckinridge would be his successor.[3]

Davis could not impose upon or ignore a man of this stature as he had previous secretaries. At the same time, Breckinridge's own background made him an ideal war minister, possessed of every qualification that his predecessors had lacked. An eminent statesman, with extensive military field experience, he had served in and knew every major theater of the war except the Gulf. He was intimately acquainted with every major commander except General Richard Taylor. He had planned and conducted his own successful campaigns and suf- fered the administrative torture of departmental command in southwest Vir- ginia, emerging with enhanced reputation from a responsibility that eclipsed most of his predecessors. Of all of those who held the war portfolio, he was also the only one—excepting perhaps George Wythe Randolph—who neither feared nor stood in awe of Jefferson Davis.

Breckinridge made his independence felt immediately. Despite ample dis- play of incompetence, General Lucius B. Northrop had been retained as com- missary general by Davis for nearly four years. Breckinridge made it clear when Davis offered him the post that Northrop's departure was a condition of ac- ceptance. It was a test of just how much authority the Kentuckian would have in office, and Davis gave him his way. A week before the president sent Breck- inridge's nomination to the Senate, the Kentuckian's old friend Eli M. Bruce temporarily relieved Northrop. Two weeks later Breckinridge personally se- lected General Isaac M. St. John as permanent commissary.[4]

Davis would declare that the function of assigning officers to command was "exclusively executive."[5] Now, however, Breckinridge took over much of the direction of general officers, their transfers and assignments. Robert E. Lee con- sulted Breckinridge, rather than Davis, in the matter of replacements for generals. It was Breckinridge, not Davis, who ordered General John B. Hood transferred to the Trans-Mississippi in March 1865. Henceforward all recommendations for promotion of general officers were made by the secretary of war.[6]

The conduct of military operations and the movement of troops were functions largely denied to former secretaries of war. Breckinridge engaged in both without interference, though certainly after consultation with Davis. He advised Lee on the proper course to follow in southwest Virginia and proposed a grand strategy to defeat Sherman in the Carolinas. He counseled Beauregard on the evacuation of Columbia, South Carolina. In mid-March 1865, as Grant's line threatened to encircle Richmond, the secretary personally managed the movements of portions of Fitzhugh Lee's cavalry in attempting to keep open a route to the south. He ordered a union of the forces of Generals Daniel Adams and Howell Cobb to defend Columbus, Georgia, in April. And following Lee's surrender, Breckinridge authorized all soldiers not surrendered with the Army of Northern Virginia to attach themselves to units of their choice in the Army of Tennessee, and he directly ordered General John Echols, commanding the Department of Western Virginia and Eastern Tennessee, to move his command to link with Joseph E. Johnston's army in North Carolina. Breckinridge, on his own authority, exempted General Wade Hampton and his cavalry from Johnston's subsequent surrender and allowed Hampton to try getting his command to the Trans-Mississippi. By mid-April it seems to have been generally understood that Breckinridge was fully in command of the War Department and all of its admittedly dwindling functions. When Jefferson Davis denied Virginia governor William Smith's proposition that he be given command of all remaining Virginia forces, Smith took his case to Breckinridge.[7]

The Commissary General's Office provides a worthy case study in how the new secretary of war seized and maintained direction of the affairs of his department. "When I arrived at Richmond the Commissary department," he later wrote, "was in a very deplorable condition."[8] With the appointment of St. John, Breckinridge made the revitalization of this bureau his first priority. The two conferred daily and lengthily. To alleviate the immediate shortage in Lee's army, they devised a system of collecting supplies by appealing to farmers and shipping the proceeds directly to the army, bypassing Northrop's old bottleneck central depots. Seeing the success wrought in the Old Dominion under this plan, Breckinridge personally persuaded Governor Zebulon Vance of North Carolina to repeat the process there.[9]

Excuses, Turning Points, and Defeats

The results were dramatic. Three weeks after Breckinridge and St. John began their work, Lee sent a letter stating that his army had not been so well supplied in months. By April 1 they had collected in Virginia and North Carolina 3 million rations of bread and 2.5 million rations of meat. Breckinridge and St. John were producing supplies in quantities that outstripped the transportation facilities available to get them to the armies.[10]

Only a war minister who felt confident of his authority could venture into some of the areas traversed by Breckinridge. When complaints reached his ears from Nathan B. Forrest and others that men raising companies in the mountains of Kentucky refused to join regular volunteer service when ordered, Breckinridge sent his own cousin into Kentucky with orders that all Confederates who did not come out and join the army would be handed over to the enemy as guerrillas.[11]

Then there was management of the press. Voluntary censorship by newsmen and editors had worked successfully early in the war, but as the conflict progressed, the government felt an increasing need to regulate news. The attendant outcry was predictable. When Breckinridge took office, he agreed that continued censorship was necessary. As a result, an almost total embargo on war news was enforced by the secretary. Yet Breckinridge found himself complimented by the press for his conduct. The Richmond *Whig* declared that "if anything of interest transpires which can be published, we are confident that the intelligent Secretary of War will cause the news to be promptly communicated to the press."[12]

Under authority from Congress, the government was empowered to take over railroads and direct their operation. As soon as the law was passed, Breckinridge notified Braxton Bragg that he would use the power if necessary, and almost immediately a case presented itself. As a military necessity for the movement of supplies, Beauregard wanted the track gauge of the Piedmont & North Carolina Rail Road between Salisbury and Danville widened to that of the major Virginia roads. Governor Vance objected, but Breckinridge told him bluntly that "under the late law, I may be compelled to take possession of some of the roads." Under authority from the secretary of war, instructions had earlier been given for Joseph E. Johnston to take over all rail facilities within his command, and while Breckinridge was negotiating with Vance, orders went out taking over the western portion of the South Side Rail Road. The war ended before the work was fairly begin, but it was one more indicator of the self-confidence and security that the new secretary felt in his office.[13]

As all of this was taking place, Breckinridge was busy organizing what must be described as a small-scale campaign—the evacuation of Richmond. On February 23 Assistant Secretary of War John A. Campbell advised Breckinridge to make plans for the almost inevitable evacuation, but the Kentuckian was considerably ahead of him. From first taking office, Breckinridge had seen what would have to happen and had already been in correspondence with Lee on a possible route of retreat from the capital, at the same time making preliminary arrangements to have supplies waiting for the retiring army at its destination. Breckinridge gathered intelligence from southwest Virginia, through which Lee would probably retreat; held stores in some depots in North Carolina to await him; and quietly but firmly alerted commanders along the way to "gather every thing up, hold it well in hand and not let the enemy advance." Confidentially he told them, "The country towards the S. west may soon become of vast importance."[14]

Breckinridge conferred frequently with Lee. The secretary tried to pinpoint how much time was available for preparation. Even before receiving a reply, he ordered his bureau chiefs to ready their archives and public stores. At the same time, he brought the matter before Davis and the cabinet on February 25, to no avail. "Nothing has been done," he lamented to Lee. "Do you advise that I go to work at once?"[15]

Breckinridge conferred with representatives of the general assembly, saw to the strength of the Richmond reserves, and made tentative plans for the destruction of matériel that could not be removed. In two days the secretary had the evacuation planned and all arrangements made for its execution. In an interview with Lee, Breckinridge promised that the movement could be completed within ten or twelve days. On April 2 when word came that Lee could hold out no longer, it took Breckinridge less than twenty-four hours to complete the evacuation of the government. Whereas in former days Davis would certainly have taken a guiding role in organizing and conducting such an important operation—particularly important should the Confederacy survive—now he played no part at all. From first to last it was the secretary of war who managed the evacuation.[16]

With this operation barely concluded, it was Breckinridge who further conferred with the retreating Lee and counseled him in the matter of a linkup with Johnston in North Carolina. Leaving Lee on April 7, Breckinridge began yet another minor campaign, this time managing the flight of the Confederate cabinet through North and South Carolina into Georgia. The story is well known. A salient feature, however, is the increasing amount of authority that he assumed after Lee's surrender. As Davis took less and less part in making the decisions, Breckinridge took more and more. It was to the secretary of war that Johnston turned for advice and counsel in his surrender negotiations with Sherman. It was Breckinridge who, on his own initiative, disbursed to the remaining Confederate troops the last of the treasury specie. And it was the Kentuckian who in effect disbanded the War Department at Washington, Georgia, on May 4. Indeed, among those who were with the fleeing government in its last weeks, the general feeling was, as General Basil Duke put it, that only Breckinridge "knew what was going on, what was going to be done, and what ought to be done."[17]

As far back as September 1861, before Breckinridge joined Southern ranks, he had confided to friends his belief that the Confederacy ultimately would be overthrown. What he met when taking over the War Department hardly changed his mind. On his first day in office a report of the unsuccessful Hampton Roads Peace Conference arrived. Two days later came Lee's complaint of lack of supplies and with it the warning that calamity faced his army. Replies to a circular he sent to all bureau chiefs asking the condition of their departments—he was the first secretary to bother to do so—were all uniformly discouraging. The generals in the high command, as always, squabbled, and there was no money to buy necessities.[18]

Barely two weeks after taking office, Breckinridge first voiced to the president his feeling that the cause was lost. Explaining all of the above, he declared, "It is plainly impracticable for this Department to carry on any of its operations under such a condition of things."[19] Taking an honorable peace as his goal, Breckinridge seized every opportunity to persuade the president. When General James Longstreet presented tentative plans for meetings between himself and Union general E. O. C. Ord, having the cessation of hostilities as their object, the secretary of war vocally approved the plan before Davis.[20]

On March 8, after reflecting on recent conversations with Lee, Breckinridge asked the general in chief for his written views on the military situation. After receiving Lee's gloomy reply, Breckinridge addressed another circular to his bureau chiefs. These replies, too, were pessimistic. Then on March 13 he submitted the entire correspondence to Davis, voicing his own concurrence in Lee's portent of calamity. Ostensibly the material was submitted for Davis to pass on to Congress before it adjourned. In fact, it had quite another purpose, one divined by Governor Vance and others. The secretary hoped to persuade Davis that further resistance was futile.[21]

Vance's suspicion is confirmed by the fact that Breckinridge began meeting privately with senators such as R. M. T. Hunter, discussing Lee's letter with them. A few days after sending the papers to Davis, Breckinridge called a conference at the hotel room of Kentucky senator Henry C. Burnett. Present were Louis T. Wigfall of Texas, Hunter and Allen Caperton of Virginia, and Waldo Johnston and George G. Vest of Missouri. As Vest later recorded the meeting, "Breckinridge stated his conviction that the Confederate cause was hopeless and in a very few days all would be lost." "I have wished for some time to confer with the members of the Confederate Senate . . . as to the effect of the final collapse. . . . What I propose is this: That the Confederacy should not be captured in fragments, that we should not disband like banditti, but that we should surrender as a government, and we will thus maintain the dignity of our cause, and secure the respect of our enemies, and the best terms for our soldiers." When someone asked, "How about the President?" the secretary of war replied, "That gives me more concern than anything connected with the plan." The meeting concluded, Breckinridge gave the senators a final plea. "This has been a magnificent epic," he said. "In God's name, let it not terminate in a farce."[22]

Neither Davis nor the congressmen were yet persuaded to act. Even Lee's surrender did not change the president's mind, and when Breckinridge rejoined the cabinet at Greensboro, North Carolina, after leaving Lee, Davis remained determined to fight on. By prearrangement Breckinridge obtained for Johnston and Beauregard an opportunity to present their view of the hopelessness of the situation before an April 13 cabinet meeting. They wanted to ask Sherman for terms. Davis disapproved. Supported by Benjamin, Breckinridge, Mallory, and Reagan argued for the plan, and the president gave in.[23]

Nevertheless, Davis hoped to continue the war. When the cabinet moved south to Lexington and was joined by Governor Vance, Davis took up in a cabinet meeting the idea of retreating west of the Mississippi to continue the war using General Kirby Smith's scattered army. It was obvious that Davis wanted Vance to lead the North Carolina troops out of the state with him. One or more of the cabinet members agreed with the President, and then, wrote Vance, "General Breckenridge spoke."

> I shall never forget either the language or the manner of that splendid Kentuckian. With the utmost frankness, and with the courage of sincerity, he said he did not think they were dealing candidly with Governor Vance; that their hopes of accomplishing the results set forth by Mr. Davis were so remote and uncertain that he, for his part, could not advise me to forsake the great duties which devolved upon me in order to follow the further fortunes of the retreating Confederacy.... With a deep sigh Mr. Davis replied to General Breckenridge: "Well, perhaps, General, you are right."[24]

That same evening began the secretary of war's involvement in the Sherman-Johnston surrender negotiations. Johnston specifically requested Breckinridge's presence in the talks because he felt that the Kentuckian could overcome Davis' objections and persuade him to accept whatever terms resulted. Breckinridge, having already approved in cabinet a preliminary list of surrender provisions, spoke for several minutes in advocacy of them before Sherman. One of his chief concerns was the political rights of paroled Confederates, and the influence of his "concise and statesmanlike mind" clearly showed in the finished document in its provisions for reestablishment of Federal courts in the South and the stress given to protection of the legal rights of former Rebels.[25]

Breckinridge personally put a copy of the agreement in Davis' hands, but the president, still clinging stubbornly to his hopes, asked for the opinions of his cabinet members in writing. Breckinridge gave his bluntly. "Prompt steps," he said, "should be taken to put an end to the war." This time the cabinet was unanimous, and finally Davis agreed to Sherman's terms. When Washington rejected the cartel and directed Sherman to treat only for Johnston's army, Davis and escort continued their journey south, to the last so-called cabinet meeting, at Abbeville, South Carolina, on May 2. Yet again Davis tried to persuade his military men to continue the fight west of the Mississippi. Yet again Breckinridge and others opposed him, thinking his views were, as Colonel W. C. P. Breckinridge put it, "wholly erroneous."[26]

Even here it was observed by members of the escort that of the remaining cabinet, only the secretary of war did not stand in awe of the president. After making good his escape to Cuba, the Kentuckian made yet one more plea for honorable surrender, advising all remaining Confederates to throw themselves on the clemency of President Andrew Johnson and ask for pardon. Breckinridge wanted no more blood shed for an extinct cause and so expressed himself to the press.[27] It is clear that Breckinridge regarded his efforts to bring about an honorable surrender for the Confederacy as the most important contribution of his cabinet service. "Should my friends ever know my part in the occurrences of the last three months," he wrote that May, "I venture to think it will give me an increased claim on their confidence and regard."[28]

Of course, the South would have fallen with or without Secretary of War John C. Breckinridge, but that it fell as it did, as a nation rather than as piecemeal bands led by Davis and others, owes much to this Kentuckian and his vision of the Confederacy in posterity. It is also indicative of the role that this war minister played in Confederate leadership. Unlike any of his predecessors, he exerted a major influence on civil and military policy and, equally important, upon the president. This does not necessarily mean, however, that the outcome of the war might have been otherwise if Breckinridge had been appointed earlier. Davis did consider him for the post back in October 1861 when Breckinridge first joined the Confederacy, but then the Kentuckian had almost no practical experience of the military and would have been an able but unknowledgeable administrator.[29]

When he took office in 1865, however, his appointment was received as a breath of fresh air. His energy inspired hope in many. "If we had had Breckinridge in [Leroy P.] Walker's place at the beginning," said the quotable Mary Chesnut, "what a difference it might have made."[30] Others more expert than her agreed, among them Robert E. Lee. General William Preston later recalled that, upon hearing of Breckinridge's appointment, Lee said that he was the ablest general in the Confederacy to assume such a post. "If I had an army I would at once put it under his command."[31] Three years after the surrender Lee made it clear to William Preston Johnston that he regarded Breckinridge as the ablest of the war secretaries. "He regretted that Breckinridge had not been earlier made secretary of war," Johnston wrote. "He is a great man," said Lee. "I was acquainted with him as Congressman and Vice-President and as one of our Generals, but I did not *know* him till he was secretary of war, and he is a lofty, pure strong man."[32]

That last is the real point. Breckinridge was a strong man, and his tenure in the War Department built the office of secretary into a strong one or as strong as was possible at that late stage of the war. Many factors contributed to this, not least of which was Lee's assuming some of Davis' former powers when

Excuses, Turning Points, and Defeats

he accepted the post of general in chief. It is also evident that Jefferson Davis in 1865 was physically and mentally weakened by four years of his terrible burden, not as formidable an opponent for a war secretary as in earlier days. But there is no doubt that the chief ingredient that finally brought the office of secretary of war into its own, to the near-realization of its intent and potential in the process of influencing the war and the history of the Confederacy, was the character and stature of its last incumbent, John C. Breckinridge. His lasting contribution to the history of the Confederate States is not that he might have won its independence but that he managed its defeat in a manner that lent his stature to the cause itself.

Part Four

The Confederacy in Myth and Posterity

Stonewall Jackson in Myth and Memory

IN 1932 THE ALWAYS DELIGHTFUL James Thurber wrote an essay titled "No More Biographies." In it he wrote of visiting his friend Rumsonby at the Library of Congress. The man had charge of the fictional Bureau of Publishing Statistics and Biographers' Permits, an agency created as a result of a recent glut of Warren G. Harding and Abraham Lincoln biographies. Rumsonby met Thurber with a stern warning that he had better not be thinking of doing a biography, especially of a Civil War figure. Everybody had been covered except an obscure Ohio captain. There were 92 Lees and 95 Grants in print, and 40 million copies of Lincoln books.

In fact, the library was now imposing fines for unauthorized biographies. Grant would cost $5,000; Jeb Stuart, $3,250; and Stonewall Jackson, $4,000, plus confiscation of the books. Lincoln carried a maximum fine of $50,000 and two years in prison. Even works of fiction that included anything that looked faintly biographical were suspect and could wind up with adjudication of fines and imprisonment by the Supreme Court.[1]

When it came to satire, Thurber was usually on the mark, and there was often more than a little grain of substance behind the parodies he penned. Certainly his jab at the proliferation of Civil War biographies, not to mention their increasing inventiveness and flights of imagination in the twentieth century, hit the target. Indeed, given what has been done with and to Stonewall Jackson in the years since his death, perhaps a fine of $4,000 for writing a biography of him is not enough.

In October 1864, barely more than a year after Jackson's death, a Confederate Kentucky cavalryman was moving down the Shenandoah Valley with his command and paused in Lexington, where the great general had lived and where now he lay buried. The cavalryman wrote of it in his diary. "A sacred, solemn air, the spirit of the great Jackson—seems to hang over these piny hills—which were immortalized by his footsteps, & consecrated by his presence." As the soldier entered the town, he passed Lexington's cemetery on his right. He turned aside, as he put it, to see the spot "where repose the ashes of our country's mightiest chieftain & idol—Stonewall Jackson." There was a small flagstaff marking the grave, "a simple sodded mound with a bouquet of flowers" that someone in Lexington replaced afresh every day. The Kentuckian could not but notice that the footboard was entirely gone, and missing, too, was most of the headboard. Locals told him that it was the Yankees in David Hunter's raid on Lexington in June who took away pieces of the boards, but not out of vandalism. "The Yankees . . . showed his memory the greatest respect," people told the Kentuckian. They took away those souvenirs as mementos of a man they admired despite his being their enemy.[2]

Already the myth-making had begun, and in some ways those Yankee soldiers were paying Jackson's memory better respect than would some of his associates and future biographers, for excepting Lincoln and Lee, probably no other great leader of the Civil War era has suffered so much from being mythologized and thus misunderstood. Yet people could not, and cannot, resist him.

Probably the first biography to appear was written by a Southern woman, Catherine C. Hopley. Her *"Stonewall" Jackson, Late General of the Confederate States Army. A Biographical Sketch, and an Outline of His Virginia Campaigns,* was published in London in two editions barely months after his death. Not surprisingly, it is sentimental, laudatory, and based wholly on hearsay and what the author had read in the newspapers of the time. Very soon thereafter appeared Markenfield Addey's *"Stonewall Jackson." The Life and Military Career of Thomas Jonathan Jackson, Lieutenant-General in the Confederate Army,* which came out within months of Chancellorsville. Ironically, it was written and published in the North, where curiosity and admiration for the general were already on the rise. It has little to recommend it since the author never knew Jackson or even saw him, and writing from across the battle lines, Addey could hardly consult Jackson's associates or family. Undeterred, he brought out another volume in 1864 titled *"Old Jack" and His Foot Cavalry,* being a virtual rehash of the earlier volume.

Also in 1863 John Esten Cooke published *The Life of Stonewall Jackson,* an admiring and uncritical account filled with flowery, embellished, and generally useless prose. Cooke, like so many others who would follow him, never let the truth get in the way of a good story. In this book and in another version in 1866 called *Stonewall Jackson, A Military Biography,* Cooke started a host of legends, such as Jackson's penchant for lemon sucking.

Robert L. Dabney published *Life and Campaigns of Lieut.-Gen. Thomas J. Jackson* in 1866 also, with full cooperation from Mary Anna Jackson. In fact, having been reduced almost to penury, Mrs. Jackson took sound advice and showed considerable shrewdness in her arrangements with Dabney, a clergyman whom the religious Jackson had made chief of staff for no good reason other than the fact that Jackson always trusted a minister and believed he would act with divine guidance. Dabney was a disaster as a soldier, but commissioned

Lieutenant General Thomas J. "Stonewall" Jackson from the frontispiece of his wife's memoir of his life. By the time it appeared, his mythic stature was already assured, South and North.
Mary Anna Jackson, Memoirs of "Stonewall" Jackson

to do the work by Mrs. Jackson, he produced a valuable book full of primary material nowhere else available. Moreover, he was honest with Mrs. Jackson, and stood out of the way while she arranged for publication in New York by the firm of Blielock & Co., while also arranging publication in England with another firm. She engaged a professor at the University of Virginia to translate the biography into German and French for European sale and through her attorney negotiated what appears to have been better than standard terms for her own compensation.[3]

Some thirty years would pass with no other noteworthy biographies, though several reprintings of those already mentioned occurred. Then in 1895 Mary Anna Jackson spoke out herself in her *Memoirs of Stonewall Jackson.* She had resisted all entreaties for decades to tell her own story, and now she claimed that she was writing at the behest of her family before she should die and her recollections go with her to the grave. Probably the best feature of her book are the many Jackson letters included, some of which have mysteriously disappeared in the ensuing century. Hers is the best intimate look we have at the general, and she, for a change, forbore to create or pass on legends and myths about him.

Just three years later appeared what is probably to date still the best biography, British colonel G. F. R. Henderson's *Stonewall Jackson.* He wrote with the full cooperation of Mrs. Jackson. Perhaps even more important, Jackson's old mapmaker, Jedediah Hotchkiss, had been collecting materials for a generation, himself intending to write a biography of his old chieftain. Now Hotchkiss turned all of this over to Henderson for his unrestricted use. Furthermore, Henderson had the advantage of being able to interview many who had known the general and served under him. The result is a biography—that probably should have listed Hotchkiss as coauthor but didn't—that is almost a primary resource. In the years since its first publication, it has gone through over twenty editions and has never been out of print, something that can be said of few other biographies.

As Jackson's memory came into the twentieth century, the biographies took on a more literary tone, with less of the extensive quotations of letters and reports that characterized nineteenth-century biography. Men who had not known Jackson, and who could no longer talk with those who had, now turned to the evocation of language to replace that of direct recollection. Allen Tate published *Stonewall Jackson, the Good Soldier* in 1928. He was no historian, but he produced a moving account. More moving still was Frank Vandiver's *Mighty*

Stonewall, which appeared in 1957. Vandiver's work was reasonably researched, though he overlooked voluminous manuscript sources. Moreover, like almost all Civil War historians of the past two generations, he had not yet learned to differentiate between the truth and the nonsense and lies that permeate so many of the published recollections of leading men of the war era, especially among some of Jackson's associates like Henry Kyd Douglas. As a result, *Mighty Stonewall* perpetuates much of the Jackson mythology. It is redeemed, however, by the beautiful prose of which few beside Vandiver are capable. Two years later, in 1959, Lenoir Chambers produced a two-volume *Stonewall Jackson*. Many still regard it as the closest thing to a definitive biography that we have. Chambers was an indifferent historian, but his research went somewhat beyond Vandiver's, and his prose was nearly as good. And while not strictly a biography of Jackson, Douglas Southall Freeman's *Lee's Lieutenants*, published in 1945, was and is a vital reference on "Old Jack," though it suffers the same weakness as Vandiver's and Chambers's books where reliance on suspect first-person accounts is concerned.

Meanwhile a number of much lesser works have appeared, and continue to appear, that deserve neither specific mention nor reading. Jackson has always been an easy target for the potboiler school of slapdash writer who simply rewrites or paraphrases a few previous biographies and some of the memoirs and calls the result a book. Indeed, from among this crowd one appeared in the late 1980s that gave Jackson a unique distinction. John Bowers, a journalist, produced a thoroughly useless life of the general that was crowned by a book jacket displaying as the title character a photograph of a Yankee cavalryman and an enlisted man at that! The author was so ignorant of the subject, and learned so little in the course of writing, that he didn't even know what Jackson had looked like or, apparently, which side he had been on.

Thus, the Vandiver and Chambers biographies have remained the standards until the anticipated 1997 appearance of James I. Robertson Jr.'s massive two-thousand-page biography, five years in the research and two years in the writing. Its revelations and its corrections of much of what has passed for history are going to make it a milestone in American biography. Much of the Jackson mythology will be laid to rest permanently.[4]

Most of that myth, much of what we *think* we know about the mighty Stonewall, is due to men who knew him—often not as well as they claimed—and who in some way, perhaps subconsciously, sought to aggrandize themselves by exaggerating their intimacy with the general. John Esten Cooke wrote repeatedly about Jackson in several books. With Cooke it is always hard to tell where his actual recollection leaves off and his novelist's imagination takes over. He is the first to bring up the notion of Jackson's peculiarity for sucking on lemons. What Cooke, and others to follow, fail to appreciate is that Jackson loved fruit of all kinds and ate it whenever possible to relieve—or so he thought —his dyspeptic stomach. Jackson was undoubtedly a hypochondriac and believed that citrus was especially helpful. He ate everything he could get but was especially fond of peaches and melons. As for the lemons, some varieties of that fruit are almost as sweet as an orange and make wonderful eating all by themselves. Viewed in this light, was Jackson sucking on a lemon necessarily such a peculiar thing for him to do?

If Cooke is hard to trust, John D. Imboden is even worse. He never wrote a book about Jackson, but he penned several articles for *Century Magazine* that later found their way into the still-influential *Battles and Leaders of the Civil War*. *Battles and Leaders* is a classic work still much read, and still in print, but historians have learned over the last couple of generations to place very little trust in it. The articles are written twenty years after the fact and usually by generals and lesser field grade officers. One maxim of military history is that the higher a man's rank is, the greater is his concern for his own reputation, and the more defensive he becomes in any controversy over his performance. *Battles and Leaders* is written chiefly by men defending their reputations, and Imboden, who was never more than a mediocre commander, is one of them. When he writes about Jackson, he consistently glorifies himself, and along the way adds pure inventions, such as the episode at Harpers Ferry in 1861 when he has Jackson shrewdly adjusting the timetables of the Baltimore & Ohio Railroad so that most of its engines and rolling stock are passing within his command all at the same time, and he then ordered Imboden to capture them all. This never happened. Jackson did take a lot of the B&O's rolling stock, but without any such stratagem.[5]

Even worse is Henry Kyd Douglas. His *I Rode with Stonewall* has been an accepted classic since it first appeared in 1940. Douglas' egotistical self-aggrandizement has led Robertson to suggest that the title really should be *Stonewall Rode with Me*. Jackson seems to seek and take his staff officer's advice at every turn. Douglas is right there in every great moment, implies that he acts as Jackson's chief of staff, and after Jackson's death is still at the center of Second Corps power as chief of staff to Jubal Early. The facts are, however, that in the entire course of Jackson's career, Douglas spent less than six months on his staff and much of the time was not with him at all. Moreover, he was never at any time Jackson's or Early's chief of staff, that position being filled chiefly by Colonel Sandie Pendleton. Douglas wrote his memoir some years after the war—apparently basing it on a diary that is still rumored to be in existence in family hands—but no one would publish it.[6] He tried one publisher after another, and there is some evidence that each time it was rejected, he rewrote it or major portions of it to make himself an increasingly important figure in the Jackson story in the hope that this would attract a publisher. By the 1890s his memoir was well known among other old Confederates, and Early, at least, seems to have read some of it, for he told Jedediah Hotchkiss that he could not even *remember* Douglas, much less that he had ever served on his staff.

Yet Douglas has been one of the single most influential sources of the Jackson legend. He, too, makes a point of the peculiarity of the lemons. Yet from what we know of Jackson now, only a man not very familiar with him at all would regard the lemon thing as a peculiarity, and much the same is to be said of other bits of the Jackson myth. The story that he avoided pepper because it made his left leg ache is a fabrication. The story that he was so punctilious about orders that when told to march at noon, he would keep his command standing in the street of Lexington until he heard the clock chime is also a falsehood.

Of course, he was peculiar. He was a hypochondriac for instance, but keep in mind that this was in an era when a great proportion of the population suffered more or less constantly. The modern concept of a healthy diet was nonexistent, and there was not a single efficacious medicine available for treating any disease or condition. The remedies people took, in addition to being ineffectual, were often instead harmful, even dangerous, and increasing rather than lessening discomfort. They had no understanding of internal medicine at all. Anything that seemed to relate to the lungs was consumption. Anything that seemed to bother the stomach and gastric system was dyspepsia. Anything troubling the spine or musculature was rheumatism. And any affliction that seemed to be inside the head was neuralgia. With nothing effective available from a doctor or an apothecary, people literally created their own medicines and experimented on themselves. Homeopathy was in full swing.

Is it any wonder, then, that people of the time showed what to most of us today would seem to be an excessive and unhealthy preoccupation with their health? Many of them, much of the time, did not feel well, and having no sci-

The Confederacy in Myth and Posterity

entifically based idea of why, they had little option for causes to blame but what would appear to us to be superstition. Look at Lincoln, Jefferson Davis, Robert E. Lee, indeed many other men and women great and small of the era, and you will find the same seeming hypochondria and the same, to us, odd superstitions related to health. In Jackson's case, he would not have avoided pepper unless he liked it, for his particular medical quackery was the notion that if he really liked something to eat, it was probably bad for him, and thereafter he would do without. He actually experimented once with bread, trying several slices with butter and others without. Deciding that he preferred the taste of bread with butter, he thereafter ate his bread plain. Indeed, the only luxury he seems to have allowed himself was his fruit.

Much the same kind of explanation helps us to gain a better—and myth-free—understanding of the great general when we look carefully at the full story of his life and the context in which he lived it. For instance, how strange it seems that when Jackson was twenty-seven and complained to a friend of trouble eating, a constriction in his chest, an inability to keep his mind on his work, and more, his friend had to tell him that the reason was that he was in love. How interesting, too, that all who knew Jackson recalled his utter inability to "get" a joke. Men tried again and again to tell him funny stories, but invariably a punchline left him with a blank stare on his face. Tell Jackson that a chicken crossed the road "to get to the other side," and he would only nod his head and then ask why the chicken wanted to get to the other side. And on those rare occasions when Jackson did laugh, he threw his head back, opened his mouth . . . and emitted no sound whatever. Just as he did not know when he was in love, so he did not know how to laugh. Douglas and Cooke and a host of others have seen these as Jackson's peculiarities, and so they have entered the legend.

But are they peculiar? Consider what we now know of Jackson's childhood. Before he was four years old—the age at which psychologists now tell us our emotional futures are pretty well set—he had seen his father and brother die. He had been taken from his mother to be raised by an uncle who was a thorough scoundrel; brought back to see his mother only once, and that when she was on her deathbed; and thereafter raised in an atmosphere of cold aloofness by a distasteful and untrustworthy man in a house entirely devoid of affection. Some today complain of what they call "psychobabble" in biographies, but only a fool would ignore the effects such a childhood can have. It is any wonder that Jackson did not get jokes or could not laugh? What had he known in his formative years that there was to laugh about? Is it really surprising that someone else had to tell him that he was in love when he experienced those disturbing sensations in the presence of his future wife? Until that moment, he had never known love or affection.

Consider these things in the context of Jackson's youth, and suddenly he seems not peculiar, but sad, pitiful, a character who draws our sympathy. Put him on the couch, so to speak, and he becomes a very familiar twentieth-century character.

Religion is the surest guide to understanding Jackson in his last ten years, and it is the failure to deal intelligently with this aspect of the man that has led more than anything else to the myths that have grown around him as an oddity or a congenital eccentric. When viewed through the lens of his intense Calvinist faith, his behavior is in fact quite consistent.

Growing up as he did rootless, loveless, Jackson lacked an anchor. The military gave him that, and he strove to excel in it as he did in all things by his single-minded dedication to purpose. Then in the 1850s he found God. In fact, he consciously looked for God, trying several denominations before he settled on so-called Old Light Presbyterianism, a brand of the faith whose deity was all powerful, all knowing, infallible, and not a little terrible. Jackson immediately poured himself into his faith. He read Scripture incessantly. He attended every service possible, and took the Sabbath so literally that he would not even have a secular thought on Sunday. Instead he devoted the entire day to prayer and church. His was an Old Testament God, unforgiving, ruthless to the point of cruelty in dealing with the unbeliever and the wicked. With the way Jackson had of unquestioning obedience to any acknowledged superior, it never occurred to him to question the acts of the Lord, even when inscrutable, even when seemingly inhumane.

Scholars and buffs have puzzled for generations, for instance, over Jackson's unyielding attitude toward deserters and other transgressors during the Civil War. Most generals went out of their way to commute death sentences. Jackson never did. Convinced that the Confederacy's cause was just, and that it was the cause of the Lord, Jackson could and did view any man who thwarted or betrayed that cause as a violator of the word of God himself, and death was the price exacted by the God of Jeremiah. This also explains something even more disturbing to Jackson's admirers, his call for the black flag early in the war. Without regret or remorse, he suggested taking no prisoners and by implication might even have countenanced putting to death noncombatants regardless of age or gender. Hit the enemy immediately, as hard and as ruthlessly as possible, he reasoned, and the enemy would recoil from prosecuting the war. But deeper within the man was the certainty that the Yankees were about the work of evil, that they had betrayed the people of God and thereby God himself, and that they were thus deserving of swift and merciless judgment.

So, too, can we explain some of those other supposed quirks or peculiarities of Stonewall's. Why did he so heartlessly persecute and prosecute once-trusted subordinates such as General Richard Garnet or A. P. Hill? In the military "transgressions" of each, most commanders would have seen nothing more than the exercise of good judgment under trying circumstances. But Jackson could see only that they had disobeyed an express order. It did not matter a whit that by so doing, they might have saved their commands from extinction. An order was an order. Jackson himself gave blind, unthinking obedience, and he expected the same from his men. In his rigid Calvinistic view of the world and the army, a man who obeyed an order and lost a battle was deserving of high praise, while one who used his discretion or disobeyed and thereby won a victory deserved only court-martial.

This also accounts for another supposed mystery. One of the great elements of the myth of Jackson that has made him mysterious to so many is his performance during the Seven Days, particularly during the Battle of Frayser's Farm. For hours that day Jackson sat immobile, his troops doing nothing, while hearing the sounds of Longstreet getting a beating only a couple of miles away. For one thing, of course, there is ample testimony that Stonewall was so exhausted as to be literally befuddled much of the day. He could not respond when officers spoke to him. He fell asleep sitting up at the mess fire, a biscuit still clenched in his teeth as he dozed. Much of the time he stared blankly at the ground. In such a state of physical and mental exhaustion, all he could do was blindly obey orders. But that was his hallmark anyhow, and he was obeying an order when he stayed out of the fight. Lee had told Jackson to lead his men to where they sat out the day's battle.

Of course, circumstances changed after Lee issued that order, and he would have been happy to have had Jackson join the fray, but he sent no new order. In such circumstances Jackson slavishly obeyed the only order he had. Given his condition, it was all he could do in any case. But Lee, for Jackson, was becoming a living embodiment of the Almighty. Jackson believed that he owed unbending duty to God alone. But since the Confederacy was the Lord's chosen cause in this contest, then the Almighty must necessarily have imbued the leaders of the cause with his own infallibility. As a result, Stonewall Jackson would no more disobey or "interpret" an order from Robert E. Lee than he would deny Jehovah himself. Lee was God's champion on earth.

The more we look at Jackson stripped of the mystery and nonsense given us by those who claimed to know him, yet who in fact only used him, we see a man not at all hard to understand. This does not mean that we necessarily like him. Even James I. Robertson has to admit that for associates the general was not a lot of fun to be around. He was humorless, religiously fanatic, utterly lacking in understanding or sympathy for those weaker than himself. While there were no measurements for such things as IQs in those days, had there been, it is likely that Jackson would not have measured much above the average. It has often been said that "a foolish consistency is the hobgoblin of tiny minds." Those not adept at thinking find comfort in situations where they do not have to think. Certainly an unbending consistency characterized Stonewall Jackson. Certainly, too, he was no quick study. He got through West Point only by rigid application, constant study, and rote memorization. Later as a professor at the Virginia Military Institute, he had to commit every day's lectures to memory the night before, and it completely unsettled him if any student interrupted the monotonous recitation of it the next day with a question. Jackson could deal with or impart information only in a certain prearranged order. He could answer questions only by repeating word for word what he had just said, and sometimes he had to back up clear to the beginning of the lecture and go through it all over again before he found the appropriate passage.

He read nothing much in the way of literature to leaven his personality. He was utterly tone deaf and unable to appreciate music, though he seemed to like it. When he sang, he wreaked chaos on any song sheet. He lacked a gift for conversation and spent hours in company without opening his mouth. Nor could he visualize things well. Even his most loving admirers admit that he was unable to read either map or terrain, nor could he look at the one and apply it to the other. Only his discovery of Hotchkiss, one of the war's most gifted cartographers, saved Jackson from being defeated by geography. Hotchkiss taught him slowly how to read a map and see on its smooth surface the great mountain of Massanutten, the passes at Luray and New Market, the valley turnpike and the passes of the Blue Ridge, that enabled Jackson to electrify the world in 1862.

Yet therein, in that dramatic valley campaign, lies the evidence that the man did have a good brain, that he could think. For no one gave him orders on how to save the valley, only that he was to do so. The brilliant campaign by which he defeated several armies, all superior to him in numbers, came exclusively from Hotchkiss' maps, the valor and determination of Jackson's "foot cavalry," and his own imagination. However much we may conclude that Stonewall lacked personality, there can be no doubt that he did possess an imagination. As to his intellect, his "genius" may simply have been that of an instinct for waging war. We cannot know.[7]

If generations of Southerners and other Americans had not thus misunderstood much of Jackson the man and general, would they still have taken him to their bosoms? Of course. His deeds either excused or justified his seeming peculiarities. Indeed, for some of us his eccentricities actually explain his performance, his peculiar form of inspiration. Whatever the case, it was with seeming light speed that Jackson became not just a sectional hero but also a national and even international figure of admiration. During the war, at the instigation of A. J. Beresford-Hope, a member of Parliament, the British struck a Stonewall Jackson commemorative medal. Back in the Confederacy, when inflation made a new $500 treasury note necessary, Richmond put Jackson's portrait on the front, making him the only general so honored. Not even Lee would appear on a Confederate note. Though never officially issued, experimental designs also used his bust on Southern postage stamps. And of course, in 1864 when a formidable new ironclad steam ram was built for the South abroad, the Confederate Navy Department named it *Stonewall.*

Scarcely was the war concluded before the Jackson mystique spread. An editor wrote, "The future historian of the great war of secession will dwell with pleasure on the splendid achievements and exalted character of Stonewall Jackson; and all America will one day claim the honor of being the country of this great captain and simple hearted Christian hero. . . . All Americans will one day be proud of the fame of Stonewall Jackson, and will enroll his name on the proud list of American heroes and soldiers." The writer was Ben Wood, editor of the New York *News,* and he wrote this in December 1865. That same year when word reached the North that Jackson's widow was struggling to support herself and his daughter on a mere $150 a year, a movement started in the North to raise a collection for their benefit.[8]

In fact, scarcely known to anyone, the Union passively honored Jackson just two months after his death and while the war was still in full sway. On or before February 24, 1863, the Union gunboat *Tahoma* captured the thirty-ton schooner *Stonewall,* used as a pilot boat. On July 24, 1863, at a Key West prize court, the U.S. Navy formally purchased the schooner and put it into service as a tender for warships in the Gulf Blockading Squadron. The navy kept the name unchanged, and thus a vessel called *Stonewall* fought for the Union. Twice more after the war the U.S. Navy would pay tribute to Jackson. During World War II the USS *Stonewall* plied the Pacific as a fuel ship, and years later, in late November 1963, the Polaris missile submarine USS *Stonewall Jackson* was launched at Mare Island, California. Later converted to carry Poseidon missiles, the submarine only recently went out of commission.[9]

Nor did the United States neglect to honor Jackson in other ways reminiscent of his Confederate honors. In the 1930s the United States Post Office issued a Civil War commemorative series. Jackson and Lee appeared on a stamp, the first time that the nation would so honor anyone who had once fought against it. And in June 1995 the United States Postal Service issued a commemorative sheet honoring the Civil War. Jackson sits prominently on the sheet, along with other great commanders such as Lee, Stuart, Grant, Sherman, and Sheridan. An oddity in the sheet is the inclusion among these *fighting* generals of Joseph E. Johnston. Only the post office can explain that one.

Even what we would term *popular culture* has adopted Jackson in a limited way. Some twenty years ago or more the McCormick's distillery issued a series of commemorative Civil War decanters in the form of porcelain statues of Grant, Lee, Lincoln, Davis, Jeb Stuart, and Stonewall Jackson. There is an irony, of course, in the fact that a single Jackson bottle holds more whiskey than the general consumed in the entire course of his life. He liked whiskey, he explained, and therefore avoided it. And of course, in that pivotal cultural experience for all of us that we call Watergate, his nickname became a verb for all time when a Southern senator told one of those charged in the conspiracy to "stonewall it."

Not only did men of his own time create and perpetuate legends about the mighty Stonewall, but also those of later times who never knew him created new ones of their own. It is a commonplace today that General George Patton and Field Marshall Erwin Rommel studied and emulated Jackson's campaigns in their own. Certainly Patton did study Jackson, as did every student at the Virginia Military Institute. But that story about Rommel is almost certainly pure invention. If you want to measure the continuing presence of Jackson's memory—as often representing the myth as much as the reality—drive the highways and back roads of Virginia and count the Stonewall Restaurants, the Lee-Jackson Motels, the innumerable shops and souvenir stands. Some Southern states, especially Virginia, observe the new federal holiday Martin Luther King Day only because it falls on an older state holiday, Lee-Jackson Day, a date honoring the birth of both generals and unknowingly mistaken about the birthday of Jackson himself. Yet one more myth.

But of course, we create and pass on myths only about those whom we love or admire or those who have made some kind of indelible impression on our personal or national consciences. Certainly that applies to Jackson. Indeed, it applies to him in a way that we have attached to no other American. For there still flourishes the greatest of all myths. If only he had lived, it says, if only those shots in the darkness at Chancellorsville had missed him, then he and not Richard Ewell would have led the old Second Corps at Gettysburg. He, unlike Ewell, would have pressed on unyieldingly on July 1, following his orders at all costs, to take Cemetery Hill. That, says the myth, would have won the Battle of Gettysburg for the South, and that victory, says the myth, would in the end have brought Confederate independence. Try to name any other man whose death, if prevented, can be presumed by so many to have had the power to so climactically affect American history. You cannot. It matters not that the myth is just that, a myth. It is the fact that so many of us believe it that gives it significance.

In a perverse way the very exaggerations and misunderstandings and falsehoods and myths that have helped obscure the real Stonewall Jackson from us for so long have also been in large part responsible for drawing us to him. We have allowed him to be peculiar because we like peculiarity in our heroes, especially in his case, because we need his peculiarity to give some color to an otherwise colorless man. And in the end we have invested him with an invincibility that even he could not have lived up to. In our hearts and our collective conscience truly the only way to "lick" Stonewall Jackson is to put him on a postage stamp.

There has been too much written about him, as Rumsonby, the keeper of the Bureau of Publishing Statistics and Biographers' Permits, would argue. But that is only because too much of it has missed the man in the race for the legend. Yet we don't need the myths when we have the reality, and now in our generation, when the full reality of who Thomas J. Jackson really was is coming to light, we can be in a way discoverers, for we will have the opportunity to be the first to *know* him in over a century. If James I. Robertson or any other future responsible biographer has to pay a fine for writing about Jackson, it will be money well spent.

Myths and Realities of the Confederacy

FOR THOUSANDS OF YEARS myth has been one of the most powerful forces in all of world culture. Spoken today, the word naturally conjures images of classical mythology, of the gods and heroes of ancient Greece and Rome. Myth is regarded as something from the distant past, used to amuse or celebrate rather than to serve social or psychological purposes. Nothing, in fact, could be further from the truth. Mythology surrounds all peoples in all times, as it does today. Indeed, we all participate in it ourselves. We create our own myths, encourage the myths of others by accepting them uncritically, and enhance myths by passing them along, often with embellishment.

Myths are not "lies," not, at least, in the sense that they are consciously created to mislead by intent. Myths are not falsehoods. Somewhere at the root of almost every myth there is some tendril of truth or fact or *perceived* fact. It is the way that slim basis is magnified and elaborated to fit personal, cultural, ethnic, or national needs and aspirations that produces a myth. Mythology sprouts like crabgrass whenever strong passions on important issues command the attention of large numbers. Thus, we should hardly be surprised that a cataclysmic event like the Civil War would produce uncountable myths great and small, touching every aspect of the conflict and the people who endured it.

Moreover, the Civil War offers another example of a related phenomenon. Out of any conflict, the losers create more myths than the winners. It is hardly a surprise. After all, winners have little to explain to themselves. They won. For the loser, however, coping with defeat, dealing with it personally and explaining it to others, places enormous strains on the ego, self-respect, and sense of self-worth of the defeated. The man who loses a scuffle rarely says that the other man was a better fighter. Rather, the light was in his eyes, or his opponent cheated. The person who loses a job hardly ever admits to himself and others that he really did not deserve it. Instead the successful applicant had "pull" or was a favorite of the employer or was better looking. These are the everyday battles fought by most people, and when we win, it is because we deserved it,

The Confederacy in Myth and Posterity

and when we lose, it is usually because of something beyond our control and often imaginary.

The impulse is the same whether that loser is an individual or a host of millions. Thus, Captain John Winslow felt no need for myth to explain his defeat of the CSS *Alabama* off Cherbourg, France, in June 1864. He met the enemy and overpowered it, and that was all there was to it, and he was right. But Admiral Raphael Semmes did not explain his defeat by saying that Winslow fought better or the *Kearsarge* was a better ship. He lost, he said, because Winslow cheated by not telling Semmes beforehand what he intended to do in the battle! In offering probably the most ridiculous excuse for defeat to come

Admiral Raphael Semmes, mythmaker, holds the
record for the Civil War's silliest excuse for defeat.
Author's collection

out of the war, Semmes said he would not have fought Winslow if he had known his foe's intentions.[1] It seems not to have occurred to Semmes that *he* never revealed *his* intentions to any of the vessels whose capture made his reputation. The only armed Yankee warship that he ever defeated, the USS *Hatteras,* was just as outclassed by the *Alabama* as that ship had been by the *Kearsarge,* yet Semmes thought his victory over the *Hatteras* glorious even though he took it by surprise, only identified himself at the last moment, and announced his intent by a broadside.[2] In other words, in the personal myth he created to deal with his defeat, Semmes condemned as ungentlemanly and unchivalrous in others exactly the same behavior that he saw as acceptable in himself. This did not make him a liar and a hypocrite, just a victim of the inconsistencies into which his own myth forced him in order to be at peace with his defeat.

Most of the more important surviving Civil War myths are those created by the Confederates and fostered and nurtured by their lineal and spiritual descendants as a means of exonerating the South from any responsibility in bringing on the conflict and helping Southerners then and later cope with defeat. All peoples part with their myths reluctantly, and historians are at some risk when they try to dismantle those of the Confederacy. To attack Confederate myths is somehow seen as an attack on the South itself. This is untrue, or at least it is not the intent of most of those who examine legends versus reality. Nevertheless, it can produce some extreme reactions. In 1989 when the magazine *Civil War Times Illustrated* published an article titled "The War We Never Finished," its dissection of some of the canon of Confederate mythology produced a hysterical flood of protests. The author was accused of being "a Marxist of the crudest and most vulgar sort," while other letter writers suggested that the magazine must be in the pay of the NAACP or even a part of some international Jewish conspiracy. One argued that another civil war was needed to eradicate the kind of people who would challenge Confederate orthodoxy.[3] Such fulminations are not necessarily the paranoid ravings of a lunatic fringe, either. These feelings are widely held and represent the extremes to which the tampering with treasured myths can drive otherwise presumably reasonable people. And such sentiments came from north and south, east and west.

It is vital to our relationship with the past that we understand that in attacking a myth, we do not necessarily attack the cause or individuals who gave birth to that myth and that in revealing the holes in old misconceptions, we are not necessarily impugning the people who have believed those things.

The Confederacy in Myth and Posterity

Myths simply throw roadblocks in the path to enlightenment, and it is from the truth that we have the most to learn. One man's truth, however, can be another's myth, and only through dispassionate and disinterested dissection of such stories can we tell the difference. The Confederate experience is dotted with episodes that are not particularly admirable. One thing that examination reveals about them, however, is that there is nothing particularly Southern or Confederate about what produced those events. Rather, they emerged out of combinations of circumstances that are inherent in *all* human endeavors. If exposing Confederate myths implies condemnation of any sort, then it is not of our regional foibles but of our human ones.[4]

Many of the myths are simply frivolous and none more so than that suggesting that ever since the conclusion of the Civil War, we have been calling the conflict by the wrong name. During the war it was known by several titles. The North called it the Civil War or the Southern Insurrection or most commonly just the Rebellion, the last two reflecting a definitely regional viewpoint. The Confederates usually just called it the war, or occasionally the War for Southern Independence. In the years after the conflict these and other terms were used, and Alexander H. Stephens' 1868 work *A Constitutional View of the War Between the States* popularized a new name that quickly gained currency in the South. Yet even the majority of former Confederates who wrote about the war in later years in books, memoirs, and letters used the term *Civil War,* which is commonly used and accepted to this day.

Another viewpoint emerged among some of the Confederate veterans, however, and is asserted actively by their descendants today. Civil War is a misnomer, they say, and on two counts. First, the dictionary definition of a civil war is "a war between two opposing groups of citizens of the same country." Interpreting this to mean "two groups fighting for control of the same nation," Confederate partisans point out that the South fought only for control of itself and not of the Union as a whole. Second, the war was not between citizens "of the same country." By its secession the South became a separate nation, and therefore the conflict was one between nations and not within a single nation. The term *Civil War,* they say, "is offensive to many and patently incorrect." They prefer Stephens' old title: War Between the States.[5] Better yet would be Lincoln's War or War of Northern Aggression. So current is this attitude in some quarters that one state branch of the Sons of Confederate Veterans enacted in the 1980s a by-law forbidding the use of Civil War in its publications, and adopting War Between the States as the official name of the conflict. Even Congress got into the act. Just after the end of World War II, as a sop to the "Dixiecrat" minority that President Truman was trying to keep in the Democratic Party, the House of Representatives passed a Southern-sponsored measure declaring that War Between the States should be the "official" name of the struggle.

Maybe the would-be name changers will one day succeed, but it is scarcely likely. The action of Congress is hardly significant in this as in so many other issues. For one thing, it is next to impossible to undo a common usage as universal and long-used as Civil War. More to the point, their arguments are based on fundamental misunderstandings of definitions. Dictionaries do define civil war as "a war between opposing groups of citizens of the same country" and similar wording. But that is all. Nothing is said or implied about them fighting for control of the *same* country, for all of it or part of it. A civil war, in short, by universally accepted definition, is any conflict in which citizens fight among themselves.

But then there is the assertion that these people were *not* citizens of the same country because the Confederacy was a separate nation. Consult any diplomatic history or text published anywhere in the world, and there appears a remarkable unanimity on what constitutes nationhood. The accepted definition in the 1860s, as now, requires that a people sets up and maintains a working civil government, is able to protect territorial integrity, and is recognized as a nation by the other leading nations of the world. Of these three key elements, the Confederacy achieved only the first, the operation of a working, if rickety, civil government. Territorially the Confederacy lost ground in huge chunks almost daily and from the outset. As for recognition, not one single nation, large or small, granted formal diplomatic relations or exchanged ambassadors. In the absence of two of the three requisite standards of nationhood, and especially the vital recognition, the Confederacy cannot be regarded as anything more than a very organized insurrection or separatist movement, just as in the eyes of the world the internal strife in Palestine in the 1940s was nothing more than that until the United States formally recognized the independence of Israel. Then and only then did Israel become a nation.

And when in history has the name of a war been selected by the losers? We call our war for independence the American Revolution, but the British might see it another way. The Mexicans would never call our conflict of 1846–1848 with them the Mexican War. They call it the War of American Intervention, which shows a very different point of view, but do we adopt their name for it? Even if the name changers refuse to acknowledge the compelling logical reasons

The Confederacy in Myth and Posterity

for leaving the Civil War as the Civil War, they must give up the wrong name myth and accept a universal fact of life that winners pick the names. Of course, that would require that they admit that the South really lost the war, and that gets to another myth.

Far more important is the issue of what caused the war, and at the outset it is vital to make a distinction between what led the sections to war and why men subsequently fought that war, for these are two entirely different things in myth and reality. For generations we have heard, both from former Confederates themselves and from their descendants today, that the central issue was state rights. The South, so the myth goes, left the Union to protect sacred sovereign rights that the states had never yielded to the central government when they ratified the Constitution, and which rights were being threatened in 1860 with the election of Lincoln. Yet when asked to enumerate those rights that were thus threatened, champions of secession at the time and defenders of the state rights excuse today are silent. A reading of the congressional debates for the decades prior to the war, of the editorials in Southern newspapers, of the speeches of leading regional statesmen, produces no list of rights endangered; only one right. Slavery. No one at the time complained that the federal government was interfering in state taxation, road building, internal commerce, militia, elections, civil or military appointments, external trade, or anything else. In fact, the state rights defense of secession in 1860–1861 did not really appear in force until *after* 1865 as builders of the Lost Cause myth sought to distance themselves from slavery.

In the past Southern politicians had shown themselves rather indifferent to the whole business of state rights in any context in which slavery was not involved. In 1814 when New England states met in the so-called Hartford Convention to protest the War of 1812 and federal interference with their militias and other state issues, the South stood almost united in opposing the New Englanders for raising the issue of state rights. Later patron saints of secession, such as John C. Calhoun, came forth as champions of nationalism over state rights. Calhoun supported a much greater challenge to the local rights of the Southern and other states in the 1820s when he joined with Henry Clay in pushing a program of internal improvements that used federal money to build roads and canals and improve rivers and harbors. That scheme represented the biggest challenge to state rights ever seen, yet the South did not feel sufficiently committed to the sanctity of state rights ideology in these instances that it went to war or seceded or even threatened to secede. Indeed, the only regional matter other than slavery in the territories that really irritated the fathers of secession was the tariff. Ardent fire-eaters such as Robert B. Rhett became almost apoplectic over what they perceived as an inequitable tariff that discriminated against the South, yet time after time Rhett could not arouse sufficient interest in the subject in his region to organize a unified protest, let along secede or go to war over the issue.

Time after time, year after year, the state rights argument always boiled down to the single issue of slavery and not so much over the right to own slaves as over the right of a slaveholder to take such property into federal territories. It was argued with considerable logical justification that those lands prior to admission to statehood had belonged to *all* the people of the United States and that therefore to exclude slavery in them constituted a de facto exclusion of slave owners. Exclude the slave owners from residence, and when the time came to form a new state, there would be no chance that the new star in the flag would countenance slavery. That being the case, the existing slave states would be doomed to an ever-smaller voice in Washington. It was, in the end, a mat-

The Civil War really began in the fears and ambitions of men like John C. Calhoun, whose Charleston grave would one day open up to swallow the whole South.
U.S. Army Military History Institute, Carlisle, Pa.

The Confederacy in Myth and Posterity

ter of power, not only the ability to maintain parity in national counsels in Washington but also, and more important, to ensure that in the future a strong antislave majority in the Capital would not move to abolish slavery in the states where by law it existed.

Yet only a few Southern leaders would actually argue their case in terms of slavery itself. They used state rights as a synonym, and it is not hard to understand why. Even then slavery was a distasteful word representing an institution with which possibly even a majority of Southerners were not entirely at ease. Unfortunately, in 1860 it was a system they were stuck with. One-third of the Southern population was slaves. That represented an enormous capital investment. If enforced abolition ever came, freedom could bankrupt much of the wealth-producing portion of Southern society. Then how was it to replace that labor force? Economically profitable, though inefficient, slavery as a labor system seemed cheaper in the long run than wage labor, and paid labor required hard cash, which was always in short supply in the South. Most threatening of all was the social problem raised by the prospect of almost 4 million free blacks turned loose on Southern society and economy, with a consequent threat of competition for jobs, civil control, and even fears of what Americans of the time called racial "amalgamation."

Southern leaders in 1860 were by and large men as good and honorable as their Northern opponents; they were simply caught in a trap unwittingly set for them by their forefathers and with no way out should the growing antislave majority in Congress decide to tamper with slavery. The best they could do was take the high ground in the debates by standing on a seemingly elevated constitutional platform like state rights rather than argue that they were simply trying to keep their slaves in bonds. For a parallel we need look no further than the court cases in the 1970s in Tennessee and elsewhere as state courts sought to convict the actors in X-rated films under state pornography laws. The defense did not claim it was the players' right to make dirty movies but sought to stand instead on the loftier ground of the constitutional principle of freedom of speech. In both cases those on the defensive sought a politically and culturally acceptable way of defending, euphemistically, what each realized privately was an unwholesome business, and that led to the creation of a myth.

In short, it is impossible to point to any other local issue but slavery and say that Southerners would have seceded and fought over it. However, if slavery is the reason secession came, that does not mean that it is the reason 1 million Southern men subsequently fought. In fact, study reveals that the two had absolutely nothing in common. Probably 90 percent of the men who wore the gray had never owned a slave and had no personal interest at all either in slavery or in the shadow issue of state rights. The widespread Northern myth that the Confederates went to the battlefield to perpetuate slavery is just that, a myth. Their letters and diaries, in the tens of thousands, reveal again and again that they fought and died because their Southern homeland was invaded and their natural instinct was to protect home and hearth.

Before we leave the subject of slavery, there is one more myth of the apologists that deserves a glance. Time and again antebellum Southerners and their defenders today try to divert a discussion of Southern adherence to slavery by

And the war began here in the slave pens of Alexandria and in a hundred other cities and towns where the sore of slavery festered.
Courtesy of Robert J. Younger

bringing up the old chestnut that, as one has put it, of all the ships that imported slaves to America, "practically every one of them was owned and operated by Northerners." The money-grubbing Puritans and their descendants profited by selling slave cargoes to Southerners and then hypocritically condemned them for practicing slavery. Worse, even after the slave trade was abolished in 1800, Yankee traders continued to import illegal cargoes. The unsaid, yet implicit argument is that if not for Yankee greed, there would not have been Southern slavery and therefore no civil war.[6]

While no one has systematically studied eighteenth- and nineteenth-century newspapers for major Southern ports like Charleston and New Orleans to analyze the announcements of arriving ships, their cargoes, and their home ports, such a search would probably find that the Southern carrying trade in slaves was more substantial than the myth admits. Then, too, arguments about the Yankees illegally continuing the slave trade after 1800 conveniently ignore the fact that Southerners did, too, including such regional heroes as Jean Lafitte and James Bowie. But even if we set all this aside, the obvious silliness of the whole basic insinuation needs to be challenged. We had slavery because the Yankees sold us slaves, it suggests, and therefore it was the Yankees' fault. That is tantamount to saying that we have a drug problem in this country only because we have drug dealers. Such logic turns free enterprise upside down. As a result, we should as readily conclude that people buy groceries only because we have supermarkets! The argument is, of course, nonsense. Whether we are dealing with canned corn, crack cocaine, or chattel slaves, if there was no demand, there would be no supply.

There is one other slavery myth that needs to be addressed, and this is in defense of the South and the Confederacy, though not in any way in defense of slavery itself. Thanks to *Uncle Tom's Cabin* there arose an impression that slaves felt overwhelmingly oppressed and resentful toward their owners and that during the Civil War they could not wait to see the Confederacy defeated. Moreover, slaves were willfully and systematically mistreated, a myth that, once begun, became a mainstay of more than a century's worth of potboilers of the *Mandingo* stripe.

The reality is markedly different. There was abuse and some of it sickeningly brutal, as will always happen when one person holds absolute authority over another. Two of Thomas Jefferson's nephews, for instance, brutally murdered a slave by chopping him to pieces bit by bit with an ax. But they were an aberration, and they became instant fugitives from the law. A master might own a slave, but cultural custom and statute law prescribed how he might treat such "property." Virtually every slave state had early laws on the books protecting slaves from unwarranted brutality by masters. "In some respects slaves may be regarded as chattels, but in others they are regarded as men," said a Mississippi State Supreme Court justice. "They are men and rational beings," he went on. "Because slaves can be bought and sold it does not follow that they can be deprived of life." In so saying, he condemned to be hanged a white man who had killed one of his own slaves.[7] Moreover, social stigma attached itself to any master who willfully mistreated his slaves, acting as a stay on those whose brute passions were susceptible of control.

As for slaves in the Confederacy, their activities hardly bear out the story of their resentment of their white rulers. The correspondence of President Jefferson Davis, especially in the early months of 1861, is replete with entreaties from the South's blacks, free and slave, to be allowed to enlist in the Confederate Army and even to raise whole companies for the cause. Others bought treasury bonds and contributed funds and foodstuffs to the war effort and continued doing so.[8] Of course, in the last weeks of the war in 1865 the government actually did start raising black troops and found men willing to join even at that late date. Moreover, the Confederacy could not have survived as long as it did if the black population behind the lines had refused to aid the war effort. With white men mostly off in the armies, trusted slaves ran or helped white women run the large plantations, just as President Davis' own plantation, Brierfield, was run by his slave Isaac Montgomery. Had the blacks mounted a serious resistance or work stoppage, they could have crippled the Confederacy.[9]

Certainly many slaves, probably even a majority of them, entertained feelings ranging from a faint interest to a passionate desire for freedom. If asked, maybe a majority would have said they hoped to see the Confederacy fail. But perhaps not. Remember that in our own century before the Holocaust got into full swing, some German and Austrian Jews tried to enlist in the Wehrmacht. Certainly it was not because they approved of the institutionalized anti-Semitism of the National Socialists. Rather, they were patriotic native Germans and Austrians who perceived a threat to what was, after all, their country, too, or so they thought. They wanted to defend their homeland. Similarly, the thousands of slaves who were willing and anxious to aid the Confederacy had motives other than the preservation of their own bondage. Many must have hoped that a good showing for the cause would improve their lot in an independent Confederacy. Many more simply felt that they were patriotic Southerners before they were blacks or slaves. They were always a minority within a minority, but the extent of their numbers belies the pat notions of a unified feeling of oppression and opposition among the South's blacks.

Of course, there is a myth about secession itself. Southerners then and later argued that it was a right inherent in the Constitution and in the Declaration of Independence. In the latter document Jefferson had written, "Whenever any form of government becomes destructive to these ends, it is the right of the people to abolish it, and to institute a new government." Even Lincoln in 1848 had declared that "any people, anywhere, being inclined and having the power, have the right to rise up and shake off the existing government, and form a new one that suits them better."[10] Of course, he stipulated that such revolution should only be in a just cause, and justice, like beauty, lay in the eyes of the beholder. He and millions in the North saw no just cause for disunion, especially in defense of slavery; Confederates saw every justification. As for the Constitution itself, nowhere does it explicitly provide for secession, and nowhere does it prohibit it either.

Legalistic Southerners tried to view the Constitution as a contract. Unfortunately, that viewpoint breaks down when viewed as a lawyer views a contract. There are very few ways to legally break a contract unilaterally. One is if the agreement contains a specifically stated means of withdrawal or a time limit. Others include duress, fraud, mutual mistake of material fact—none of which applies to the Union in 1860 or to the Constitution. If one party is guilty of noncompliance with the terms of the agreement, a withdrawal is possible, though questionable, unless the contract contains a noncompliance clause, which the Constitution does not. Nor at the time of secession was the Washington government guilty of any noncompliance. As of December 1860 when South Carolina voted to secede, the federal government had done nothing to interfere with slavery or any other right, nor would it do so until two years after South Carolina had acted. Moreover, Lincoln repeatedly promised in his speeches that he would make no attempt to interfere with slavery where it then existed. While there may have been no reason for Southerners to believe Lincoln, at the time of secession there was no overt reason not to believe him. In short, the South seceded out of a fear of future noncompliance, which any lawyer would testify is a legal position so perforated with holes as to be transparent.

And even apart from these arguments, there is an elemental point that almost everyone seems to miss, though as was so often the case, Lincoln put his finger on it in his 1847 quotation. "Any people," he said, *"having the power"* had the right to rise up. The fact is and always has been that there are no basic, inherent, universal "rights." There are only those freedoms that people perceive to be worth asserting, and if necessary defending, and if they are maintained successfully, then they become rights. In this context might does make right and rights. Secession was legal only if the Confederacy tried it, successfully defended it, and thus established a precedent, just as our legal codes today are full of provisions that were not lawful until someone tried them and won the case. As of this moment secession is not and never has been a right inherent in the Constitution, but that is not to say that someday it will not become a right if attempted again and successfully.

These myths interlock and often support each other. Unraveling one tends to undermine the next. If slavery and not state rights led to secession, and if secession was not a legal right, then what does this say about the argument that the Union itself was responsible for the outbreak of hostilities when it attempted to reinforce Fort Sumter, forcing the Charlestonians to open fire on the fort? It says rather plainly that this, too, is a myth and one like so many others founded to relieve the Confederates of their share of responsibility for the war that followed.

Of course, in many minds the mere fact that the Confederates fired the first hostile shots is enough for most people to decide responsibility for turning a confrontation into a war. But there are those who argue that Lincoln maneuvered Davis into being the aggressor and therefore that the Union president bears the responsibility. Certainly he made it clear from the day of his inauguration that if war came, Southerners would have to fire first, and to some degree he put them in a position from which they either had to shoot or back down. His oath to "protect and defend" the Constitution gave him no other choice. Franklin Roosevelt did somewhat the same thing with the Japanese in 1941, and there are those who argue that he forced them to attack Pearl Harbor. If one wants to accept the notion that the United States was responsible for the war in the Pacific in 1941–1945, then one could accept that the Union brought on the Civil War, making it truly the War of Northern Aggression.

Set aside the argument of who fired first, however. Well before Fort Sumter, secessionists had seized federal forts and arsenals all across the South. When John Brown tried to seize Harpers Ferry and its arsenal in 1859, Virginians and Southerners generally called it treason and insurrection. Was it not the same thing when state militias in 1860–1861 forcibly took federal property? The fact

The Confederacy in Myth and Posterity

that they acted on the authority of their state legislatures made the difference, they would argue, but when in our history have *state* assemblies had recognized power over *federal* installations? Never. But they were merely resuming control of state property, they would say. Not so. Those forts and arsenals were built on ground ceded to the federal government, funded by federal tax monies, and stocked with material paid for out of *all* the people's Treasury (and the overwhelming majority of that tax money was paid by Northerners, as it happens).

The Confederates would then plead that they were merely taking possession of what already belonged to them before they surrendered their sovereignty and were admitted to statehood. Virginia, North Carolina, South Carolina, Georgia, Texas, and possibly Tennessee could say this; but Florida, Alabama, Mississippi, Louisiana, and Arkansas certainly could not. They had never been independent entities prior to statehood. All had belonged to the federal government first as territories acquired by the national government either by treaty, purchase, or conquest. They never had any local sovereignty to reclaim. Consequently, their actions in taking at gunpoint the arsenals, customs houses, fortifications, and other federal property within their borders were clear and unmistakable acts of hostility and aggression, every bit as much as John Brown's seizure of Harpers Ferry. Jefferson Davis did not need to open fire on Fort Sumter on April 12, 1861, to begin the war. Armed insurrection began on December 27, 1860, when South Carolina state forces seized Castle Pinckney and Fort Moultrie and the U.S. revenue cutter *William Aitken*.

Given the circumstances of the time, the hysteria of the moment, and the generation and more of growing paranoia in the slave states as they saw themselves becoming increasingly a minority in the struggle for power in Washington, it is hard to see what else Southerners were to do. It is incumbent on historians and Americans in general to try—impossible as it truly is—putting themselves in the position of the men and women of the time before judging them. We can say from hindsight that Lincoln might not have gone back on his word to leave slavery alone where it existed. We can see how a war may not have been necessary. We can posit scenarios of compromise that might have averted the crisis and the calamity that followed. But that is all immaterial. All that counts is what the people on the scene felt and believed, however right or erroneous, and what they could see as legitimate options.

The leaders in the South in 1860–1861 believed that their rights of property, self-government, the underpinnings of their culture and economy, all were mortally threatened by a Republican victory at the polls. Many also believed that a weak-willed Northern body politic would let them go without an attempt to coerce them into staying in the Union, and if a weakling like James Buchanan had been sent to the White House in 1861 instead of Lincoln, they might have been right. Many of them believed quite sincerely that secession was merely the exercise of a self-evident American right. Hindsight reveals them to be mistaken on all counts. That does not mean that they deserve to be charged with malign intent in the choices they made. Neither should their apologists be allowed to excuse them of their rightful share of responsibility. There is plenty of blame to go around for what happened in 1861–1865. Lincoln himself declared, "We cannot escape history."[11] Neither can the North or South escape a full measure of responsibility for the war.

The Confederacy paid well for its portion of the blame. Incredibly, there is a notion among some that the South really was not beaten by the Union. A few years ago a quiz at a Sons of Confederate Veterans meeting contained a question referring to April and May 1865 as the period at which "the Confederacy withdrew from the war." *Withdrew?* Somehow that conjures recollections of the worst days of the Vietnam War, when some wag suggested that President Richard Nixon simply declare, "We win" and bring everybody home, regardless of what was actually happening. When a contestant's industry is destroyed. When the will of its people to continue the fight is crushed. When its armies are surrounded or on the run and are dissolving rapidly through desertion. When its ports are closed and its territory carved up into uncoordinated bits. When its economy is shattered, and it cannot feed its people in uniform, or keep them from simply going home. When its armies have nowhere to go, no one to turn to, and cannot muster enough men at arms to meet a foe at odds even as bad as one to two. And when the men leading those armies have long since concluded that they cannot win. When all that happens, a combatant does not "withdraw" from a war, as if to say, "Well, we fought for awhile, but we're tired now, and we'll just pretend that nothing ever happened." The Confederacy was utterly, crushingly, devastatingly defeated, and to suggest anything else is not just myth but pure fantasy.

Myth-making about the Confederacy, pro and con, continues to the present and will into the future. The past decade has seen civil rights advocates protest the display of the Confederate battle flag and its use in the banners of some of the Southern states. They claim that it represents a racist symbol of white supremacy. Southerners who disagree say that it is there as a symbol of pride in their Confederate heritage. Both sides are mistaken, betraying an ignorance of history that has never stopped myth crafters and never will. The blue St. Andrew's cross on a red field that constitutes the battle flag did not become a part of state flags in the South until the 1950s, and it did so not as an expression of pride in heritage but as a direct reaction to and defiance of *Brown* v. *Board of Education* and the forced desegregation of schools. To that extent it does represent white supremacy and opposition to civil rights. The trouble is, that the men who put it there used the wrong flag. They should have used the so-called Stars and Bars, the actual national flag of the Confederacy, which was nothing if not a nation created by secession that was itself a direct result of slavery.

But the battle flag is something different. It was not a governmental banner. It was the flag of the men in the ranks in the Confederate armies, the average Johnny Reb's, 90 percent of whom never owned a slave, had no stake in a slave economy, and were not at all fighting to preserve slavery. They were fighting for purely *American* values that millions of other men and women, north and south, white and black, have fought for for generations—defense of home and hearth and what they perceived as their country. The battle flag is not a symbol of racism but of motives that represent the best that all of us have to give—courage, patriotism, self-sacrifice. As such, it is viewed with justifiable pride not just by Southerners but also by Americans of all sections. Those who cheapen it by putting it on underwear and license plates and flying it at white supremacist rallies do the flag and those who followed it a disservice. Likely many of our Confederate ancestors would be ashamed of them, but such antics cannot diminish the fact that the battle flag stands for much of what is best in all of us.

Myth is a rich part of any culture and should be treasured and enjoyed. But it should also be understood for what it is and not allowed to blind us to realities. In some ways our Confederate ancestors dealt with and accepted their defeat more maturely and manfully than have many of their descendants. They neither excused nor apologized, nor did they need to. They *lived* the Confederate experience, and win or lose, for most of them that was enough. Moreover, the real story they left behind is ever so much richer than any legend. The best way to honor their memory lies neither in glorification nor recrimination but in a simple search for the truth.

The Civil War and the Confederacy in Cinema

THE CIVIL WAR HAS HAD a long and occasionally distinguished history on American cinema and television screens, one sometimes befitting, and at other times at odds with, its continuing status as the single most studied episode in our past. In a number of other fields its predominance is unchallenged. It so fills our literature that the number of publications dwarfs every other nonfiction topic. Our museums bulge with paintings and portraits of battles and leaders. The major eastern cities sprout a host of parks centered around or named after the great generals, including their larger-than-life equestrian statues, and virtually every county seat, even in the once-impoverished South, has its specially commissioned or mass-produced statue of a standing soldier.

Influences that we do not even recognize surround us. How many know that the canned ham we lazily heat and eat for a Sunday meal is the lineal descendant of the tinned meats sent to Yankee soldiers during the war? How many realize that "contented cows" first started contributing condensed milk for soldiers' coffee? Do we remember that Lincoln wore Brooks Brothers shirts and scribbled some of his immortal lines with a Dixon pencil not markedly different from the Ticonderogas that we all used and still use in school? Long before a bouncing ball got television watchers to sing "The Yellow Rose of Texas," Confederate soldiers sang it in their camps. And when that greatest of all cultural icons, Elvis Presley, scored one of his greatest hits with "Love Me Tender," he was simply singing the Civil War love song "Aura Lee" with different words. The Mormon Tabernacle Choir still sends shivers up our spines with the power of "The Battle Hymn of the Republic." Step out onto the street in New Orleans, Louisiana, or Missoula, Montana, and passing auto horns sound "Dixie." The Civil War remains for us, as it has always been, a great human experience that is uniquely our own. Even other nations try as they may to adopt a bit of it. Those "Dixie" horns are also heard in County Tipperary, Ireland, and a speaker

The Confederacy in Myth and Posterity

signaling that it is safe for the sight-impaired to cross a downtown street in Yokohama, Japan, plays "When Johnny Comes Marching Home."

Interestingly enough, given this mammoth cultural impact, the story has been somewhat elusive in our most distinctive cultural form, the film. Not that it has been absent. Quite to the contrary, Civil War scenes were being projected not very long after the invention of commercial cinema itself and have appeared with an intermittent regularity ever since. The question is not so much that we have not depicted the war on screen as it is that we have never known exactly quite what to do with it or how to do it.

The war went onto "film" even before it was invented. From the tin positives and glass negatives of wartime photographers like Timothy O'Sullivan, it was only a few years and a little technology to *The Birth of a Nation* and *Gone with the Wind*.
U.S. Army Military History Institute, Carlisle, Pa.

The Civil War and the Confederacy in Cinema

The natural affinity of film for a story like this has never been questioned. The biggest event in our history belongs on the biggest canvas humans can devise. Certainly the characters do. Of all historical figures in our past—and perhaps in the human past—none has been portrayed as many times as Lincoln. As of 1991 actors had presented him some 187 times on film and television, and the number has increased since then. That is natural in light of Lincoln's stature as the greatest of all American leaders. Yet the president who stands just behind Lincoln—though a distant second—was in reality one of our worst, Ulysses S. Grant. He has been portrayed at least sixty-eight times and obviously not for his wit and wisdom. He is shown time and again for the brief four-year period in which he achieved greatness and usually as a result of interacting with Lincoln.

We all know of *Birth of a Nation,* the great D. W. Griffith epic of the Civil War and Reconstruction, based on a highly erroneous portrait of both in a popular novel, *The Klansman,* by Thomas Dixon. But it was by no means the first Civil War film. Dozens of silents were made early in this century presenting small vignettes of fictionalized Civil War drama, almost always working a simple soldier, the girl he loves, and Lincoln into a maudlin story of daring and humanity. And it is in those earliest days that our first screen depictions of the Confederacy appear, romanticized and heavily fictionalized. If in the long run the South won the battle for time on the big and small screen, not so its leader. It is in silent film that we find the only two big-screen depictions of Jefferson Davis. The actor, like the films themselves, was eminently forgettable. There Davis' film "career" foundered for generations until the 1980s when Lloyd Bridges briefly portrayed him on television.

Yet *Birth of a Nation* did set a different tone, and attempt to fill a greater stage, than these two Rebel melodramas. It ran 160 minutes, the longest film ever made when it appeared in 1916. Forget for a moment the grossly biased and outrageously racist point of view it expressed, and just look at it for its sweep and scope. Griffith could and did engage living Confederate veterans to tell him how to stage his battle scenes, with the result that despite all the weaknesses of silent film to our eyes today, *Birth of a Nation* still offers perhaps the most convincing look at Civil War combat ever filmed until the appearance of *Glory* some seventy years later.

But then when the cinema had at last established the Confederacy as the stuff of screen epic, what was the next great film? A Buster Keaton comedy called *The General,* based loosely on the celebrated Great Locomotive Chase.

The Confederacy in Myth and Posterity

Make no mistake, *The General* is a great film. It is so recognized internationally that in 1991 the British Broadcasting Corporation aired it as prime-time television. It is a classic comedy and a masterpiece of film by any definition. But how could the Civil War and the Confederacy go so quickly from a historical epic to a slapstick farce? Quite clearly, we had no sure or settled sense as yet of how to handle it or of what was an appropriate fictional story to drape over such a magnificent framework. The Confederacy had yet to be typecast.

It had to wait until 1939 and *Gone with the Wind*. To be sure, the film wears a bit thin when seen more than half a century later. It shows its age and by modern standards is more than a bit maudlin and even corny. One European film critic recently referred to it as "'Dallas' does Atlanta." But it grasped a hold on Americans that it still clings to tenaciously today. Yet observe that except for a hospital scene, a few Confederates marching down a road, a leering Yankee threatening to ravish Miss Scarlett, and the burning of some buildings in Atlanta, *Gone with the Wind* portrays almost nothing of the Civil War itself. It tells nothing of the causes, presents a distorted and one-sided view of the consequences, and barely hints at a few events in the conduct of the war. It is a love story to which the war and the Confederacy are quite peripheral. Yet it remains in the American consciousness as *the* Civil War film of all time. Its most lasting impact has been to create in the minds of millions here and abroad a mostly fictitious "moonlight and magnolias" portrait of the Old South and the Confederacy.

After *Gone with the Wind* little of much substance appeared for a number of years, but at least filmmakers started to approach genuine events in the Confederate experience. They presented *Tap Roots,* telling the story of the so-called Free State of Jones, the Mississippi county that tried to opt out of the Confederacy. In 1954 we got *The Raid,* a depiction of Bennett Young's adventurous foray with Canada-based Confederate cavalrymen into the Vermont town of St. Albans, which they captured for a few hours, robbing its bank. There was even *The Dark Command* in 1940, the loosest of them all with facts. It ostensibly portrays the story of William Quantrill's raiders during the days of Bleeding Kansas, the sacking of Lawrence, Kansas, and Quantrill's ultimate death. Everything about it is wrong, starting with the heavy being named Will Cantrell. Worse, the casting is incredible, having the psychopathic terrorist played by, of all people, Walter Pidgeon. Nevertheless, Republic Studios was actually proud of its historical achievement, premiered the film in Lawrence, and cooperated with the Kansas Department of Secondary Education in publishing a schoolroom "Guide to the Discussion of the Photoplay."[1] It was really just a Western in uniform.

By the 1950s a change had become evident. Films were getting bigger and bigger. The term "cast of thousands" became a cliché in the advertising of such major costume epics as *Captain from Castille* and *Quo Vadis*. But to producers this also meant that the Civil War film was on its way to being priced out of production. It simply cost too much to make one. In a Western any old guns in the property department would suffice. But a Civil War film that depicted any real action required very specific types of uniforms and even more specific weapons and paraphernalia, most of which would have to be manufactured. It was the beginning of an era, in which we still live, in which production costs defeated almost every proposed film dealing substantially with the military side of the war and the Confederate experience.

No better evidence of this is needed than the first picture done in the decade and still considered among the finest Civil War movies of all. When director John Huston decided to film Stephen Crane's *Red Badge of Courage,* even a man with his track record of success could not raise the money from the studios to finance the film. He had to make it with his own money, film it on his own southern California ranch to save paying for a film lot, and cast it entirely with amateur and unknown actors who could command little pay. It is also one of the shortest feature films ever made, at only about seventy minutes. He could not afford to make it longer and had to do it in black and white and thirty-five millimeter, when other screen epics of the time were using Technicolor and wide-screen Cinemascope.

In spite of all, *The Red Badge of Courage* was a major critical triumph, but its length and other limitations prevented it from having much of a chance at the box office, a result that seemingly proved the growing feeling in Hollywood that the Civil War was a subject best not touched, that it was a money loser. As a result, during the next forty years only a small handful of serious attempts to make a Civil War film of real stature and scope would be made. Hollywood opted instead for the "mood" and "period" piece depicting a small personal story loosely dressed in the context of the war that was somewhere just out of sight. Such was William Wyler's 1956 *Friendly Persuasion,* probably the best of the lot. More typically we got mush like *Raintree County,* notable only for the fact that even Elizabeth Taylor is terrible in it. In 1965 the dramatic real-life Confederate adventure of General Wade Hampton's 1864 "Beefsteak Raid" on a Yankee cattle herd in Virginia was turned into a fictionalized account called

The Confederacy in Myth and Posterity

Alvarez Kelly, complete with Richard Widmark apparently getting so frustrated at his abominable attempt at a Virginia drawl that he shoots off one of William Holden's fingers.

A few films made a better attempt at accurate portrayal. Walt Disney Studios managed a creditable, if simplistic, docudrama called *The Great Locomotive Chase,* based quite accurately on the famous Andrews railroad raid of April 1862. Even better were a pair of John Ford efforts. In 1959's *The Horse Soldiers* he depicted the 1863 cavalry raid through Mississippi and Louisiana of Colonel Benjamin Grierson, one of the great mounted operations of the war. A few names were changed, but the basic story—other than the addition of a pointless romantic interest for John Wayne—was filmed largely as it happened and most of it in Mississippi rather than on a Hollywood lot. Holden costarred and this time managed to keep all his fingers, fortunate since he played a surgeon. The abominable Southern accent came this time from the love interest, Constance Towers. Ford also directed a Civil War segment of the Cinerama epic *How the West Was Won,* depicting a part of the Battle of Shiloh. This time the historical characters kept their real names, and the brief episode packed both drama and convincing action, while staying pretty faithful to the record.

In the next two decades, however, the genre hit almost rock bottom. In 1964 Columbia Pictures released *Major Dundee,* based on "a true and unusual" episode in 1864 that, in fact, never happened. It was simply an excuse to make a typical Western cloaked in the trappings of a fictional Civil War story. Soon thereafter Universal released Andrew McLaglen's *Shenandoah,* a portrait of one Southern family caught in the war and forced to choose sides. It has achieved a minor cult status for being so terrible that even James Stewart could not save it. McLaglen himself swore afterward that he would never do another Civil War picture.[2] Then came the lowest ebb of all, in 1977, with the release of *The Lincoln Conspiracy.* It purported, in docudrama format, to establish that Lincoln had been murdered by a high-level conspiracy of politicians and military leaders in his own government, who then engaged in a massive Watergate-style cover-up. The whole thing was based on forged documents and shabby research that the producers were only too happy to accept as genuine without looking too carefully for flaws. Given their previous record of such films as *The Search for Noah's Ark, The Bermuda Triangle,* and *In Search of Ancient Astronauts,* it was no surprise that the matter of historical truth and accuracy rated rather low on the producers' list of priorities.

The Civil War and the Confederacy in Cinema

For more than a decade after *The Lincoln Conspiracy* the Civil War was absent from the big screen. Then came something the public had been conditioned not to expect—a beautiful, accurate, detailed, and large-scale motion picture called *Glory*. Despite a few, and minor, flaws, it is probably the most historically sound and reliable dramatization of genuine events yet put on the screen. It tells in rich color and scale the story of Colonel Robert G. Shaw and his black Fifty-fourth Massachusetts Infantry and their heroic, yet doomed attack on Battery Wagner during the siege of Charleston. Unfortunately, after spending a lot to make it, the producers fell prey to the old conservatism again and spent rather little on promoting the film. As a result, the old self-fulfilling prophecy that audiences would not respond to a Civil War picture came true yet again. *Glory* got a respectable reception at the box office, but in many areas of the nation it never played at all. The critics loved it, and so did the overwhelming majority of the audience it did attract. But in the end probably only video sales will return it a decent profit.

And so once again Americans were left asking why it is that we who largely invented film cannot or will not translate our greatest national event to our most distinctive national art form. It can be done. We have only to look at the British, who have done it repeatedly. In 1965 Cy Endfield produced probably the most accurate, yet compellingly dramatic historical film ever made, *Zulu*. It instantly achieved minor cult status among history buffs around the world and played continuously in one or another of London's cinemas for years. It still reaps millions from the sale of videocassettes and sound track albums, not to mention the fact that it launched the film career of Michael Caine.

Our performance with the Civil War on another distinctly American medium, the small screen, has been no better. By definition, television must look for small scale. No sense in spending millions to film the Battle of Gettysburg when the tube will inevitably reduce Pickett's Charge to something the size of a fish tank. Instead television consistently went for the smaller, more intimate story, using the Civil War as an excuse for the drama but hardly a real part of it. Probably the first attempts in the early 1950s were the "You Are There" stories, half-hour segments that presented Walter Cronkite reporting on the death of Stonewall Jackson and the Lincoln assassination. Only twice would network television attempt to field a weekly series. One, *The Gray Ghost*, came out in the mid-1950s, aimed largely at a juvenile audience, and was little more than a Western masquerading as an account of Confederate John S. Mosby's partisans. The other series was a dismal attempt to cash in on the Civil War centennial; in 1962 a series called *The Blue and the Gray* offered weekly adventures of two brothers divided by the war. The war lasted four years; the series did not finish its first season, but then it ran opposite *Bonanza,* which offered three brothers instead of two and a Chinese cook as well.

The "You Are There" episodes effectively set the style for all but a few of the future attempts to present the war on the box for the next thirty years. The term *docudrama* had not yet been coined, but that is the approach television chose to take. During the centennial a series called *Appointment with Destiny* broadcast a creditable episode dealing with Grant and Lee at Appomattox. *American Heritage* magazine lent its name to another series, which included an episode on Grant and Lee in the Wilderness. Another producer dramatized the famed story of the "longest shot" of the war, when a Yankee sharpshooter killed a Confederate general in Louisiana with a rifle shot of more than a mile. The fact that the story is a total fabrication did not keep it from being presented under the aegis of *True* magazine.

Then came the docudrama miniseries. The first was CBS's *The Blue and Gray,* a positively stupid fictional story, filled with clichés, that nevertheless depicted a fair amount of action and historical background and did it more effectively than anything before. The producers engaged distinguished historian E. B. Long to go over the script and hired others to observe the filming for accuracy. Everyone involved really tried, and though there were still a few glaring inaccuracies, it was still the best television had done to that date. Ratings were not overwhelming, but they were good enough to encourage producers to think of doing more. Soon Hal Holbrook was appearing several nights in a row in *Sandburg's Lincoln,* based on Carl Sandburg's six-volume biography and no more accurate than the books. It did not help for a start that Holbrook was six inches shorter than Lincoln. The sixteenth president was also the central figure in a 1980s series called *Gore Vidal's Lincoln,* a dismal production that said a lot more about Vidal than Lincoln. We hit rock bottom with *North and South,* which was little more than *Dynasty* with hoop skirts.

The war also started to make it into another new form, the somewhat oxymoronically dubbed "made-for-television movie." In 1975 another attempt at *The Red Badge of Courage* appeared for the small screen, this time casting *The Waltons* star Richard Thomas as the central character and leading some critics to title the picture "John-Boy Goes to War." It was longer than Huston's film version and infinitely inferior, suffering terribly from one of the presumed benefits of television over film, economy. The picture was done so cheaply that the prop master had no funds for new costumes or weapons. The uniforms used were rented from a costumer whose stock had been used as far back as *Gone with the Wind,* while the rifles used were mostly breech-loaders not even invented until the decade after the war. The poor fellow was allowed money for no more than one hundred actual live black powder paper cartridges for the filming. As a result, he had to have several cameras at different angles filming the loading and firing of those precious rounds in order to get maximum footage. The rest of the time when soldiers were seen biting into a paper cartridge and ramming it down the muzzles of their breech-loading guns, they were actually biting into feminine tampons colored to look like cartridges. Not even worth mentioning was another production remaking the old *Prisoner of Shark Island,* which in 1935 starred Warner Baxter and Barbara Stanwyck and told the story of Confederate doctor Samuel Mudd and his imprisonment for involvement in the Lincoln murder. Dennis Weaver played Mudd in this new version and should have changed his name to just that for appearing in it. *Iron-clads,* a terrible production about the *Monitor* and the *Virginia,* had absolutely nothing to recommend it except some good recreations of shipboard scenes on those historic vessels.

In spring 1991 the perennial Lincoln came back to the small screen, this time in *The Perfect Tribute.* It is a fictionalized account of the events leading up to the Gettysburg Address, this time starring Jason Robards, who is even shorter than Holbrook. *The Perfect Tribute* probably expended the greatest effort to date of any production in its attempt to achieve accuracy. Its faithfulness to detail is perhaps the most notable feature of the drama.

Then came 1993 and the Ted Turner production *Gettysburg.* Once again after a long hiatus the Civil War not only returned to the big screen but also positively leaped onto it. Based on Michael Shaara's Pulitzer Prize novel *The Killer Angels,* the film started out intended for television, but when the producers saw the epic proportions of what they were making, they opted to release a shortened version of the six-hour film in theaters. It told the story of the epic battle of the Civil War, chiefly through the experiences of a few characters, Robert E. Lee, James Longstreet, John Buford, Joshua L. Chamberlain, and others. Once again for the first time in decades the term "cast of thousands" was heard. Nearly 7,500 reenactors assembled to do the battle scenes, offering the economic advantage of already having their uniforms and weapons and animals, the most expensive part of any Civil War movie. The climactic July 3 Con-

The Confederacy in Myth and Posterity

federate assault was filmed at almost half-scale. The artillery barrage is stunning. Some of the actual landscape of the battle was used in the location filming. Dramatically, the film is contrived and self-conscious. The casting is sometimes controversial, especially Martin Sheen's portrayal of Lee, for some reason. The makeup can be hideous, particularly the restless beaver apparently cast to be Longstreet's beard. The worst feature of the film is its historical viewpoint. Shaara was no historian and wrote a great novel that is deeply flawed by heavy reliance on discredited sources, and the film follows his lead. But cinematically it remains a stunning achievement. Better yet, it made money and is still making money and showed that the Civil War *can* be brought to the screen in real scale and for real profit.

But that does not mean that we can necessarily expect to see more such epics. One problem is the very thing that plagues even the best work. The question of accuracy, and the public response to carelessness with the facts, bedevils producers. We will accept horrendous flaws in depictions of almost any other historic era, but we become a nation of critics and letter writers whenever a Confederate soldier's jacket has the wrong buttons. More Americans consider themselves expert on some aspect of the war than for any other period in our past, and we can lose entirely our sense of perspective—and humor—when Hollywood is careless or takes liberties. As a result, moviemakers avoid the subject in part to avoid its scholars and buffs. McLaglen's oath never to make another Civil War film after *Shenandoah*—an oath he broke to direct *The Blue and the Gray*—came because he got sick and tired of the letters and calls he kept getting for years after the film was released, all complaining.

Complaint is all too often justified, for Hollywood, big screen and small, has an unenviable reputation for accuracy. *Gone with the Wind* had to virtually custom make most of its costumes and apparently did not consult any surviving originals. As a result, some Confederate soldiers wore uniforms that touched every hue of the rainbow, even purple. Perhaps regular Confederate gray and butternut were too dull for this first color epic. Unfortunately, those costumes went into the vaults of the wardrobe outfitters and would be brought out again and again, as late as forty years later in *The Blue and Gray*. Accuracy also plagued *The Great Locomotive Chase,* when Disney used locomotives that were vintage 1880s and not Civil War in appearance at all.

As usual, it remained for television to do the worst. Besides the problems with the *True* program that was definitely false, there was the Appomattox episode of *Appointment with Destiny,* which had Lee emerge from the McLean house after the surrender, mount Traveler, and ride off—toward Union lines. He would do the same thing twenty years later in *The Blue and Gray.*

Some producers, to their credit, have expended commendable effort to get it right, and, interestingly enough, much of this effort stems from the interest of the players themselves. Gregory Peck, George C. Scott, Richard Dreyfuss, John Wayne, Jason Robards, Rip Torn, Stacy Keach, Charleton Heston, and many more have at least one thing in common besides their profession. They are all to some degree Civil War buffs, and when called on to play a part, they bring to it more than the producers expect. In *The Blue and Gray* Peck played Lincoln and had special contact lenses made to turn his blue eyes gray like Lincoln's, even though wearing them was painful and they could be kept in only half an hour to avoid damaging his sight. When a typist inadvertently got a preposition wrong in the Gettysburg Address, it was Peck who spotted the error. Left-hander Rip Torn played Grant, and recalled after shooting a scene in which he wrote a message announcing Lee's surrender that Grant was *right*-handed. Torn refused to do his next scene until that one was reshot properly. He even arrived on the set with his own uniform.

The Perfect Tribute came even closer. Many of the lines in the script were direct quotes from original sources, modified only for brevity. All the sets were constructed based on period photographs, including a wonderful recreation of Lincoln's White House office. During filming the director repeatedly stopped the cameras to ask historical consultants whether a scene was set properly. Historically, it is the most accurate drama television has done to date.

And television is probably the only medium that will deal with the war in the future. The costs of everything associated with the cinema have escalated so much that even another *Gettysburg* will be difficult to film, especially since the budgets required to make the blockbuster pictures are spent only on movies aimed at a youth audience. In 1982 *The Blue and Gray* cost $14 million for eight hours. *The Perfect Tribute* nearly ten years later cost almost the same for only two hours. It took more than a decade, and a long trail of failed deals, to bring Shaara's *Killer Angels* to the screen. Frank McCarthy, Academy Award– winning producer of *Patton* and *MacArthur,* fought unsuccessfully for twenty years to find funding for a far less ambitious picture about the 1864 Battle of New Market and the Virginia Military Institute cadets.

Television, with its reduced scale, would seem to be the only alternative, yet

The Confederacy in Myth and Posterity

even there the prognosis is uncertain, being hostage to ratings like everything else, except on the noncommercial networks. But by definition television producers will not have the kind of funding needed to make a major event series like *The Blue and Gray,* so almost inevitably they will have to opt for the documentary format.

Civil War documentaries have been very few. One or two were actually done for the big screen in the earlier years, most notably a now forgotten half-hour film on Pickett's Charge done in the 1950s and shown in theaters in the days when so-called short subjects still filled the now-extinct interval between films at the now-extinct double feature. There is a compelling logic for wedding the documentary with television. Expensive sets and actors are not needed. The director needs a camera and a small crew, a battlefield or other location(s), and a narrator, and then he or she starts filming. Neither are expensive props or costumes required. Live battle footage is abundantly available today thanks to reenactors, and more can be had every weekend.

Ironically, then, the first really good documentary of scope, depth, and visual richness was done by the English, who are far more interested in our Civil War than in their own. The independent television network Channel 4 several years ago produced *The Divided Union,* a five-hour documentary, with the obligatory companion book and sound-track album, that was later broadcast in America first by a pay-for-view network and later on the Public Broadcasting Service. It was thorough, penetrating, informative, very well balanced, and almost hopelessly dull. It suffered from one of the chief evils of documentaries of all kinds, what is known in the industry as "talking heads." The director simply put a succession of often less than cosmetic academics in front of the camera, giving viewers a series of two- or three-minute vignettes of bearded, graying men in tweed pontificating on the war. Documentaries do not have to be made this way, but they usually are, revealing more a lack of funding or a want of imagination on the part of the producers than any inherent weakness in the form. The absence of vintage live footage adds to the challenge faced by producers, of course. Still photographs exist in abundance—hundreds of thousands—but they are just that, still, which is not exactly captivating on the screen.

There matters stood until 1990 when the Ken Burns ten-hour series *The Civil War* broadcast on the PBS network. It captured the attention and admiration of the nation for weeks. It was six years in the making and seems to have justified all the effort that went into it. The national reaction was staggering. Suddenly everyone discovered the Civil War. Publishers could not get enough books on the subject to market, national news magazines featured historians on their covers, merchandising of everything from records and videotapes to T-shirts and coffee mugs exploded. Tourist destinations like Gettysburg experienced a severalfold expansion in business and visitation. Even the BBC broadcast the series, and soon thereafter foreign-language versions appeared on the world's television screens. Every coffee table of any pretension had the companion book prominently displayed.

The series was beautifully made, a visual and aural treat. Burns is a master filmmaker. Moreover, at least in the initial stages, he assembled a panel of blue-ribbon experts covering the gamut of subject material of the war, its causes and effects, and its people. Genuinely serious effort was made to make it as accurate as possible, and in the main Burns succeeded. Of course, there are errors, and plenty of them, most minor in nature, and they crept in despite the best efforts of everyone, as things will always do in any human endeavor. Contrary to widespread misconception, *The Civil War* did not create a boom in Civil War interest or merchandising, but the overwhelming public response to the film did add an extra impulse to the already existing and long-standing boom that had begun shortly after the war ended and has never since ceased.

Buffs and historians, frequently the people who have made things so hard on filmmakers, also responded with unaccustomed, if not universal, approval. Professional Civil War historians have been generally laudatory of the series, even while pointing out its shortcomings. But there have been other sections of the audience, lay and professional, whose objections are more general and vocally expressed. The series is anti-Southern and pro-Northern in tone, they say. It concentrates too heavily on the military aspects of the war years. There is, depending on whom you listen to, either too much or too little coverage of black involvement and too much emphasis on slavery as *the* cause of the war. Already the debate has spawned one book and innumerable academic symposia.[3]

The Civil War certainly does appear to betray a northeastern establishment viewpoint, the same vantage that characterizes much of what appears on public television. This should hardly be a surprise. The producer and the author who wrote the screenplay are northeasterners. Most of the consultants to the series are northeastern academics. The National Endowment for the Humanities, which funded the series, has a long record that shows an apparent bias toward northeastern productions, just as a plurality of the more ambitious PBS productions are generated by northeastern affiliates. There is hardly a conspiracy here, though some critics have seen it that way. The northeast is where the money is and where the affiliates with a track record of producing high-quality programs happen to be located. No producer or affiliate in Alabama or Iowa or Oregon could line up the talent and money to make *The Civil War.* Naturally it would come out of the northeast, and doing so, it was unavoidably bound to reflect at least a little of the prevailing attitudes of that region.

The regional viewpoint that seems to pervade *The Civil War* is not necessarily a wrong viewpoint. The problem is that there are others not aired, making Burns' error one of omission rather than commission. If the series seems too hard on the South and the Confederates, it is chiefly because too few Southern historians were involved and no Southern production management. Had the series been made in Georgia instead of New England, there might be complaints of its being anti-Northern. As for the widely voiced complaint that the series presents slavery as the cause of the war, well, like it or not, the producers are right. Or, rather, slavery was the sine qua non behind secession, and secession was what led to the war. Does *The Civil War* spend too much time on the battlefield? Well, silly as it seems to have to point this out, the Civil War was a *war* after all. In fact, the series devotes rather less than half of its attention to military affairs, which is a lot less than the attention people at the time gave to the armed conflict. Some protest that it does not give adequate coverage to Reconstruction, but again, the title says what it is and is not about. Reconstruction is a separate subject, far more related to history post-1877 than to what preceded it. And besides, even very few historians have ever managed to get interested in Reconstruction. Interesting the American viewing public in it for any appreciable amount of airtime is a task probably beyond even Ken Burns' considerable talents.

Perspective is what is most needed with *The Civil War.* The state of American education is a sad one in the last decade of this century, with even college students thinking that Eisenhower was the president who preceded Lincoln and even that the seemingly self-evidently dated War of 1812 really occurred in the 1700s. Teachers are not teaching, or students are not learning. In such a situation, anything that arouses interest in our own history does us as a people a useful service, even if there are elements in it that fail to please everyone. *The Civil War* had a profound impact on millions who previously had known little or nothing about the subject. It opened some minds and stimulated some interests, and that is enough good work to more than make up for its flaws.

Evidence that the interest stimulated by *The Civil War* continues, and is doing good work, is abundant. In 1994 the Arts and Entertainment Network began broadcasting the Greystone production *Civil War Journal,* a weekly documentary series that to date has run fifty-two one-hour episodes. It has managed to avoid the pitfalls that caught Burns and seems to have done that most difficult of all tasks in the Civil War field, namely, pleasing almost everyone. Accurate, authoritative, yet entertaining, it has an audience clamoring for more even after fifty-two hours. Lincoln has come back to the screen again, both in dramas such as *Tad* and in documentary format. The production of local documentary television focused on the Civil War has blossomed, and more epics are under way, most recently a Turner dramatization of the McKinlay Kantor novel *Andersonville.* The return of the Civil War to the big screen may be a long way off, or may never be seen again, but television and the Civil War seem to have found a natural wedding of story and medium that will not soon come to an end. We can only wonder what changes of fortune and interpretation await in future dramatizations and documentaries. Of one thing we can be sure. Every generation of Americans has produced its own vision of the Civil War, whether in art, literature, music, or, recently, film—a vision that suited the needs, aspirations, prejudices, or even ignorance of the times. Film and television make it easier to present any such vision and to do it with an impact denied to books and magazines. Undeniably, for all future generations Americans' impressions of that era and its people are going to be dramatically influenced by this visual medium. We may carp about it and critique it and resent it even as we flock to see it. But like history itself, we cannot escape it.

Notes

Chapter One. Jefferson Davis

1. John W. DuBose, *The Life and Times of William Lowndes Yancey* (Birmingham, Ala., 1892), 2:743. The fullest and most recent biography of Davis is William C. Davis, *Jefferson Davis: The Man and His Hour* (New York, 1991).

2. Quoted on the jacket of Clement Eaton, *Jefferson Davis* (New York, 1977).

3. Colin Tarpley, *A Sketch of the Life of Jeff. Davis* (Jackson, Miss., 1851), p. 6. The Tarpley biography is an underappreciated document that shows clear signs of close consultation with Davis during its composition.

4. William Preston Johnston to Rosa Johnston, June 10, 1862, Mason Barret Collection, Special Collections, Howard Tilton Memorial Library, Tulane University, New Orleans, La.

5. Ibid., June 9, 1962.

6. Haskell M. Monroe and James T. McIntosh, eds., *The Papers of Jefferson Davis,* Vol. 1, *1808–1840* (Baton Rouge, La., 1971), pp. lxix, lxxii–lxxiii.

7. Ibid., p. lxxx; Johnston to Rosa Johnston, August 24, 1862, Barret Collection.

8. Monroe and McIntosh, *Papers,* 1:lxxix; Lynda Lasswell, ed., "Jefferson Davis Ponders His Future," *Journal of Southern History* 49 (November 1975): 520–21.

9. Johnston to Rosa Johnston, June 9, 1862, Barret Collection; Stephen R. Mallory Diary, September 27, 1865, Stephen R. Mallory Papers, Southern Historical Collection, University of North Carolina, Chapel Hill.

10. Varina Davis' memoir of her husband does not refrain from detailing several of his youthful misadventures, including his part in the celebrated West Point eggnog riot. Yet she is absolutely silent on his 1835 court-martial, suggesting that the episode was so embarrassing to Davis that she would not speak of it or that he never told her of it in the first place.

11. *Union* (Washington, D.C.), March 14, 1850.

12. James F. McIntosh, ed., *The Papers of Jefferson Davis,* Vol. 3, *July 1846–December 1848* (Baton Rouge, La., 1983), pp. 302–3.

13. Monroe and McIntosh, *Papers,* 1:406–7.

14. Thomas Watts, *Address on the Life and Character of Ex-President Jefferson Davis* (Montgomery, Ala., 1889), n.p.; *Morning News* (Dallas), April 30, 1897; Mallory Diary, October 6, 1865, Mallory Papers.

15. Theophilus H. Holmes to Jefferson Davis, August 28, 1862, and November 9, 1862, Theophilus H. Holmes Papers, William Perkins Library, Duke University, Durham, N.C.

16. Jefferson Davis to John Forsyth, July 18, 1862, Sam Richey Collection, Miami University, Miami, Ohio.

Chapter Two. Davis, Johnston, and Beauregard

1. My conversations with Major Grant took place frequently at his Escondido, California, home during the early 1960s. The most recent fuller study of the Davis-Johnston-Beauregard relationships, among others, is Stephen E. Woodworth, *Jefferson Davis and His Generals* (Lawrence, Kans., 1990). Thomas L. Connelly's magisterial *Army of the Heartland* (Baton Rouge, La., 1967) and *Autumn of Glory* (Baton Rouge, La., 1971) are still indispensable.

2. Robert McElroy, *Jefferson Davis, The Unreal and the Real* (New York, 1937), 1:19.

3. Lynda Lasswell Crist and Mary S. Dix, eds., *The Papers of Jefferson Davis,* Vol. 5, *1853–1855* (Baton Rouge, La., 1985), p. 432. The most recent biography of Johnston is Craig L. Symonds, *Joseph E. Johnston* (New York, 1992). By far the best to date, it is still rather more sympathetic than the general deserves.

4. United States Senate, *Journal of the Executive Proceedings of the Senate of the United States of America* (Washington, D.C., 1828–1887), 11:229–30.

5. C. Vann Woodward, ed., *Mary Chesnut's Civil War* (New Haven, Conn., 1981), p. 80.

6. Incident relative to Mr. Davis' telegram announcing our victory, n.d., P. G. T. Beauregard Papers, Library of Congress, Washington, D.C.

7. For a fuller discussion of the imbroglio over Johnston's rank, see William C. Davis, *Jefferson Davis: The Man and His Hour* (New York, 1991), pp. 356–61.

8. United States War Department, *War of the Rebellion: Official Records of the Union and Confederate Armies* (Washington, D.C., 1880–1901), Series I, 5:945.

9. For more on the Davis-Beauregard controversy, see Davis, *Jefferson Davis,* pp. 361–65. The best biography of the general to date remains T. Harry Williams, *P. G. T. Beauregard, Napoleon in Gray* (Baton Rouge, La., 1955).

10. Woodward, *Mary Chesnut,* p. 130.

11. William Preston Johnston to Rosa Johnston, May 19, 1862, and July 20, 1862, Mason Barret Collection, Special Collections, Howard Tilton Memorial Library, Tulane University, New Orleans, La.

12. Jefferson Davis to Varina Davis, June 3, 13, 21, 1862, Jefferson Davis Papers, Museum of the Confederacy, Richmond, Va.

13. P. G. T. Beauregard to Thomas Jordan, July 12, 1862, P. G. T. Beauregard Papers, William Perkins Library, Duke University, Durham, N.C.

14. Joseph E. Johnston to Louis T. Wigfall, November 12, 1863, Wigfall Family Papers, Library of Congress, Washington, D.C.

15. Crist and Dix, *Papers,* 8:209.

16. Woodward, *Mary Chesnut,* p. 268.

17. Dunbar Rowland, comp., *Jefferson Davis, Constitutionalist* (Jackson, Miss., 1923), 6:73–78.

18. Williams, *P. G. T. Beauregard,* p. 199.

19. A. B. Roman, *Military Operations of General Beauregard* (New York, 1884), 2:390–93.

20. *Times-Democrat* (New Orleans), December 22, 1881, and January 12, 1882.

21. Jefferson Davis to Joseph E. Davis, May 7, 1863, Lise Mitchell Papers, Tilton Library, Tulane University, New Orleans, La.

Chapter Three. Davis and Lee

This is a revised version of an essay that first appeared in Gary W. Gallagher, ed., *Lee the Soldier* (Lincoln, Nebr., 1996).

1. William C. Davis, *Jefferson Davis: The Man and His Hour* (New York, 1991), p. 197. The best and most recent full study of the Lee-Davis relationship is Stephen E. Woodworth, *Davis & Lee at War* (Lawrence, Kans., 1995).

2. Charles Bracelen Flood, *Lee: The Last Years* (Boston, 1981), p. 220.

3. Clifford Dowdey, ed., *The Wartime Papers of R. E. Lee* (Boston, 1961), p. 21.

4. Francis W. Pickens to Milledge L. Bonham, July 7, 1861, Milledge L. Bonham Papers, South Caroliniana Library, University of South Carolina, Columbia.

5. Davis, *Jefferson Davis*, p. 425.

6. William Preston Johnston to Rosa Johnston, June 1–2, 1862, Mason Barret Collection, Special Collections, Howard Tilton Memorial Library, Tulane University, New Orleans, La.

7. Dunbar Rowland, comp., *Jefferson Davis, Constitutionalist* (Jackson, Miss., 1923), 5:264.

8. Johnston to Rosa Johnston, June 9, 1862, Barret Collection.

9. United States War Department, *War of the Rebellion: Official Records of the Union and Confederate Armies* (Washington, D.C., 1880–1901), Series I, volume 12, part 3, p. 945.

10. Dowdey, *The Wartime Papers*, p. 184.

11. Ibid., p. 188.

12. Ibid., pp. 233, 238, 254.

13. Ibid., pp. 254, 259.

14. Ibid., p. 303.

15. Ibid., p. 301.

16. Davis, *Jefferson Davis*, p. 500.

17. Ibid., p. 508.

18. Stephen R. Mallory Diary, n.d., Stephen R. Mallory Papers, Southern Historical Collection, University of North Carolina, Chapel Hill.

19. Davis, *Jefferson Davis*, pp. 588–89.

20. John B. Gordon, *Reminiscences of the Civil War* (New York, 1903), p. 393.

21. Douglas Southall Freeman, *R. E. Lee* (New York, 1935), 3:544.

22. *Life and Reminiscences of Jefferson Davis, by Distinguished Men of His Time* (N.p., 1890), pp. 232–33.

23. Flood, *Lee*, p. 287n.

24. Ibid., p. 171.

25. Jefferson Davis to Joseph Davis, May 7, 1863, Lise Mitchell Papers, Tilton Library, Tulane University, New Orleans, La.

26. Rowland, *Jefferson Davis*, 7:284.

Chapter Four. The Siege of Charleston

1. E. Milby Burton, *The Siege of Charleston, 1861–1865* (Columbia, S.C., 1970), p. 6. Burton's is the fullest account of the Charleston operations. Robert N. Rosen, *Confederate Charleston* (Columbia, S.C., 1994), should also be consulted.

2. Burton, *The Siege*, p. 61.

3. Rosen, *Confederate Charleston*, p. 83.

4. Francis W. Pickens to Milledge L. Bonham, July 7, 1861, Milledge L. Bonham Papers, South Caroliniana Library, University of South Carolina, Columbia.

5. United States War Department, *War of the Rebellion: Official Records of the Union and Confederate Armies* (Washington, D.C., 1880–1901), Series I, 14:524.

6. Thomas Pelot to Lalla Pelot, September 15, 1861, and J. W. Pelot to Lalla Pelot, September 15, 1861, Lalla Pelot Papers, William Perkins Library, Duke University, Durham, N.C.

7. *Official Records*, I, 14:437.

8. Samuel Jones, *The Siege of Charleston* (New York, 1911), p. 243.

9. Russell Duncan, ed., *Blue-Eyed Son of Fortune: The Civil War Letters of Colonel Robert Gould Shaw* (Athens, Ga., 1992), p. 54.

10. Robert Brady, *The Story of One Regiment: The Eleventh Maine Infantry* (New York, 1896), p. 109.

11. In 1995 the wreck of the *Hunley* was finally discovered after more than a century of eluding searchers. As of this writing, no cause for its sinking has been determined, though a missing pane of glass in the hatch tower suggests that perhaps marines aboard the *Housatonic*, who are known to have fired at it, might have shot the glass out, and as the *Hunley* steamed away, it started taking in water through the opening.

12. Frederic Denison, *Shot and Shell: The Third Rhode Island Heavy Artillery Regiment* (Providence, 1879), p. 255.

13. Ibid.

14. Charlotte R. Holmes, *The Burckmyer Letters, March 1863–June 1865* (Columbia, S.C., 1926), p. 127.

15. Burton, *The Siege*, p. 260.

16. *Official Records*, I, 47, pt. 1, p. 38.

Chapter Five. A Different Kind of War

1. Walter P. Lane, *The Adventures and Recollections of Walter P. Lane* (Marshall, Tex., 1887), pp. 92, 93.

2. Ibid., pp. 111–12.

3. Ibid., pp. 112, 113, 114.

4. William H. Tunnard, *A Southern Record* (Baton Rouge, La., 1866), p. 101.

5. Bell I. Wiley, *The Life of Johnny Reb* (Indianapolis, Ind., 1943), pp. 6, 289.

6. Robert L. Kerby, *Kirby Smith's Confederacy* (New York, 1972), pp. 377–83.

7. Albert Castel, *General Sterling Price and the Civil War in the West* (Baton Rouge, La., 1969), p. 53.

8. C. C. Buel and Robert U. Johnson, eds., *Battles and Leaders of the Civil War* (New York, 1887), 1:311–12; Castel, *General Sterling Price,* pp. 54–55.

9. Lane, *Adventures,* pp. 90–91.

10. United States War Department, *War of the Rebellion: Official Records of the Union and Confederate Armies* (Washington, D.C., 1880–1901), Series I, volume 22, part 1, p. 83.

11. Paul W. Burch, "Kansas: Bushwhackers vs. Jayhawkers," *Journal of the West* 14 (January 1975): 92–93; Albert Castel, *A Frontier State at War: Kansas, 1861–1865* (Ithaca, N.Y., 1958), pp. 92–93.

12. Stephen B. Oates, *Confederate Cavalry West of the River* (Austin, Tex., 1965), pp. 85–87.

13. Kerby, *Kirby Smith,* p. 362.

14. Nannie M. Tilley, ed., *Federals on the Frontier* (Austin, Tex., 1963), pp. 75–76.

15. Kerby, *Kirby Smith,* p. 362.

16. Tunnard, *A Southern Record,* pp. 132–33.

17. Oates, *Confederate Cavalry,* p. 87.

18. *Official Records,* I, 22, pt. 1, p. 678.

19. Oates, *Confederate Cavalry,* pp. 145, 147; Fred L. Lee, ed., *The Battle of Westport* (Kansas City, Mo., 1976), pp. 22–23.

20. Lane, *Adventures,* p. 87.

21. Albert Castel, "They Called Him 'Bloody Bill,'" *Journal of the West* 3 (April 1964): 238.

22. *Official Records,* I, 34, pt. 1, p. 1012.

23. Lane, *Adventures,* p. 107.

24. Ely S. Parker, on Ulysses S. Grant's staff, is commonly referred to as a general, but his rank was only honorary, by brevet.

25. Kenny A. Franks, *Stand Watie and the Agony of the Cherokee Nation* (Memphis, Tenn., 1979), pp. 148, 157.

26. Oates, *Confederate Cavalry,* pp. 167–69.

27. Leroy H. Fischer, "The Western States in the Civil War," *Journal of the West* 14 (January 1975): 22–23.

28. Castel, *A Frontier State,* p. 130.

29. Lee, *The Battle,* pp. 33–34.

30. Franks, *Stand Watie,* p. 170; Tilley, *Federals,* p. 127.

31. Tunnard, *A Southern Record,* pp. 100, 103; Franks, *Stand Watie,* p. 139; Kerby, *Kirby Smith,* p. 365.

32. *Official Records,* I, 13:33.

33. Kit Dalton, *Under the Black Flag* (Memphis, Tenn., 1914), p. 54.

34. Tilley, *Federals,* pp. 97, 103.

35. Ibid., p. 102.

36. Ibid., pp. 107–8.

37. Dalton, *Under the Black Flag,* p. 54.

38. Albert Castel, *William Clarke Quantrill: His Life and Times* (Columbus, Ohio, 1992), p. 181.

39. *Official Records,* I, 34, pt. 2, p. 542.

40. The definitive account of the Lawrence raid is Thomas Goodrich, *Bloody Dawn: The Story of the Lawrence Massacre* (Kent, Ohio, 1991).

41. Thomas Goodrich, *Black Flag: Guerrilla Warfare on the Western Border, 1861–1865* (Bloomington, Ind., 1995), pp. 109–11. Goodrich's book, and Michael Fellman, *Inside War: The Guerrilla Conflict in Missouri During the American Civil War* (New York, 1989), are the most recent and best works on the general subject.

42. *Official Records,* I, 22, pt. 1, pp. 700–701.

43. Goodrich, *Black Flag,* pp. 139–41.

44. Ibid., 142–44; Castel, "They Called Him 'Bloody Bill,'" pp. 238–39.

45. Tilley, *Federals,* pp. 72, 73, 74.

Chapter Six. Forgotten Wars

1. United States War Department, *War of the Rebellion: Official Records of the Union and Confederate Armies* (Washington, D.C., 1880–1901), Series I, volume 22, part 2, p. 873.

2. Dunbar Rowland, comp., *Jefferson Davis, Constitutionalist* (Jackson, Miss., 1923), 5:183.

3. The most recent account of Sibley's raid is Donald S. Frazier, *Blood and Treasure: Confederate Empire in the Southwest* (College Station, Tex., 1995).

4. *Official Records,* I, 13:830.

5. R. J. Bell Diary, August 12, 1863, Civil War Papers, Missouri Historical Society, St. Louis, Mo.

6. Sarah Woolfolk Wiggins, ed., *The Journals of Josiah Gorgas, 1857–1878* (Tuscaloosa, Ala., 1995), p. 66.

7. Robert L. Kerby, *Kirby Smith's Confederacy* (New York, 1972), p. 53.

8. Joseph H. Parks, *General Edmund Kirby Smith, C.S.A.* (Baton Rouge, La., 1954), p. 258.

9. *Official Records,* I, 22, pt. 2, p. 873.

10. Ibid., pp. 802–3.

11. Ibid., pp. 925–26.

12. Ibid., I, 22, pt. 2, pp. 993–94.

13. Ibid.

14. Ibid., pp. 856, 857.

15. Kerby, *Kirby Smith,* p. 214.

16. Ibid.

17. *Official Records,* I, 34, pt. 2, pp. 868–70.

18. Ibid., I, 22, pt. 2, pp. 759, 781, 793, 1127; I, 41, pt. 2, p. 967; I, 41, pt. 3, pp. 466, 527–28; I, 41, pt. 4, pp. 360, 1140; I, 48, pt. 1, pp. 1017–18, 1307–9, 1357–58; I, 48, pt. 2, pp. 401–2; Kerby, *Kirby Smith,* p. 415.

Chapter Seven. Lost Will, Lost Causes

1. Clothing Account Book, Company C, 4th Kentucky Infantry, 1862–1864, Record Group 109, Chapter 8, Volume 69, National Archives, Washington, D.C.

2. Nancy N. Baxter, ed., *Hoosier Farm Boy in Lincoln's Army: The Civil War Letters of Pvt. John R. McClure* (N.p., 1971), p. 44.

3. William C. Lusk, ed., *War Letters of William Thompson Lusk* (New York, 1911), pp. 284–85.

4. James McPherson, *Battle Cry of Freedom* (New York, 1988), p. 432; E. B. Long, *The Civil War Day by Day* (New York, 1971), p. 706.

5. McPherson, *Battle Cry,* p. 600.

6. United States War Department, *War of the Rebellion: Official Records of the Union and Confederate Armies* (Washington, D.C., 1880–1901), Series III, 3:1051.

7. Ibid., IV, 3:1099.

8. Ella Lonn, *Desertion During the Civil War* (New York, 1928), pp. 150–51, 151n; McPherson, *Battle Cry,* p. 584.

9. Lonn, *Desertion,* p. 152.

10. Long, *The Civil War,* p. 706; *American Annual Cyclopedia, 1863* (New York, 1864), pp. 18–19.

11. Lonn, *Desertion,* pp. 18, 29; Bell I. Wiley, *The Life of Johnny Reb* (Indianapolis, Ind., 1943), p. 131.

12. Albert B. Moore, *Conscription and Conflict in the Confederacy* (New York, 1963), p. 224.

13. *Official Records,* IV, 2:947.

14. Long, *The Civil War,* p. 706.

15. *American Annual Cyclopedia, 1863,* p. 413.

16. Ibid., pp. 2–3.

17. Ibid., p. 407.

18. McPherson, *Battle Cry,* p. 448.

19. Ibid., p. 440.

20. Ibid., pp. 447, 691; Long, *The Civil War,* p. 728.

21. Adrian Cook, *The Armies of the Streets* (Lexington, Ky., 1974), pp. 193–94.

22. McPherson, *Battle Cry,* pp. 617–18.

23. Ibid., p. 440.

24. The most recent study of this phenomenon is Richard N. Current, *Lincoln's Loyalists* (Boston, 1992).

25. Georgia L. Tatum, *Disloyalty in the Confederacy* (Chapel Hill, N.C., 1934), p. 123.

26. Ibid., pp. 162–63.

27. McPherson, *Battle Cry,* pp. 561–62, 687–88.

28. Wilfred B. Yearns, *The Confederate Congress* (Athens, Ga., 1960), pp. 49–50.

29. C. Vann Woodward, ed., *Mary Chesnut's Civil War* (New Haven, Conn., 1981), p. 519.

30. *American Annual Cyclopedia, 1863,* p. 217.

31. John B. Jones, *A Rebel War Clerk's Diary* (Philadelphia, 1866), 2:101, 103.

32. Randall C. Jimerson, *The Private Civil War* (Baton Rouge, La., 1988), p. 238.

33. Robert Garlick Hill Kean, *Inside the Confederate Government* (New York, 1957), p. 119.

34. William D. Pender, *The General to His Lady* (Chapel Hill, N.C., 1965), p. 190; Robert Moore, *A Life for the Confederacy* (Jackson, Tenn., 1958), p. 127.

35. Jimerson, *The Private Civil War*, pp. 230, 231, 234.

36. Loren J. Morse, ed., *Civil War Letters and Diaries of Bliss Morse* (Tahlequah, Okla., 1985), p. 108.

37. Richard Beringer, Herman Hattaway, Archer Jones, and William Still, *Why the South Lost the Civil War* (Athens, Ga., 1987), pp. 245, 305; McPherson, *Battle Cry*, pp. 670–71.

38. Jimerson, *The Private Civil War*, pp. 230, 232–33.

39. James I. Robertson Jr., *The Civil War Letters of General Robert McAllister* (New Brunswick, N.J., 1961), pp. 248, 384.

40. Beringer et al., *Why the South Lost*, p. 425. This work is the major and most recent exponent of the loss of will theory and has sparked considerable discussion.

41. Ibid., pp. 31, 32, 34.

42. Ibid., pp. 81, 266.

43. Clothing Account Book, National Archives.

Chapter Eight. The Turning Point That Wasn't

1. Larry E. Nelson, *Bullets, Ballots, and Rhetoric: Confederate Policy for the United States Presidential Contest of 1864* (University, Ala., 1980), p. 14.

2. Alexander H. Stephens to Linton Stephens, May 7, 1864, Alexander H. Stephens Papers, Manhattanville College of the Sacred Heart, Purchase, N.Y.

3. United States War Department, *War of the Rebellion: Official Records of the Union and Confederate Armies* (Washington, D.C., 1880–1901), Series I, volume 37, part 1, pp. 766–67.

4. Ibid., I, 41, pt. 4, pp. 1068–69; Albert I. Castel, *General Sterling Price and the Civil War in the West* (Baton Rouge, La., 1968), p. 252.

5. The failure of DuPont's fleet against Fort Sumter in 1863 not to the contrary. DuPont was not trying merely to bypass the fort. Moreover, his fleet was ravaged not by Sumter's guns but by those of the myriad shore batteries ringing Charleston Harbor.

6. Nelson, *Bullets*, p. 61.

7. Ibid., pp. 25–26.

8. Joseph E. Johnston, *Narrative of Military Operations* (New York, 1874), pp. 362–63.

9. Nelson, *Bullets*, pp. 13–14.

10. Jefferson Davis, *Rise and Fall of the Confederate Government* (New York, 1881), 2:611.

11. Nelson, *Bullets*, pp. 70ff.

12. Ibid., pp. 89ff.

13. John W. Headley, *Confederate Operations in Canada and in New York* (New York, 1906), pp. 271ff.

14. *Official Records,* I, 43:932.

15. Oscar Kinchen, *Confederate Operations in Canada and the North* (North Quincy, Mass., 1970), pp. 131–34.

16. William C. Davis, "The 'Conduct of Mr. Thompson,'" *Civil War Times Illustrated* 9 (May 1970): 46.

17. Nelson, *Bullets,* pp. 170–75.

18. Stephen W. Sears, *Landscape Turned Red: The Battle of Antietam* (Boston, 1983), p. 167.

19. John Prest, *Lord John Russell* (Columbia, S.C., 1972), p. 395.

20. Roy P. Basler, comp., *The Collected Works of Abraham Lincoln* (New Brunswick, N.J., 1955), 7:514.

21. U. S. Grant, *Personal Memoirs* (New York, 1885), 2:146.

22. *Official Records,* I, 32, pt. 3, p. 246.

23. Grant, *Memoirs,* 2:146.

24. David E. Long, *The Jewel of Liberty* (Harrisburg, Pa., 1994), pp. 283–84.

25. Stephen W. Sears, *George B. McClellan, the Young Napoleon* (Boston, 1988), pp. 375–76.

26. Ibid., p. 375.

27. U.S. Congress, *Journal of the Congress of the Confederate States of America* (Washington, D.C., 1904), 1:66.

28. *Daily Dispatch* (Richmond), October 10, 1864.

29. Interested readers will find a stimulating and thoughtful alternative view of the importance of the election of 1864 in Albert Castel, *Winning and Losing in the Civil War* (Columbia, S.C., 1996).

Chapter Nine. John C. Breckinridge and Confederate Defeat

1. The standard biography is William C. Davis, *Breckinridge: Statesman, Soldier, Symbol* (Baton Rouge, La., 1974).

2. Burton J. Hendrick, *Statesmen of the Lost Cause* (New York, 1939), p. 324.

3. *Turf, Field and Farm* (New York), May 21, 1875; House of Representatives to John C. Breckinridge, August 23, 1862, Breckinridge Compiled Service Record, Record Group 109, National Archives, Washington, D.C.; John B. Jones, *A Rebel War Clerk's Diary* (Philadelphia, 1866), 2:425.

4. *Tri-Weekly Constitutionalist* (Augusta), February 8, 1865; Jones, *A Rebel War Clerk,* 2:395, 403; Breckinridge to Jefferson Davis, February 14, 1865, Chapter 9, Volume 99, Record Group 109, National Archives.

5. United States War Department, *War of the Rebellion: Official Records of the Union and Confederate Armies* (Washington, D.C., 1880–1901), Series I, volume 47, part 2, p. 1303.

6. Ibid., I, 46, pt. 3, pp. 1339, 1362; I, 47, pt. 2, pp. 1174, 1284, 1313, 1347, 1398; I, 49, pt. 2, p. 1166; I, 53, p. 1041.

7. Ibid., I, 46, pt. 2, pp. 1245, 1292, 1311–12; I, 47, pt. 2, pp. 1201, 1207–8, 1238; I, 47, pt. 3, pp. 795–96, 813–14, 829–30, 836, 845, 851; I, 49, pt. 1, p. 970; I, 49, pt. 2, p. 1255; I, 51, pt. 2, p. 1069.

8. Dunbar Rowland, comp., *Jefferson Davis, Constitutionalist* (Jackson, Miss., 1923), 7:356.

9. Ibid., pp. 351–52, 357; *Official Records*, I, 47, pt. 2, p. 1312; I, 51, pt. 2, pp. 1063–64.

10. Rowland, *Jefferson Davis*, 7:349–52; *Official Records*, I, 51, pt. 2, pp. 1063–64.

11. *Whig* (Richmond), March 31, 1865.

12. J. Cutler Andrews, *The South Reports the Civil War* (Princeton, N.J., 1970), pp. 529–33.

13. *Official Records*, I, 46, pt. 3, pp. 1335–36; I, 47, pt. 2, pp. 1311, 1312, 1313, 1376, 1425; Breckinridge to Zebulon Vance, March 23, 31, 1865, Secretary of War, Telegrams Sent, Chapter 9, Volume 35, Record Group 109, National Archives.

14. *Official Records*, I, 46, pt. 2, pp. 1242, 1244–45, 1252–53; I, 49, pt. 1, p. 1006; Jones, *A Rebel War Clerk*, 2:441; Breckinridge to J. Stoddard Johnston, February 23, 1865, J. Stoddard Johnston Papers, Filson Club, Louisville, Ky.

15. *Official Records*, I, 46, pt. 2, pp. 1254, 1257.

16. Ibid., pp. 1257, 1259–60, 1264–65; I, 46, pt. 3, p. 1370; Jones, *A Rebel War Clerk*, 2:454.

17. Rowland, *Jefferson Davis*, 7:354–55; Breckinridge to Chiefs of Bureau, May 4, 1865, Jeremy F. Gilmer Papers, Museum of the Confederacy, Richmond, Va., Basil W. Duke to William T. Walthall, April 6, 1878, Breckinridge Family Papers, Library of Congress, Washington, D.C.

18. *Commercial* (Cincinnati), November 15, 1887; *Courier-Journal* (Louisville), May 30, 1900; *Official Records*, I, 38, pt. 3, p. 697; I, 46, pt. 2, pp. 446, 1209–10; I, 49, pt. 1, pp. 978–79; IV, 3, p. 1064; Jones, *A Rebel War Clerk*, 2:416.

19. Breckinridge to Davis, February 18, 1865, Jefferson Davis Papers, Louisiana Historical Association Collection, Howard Tilton Memorial Library, Tulane University, New Orleans, La.

20. James Longstreet, *From Manassas to Appomattox* (Philadelphia, 1896), p. 504.

21. John A. Campbell to Breckinridge, March 5, 1865, John A. Campbell Papers, Southern Historical Collection, University of North Carolina, Chapel Hill; R. E. Lee to Breckinridge, March 9, 1865, Davis Papers, Tulane University, New Orleans, La.; Richard Morton to Breckinridge, March 10, 1865, and A. R. Lawton to Breckinridge, March 10, 1865, and Josiah Gorgas to Breckinridge, March 11, 1865, Louis T. Wigfall Papers, Library of Congress; Breckinridge to Davis, March 13, 1865, Frederick M. Dearborn Collection, Houghton Library, Harvard University, Cambridge, Mass.; Breckinridge to Vance, March 25, 1865, Zebulon Vance Papers, Department of Archives and History, Raleigh, N.C.

22. Rowland, *Jefferson Davis*, 7:577; *Courier-Journal* (Louisville), June 8, 1875.

23. *Official Records*, I, 46, pt. 3, pp. 1382–83, 1393; Joseph E. Johnston, *Narrative of Military Operations* (New York, 1874), pp. 396–98.

24. Clement Dowd, *Life of Zebulon B. Vance* (Charlotte, N.C., 1897), pp. 485–86.

25. Johnston, *Narrative,* pp. 404–5; John H. Reagan, *Memoirs, with Special Reference to Secession and the Civil War* (New York, 1906), p. 200; J. Stoddard Johnston, "Sketches of Operations of General John C. Breckinridge, No. 3," *Southern Historical Society Papers 7* (October 1879): 389.

26. *Official Records,* I, 47, pt. 3, pp. 830–31, 834; Breckinridge to Davis, April 23, 1865, Johnston Papers; Rowland, *Jefferson Davis,* 8:192.

27. William H. Parker, *Recollections of a Naval Officer, 1841–1865* (New York, 1883), p. 366; *Herald* (New York), June 27, 1865.

28. *Official Records,* I, 49, pt. 2, p. 719.

29. *Daily Dispatch* (Richmond), October 28, 1861.

30. C. Vann Woodward, ed., *Mary Chesnut's Civil War* (New Haven, Conn., 1981), p. 706.

31. *Courier-Journal* (Louisville), May 18, June 18, 1875.

32. W. G. Bean, ed., "Memoranda of Conversations Between Robert E. Lee and William Preston Johnston May 7, 1868 and March 18, 1870," *Virginia Magazine of History and Biography 73* (October 1965):479.

Chapter Ten. Stonewall Jackson in Myth and Memory

1. The essay "No More Biographies" has appeared in several anthologies, most recently *Thurber on Thurber* (New York, 1989).

2. Edward O. Guerrant Diary, October 24, 1864, Southern Historical Collection, University of North Carolina, Chapel Hill.

3. Undated clipping in O. L. Cottrell Confederate Scrapbook in possession of the author.

4. As of this writing the book is untitled.

5. C. C. Buel and Robert U. Johnson, eds., *Battles and Leaders of the Civil War* (New York, 1888), 1:122–23. Robertson's forthcoming biography explodes this myth ably.

6. The late Frederick S. Klein, who edited *The Douglas Diary: Student Days at Franklin and Marshall College, 1856–1858* (Lancaster, Pa., 1973), told the author in the early 1970s that he had heard that Douglas' Civil War diary still existed in family hands but that, distrustful of historians, family members had determined not to let it be seen.

7. These comments reflect the conclusions Robertson shared with the author during many hours of interesting and stimulating conversation over the course of his writing of his definitive biography.

8. Undated 1866 *News* (New York) clipping in Eliza Kidd Porter Album, Benjamin Porter Papers, Special Collections, Auburn University, Auburn, Ala.

9. *Dictionary of American Naval Fighting Ships* (Washington, D.C., 1976), 6:645–47.

Chapter Eleven. Myths and Realities of the Confederacy

1. Raphael Semmes, *The Confederate Raider* Alabama (New York, 1962), pp. 369–70.

2. Ibid., p. 166.

3. Richard M. McMurry, "The War We Never Finished," *Civil War Times Illustrated* 28

(December 1989): 62–71. The correspondence referred to will not be cited by name of writer in order to prevent any embarrassment, not to mention litigation. Copies of the correspondence are in my files.

4. On a personal note, the author would point out that his own career has been devoted predominantly to the study of the Confederacy, and that his ancestry is almost entirely Southern, including four forebears who fought in the Confederate Army. One of them, Private Josiah Davis of the Army of Northern Virginia, died April 7, 1865, two days before he would have been surrendered. And the author's son happens to be named Jefferson Davis. This probably will not prevent some accusations that the author is anti-Southern or anti-Confederate or even a Marxist, a Zionist, or a tool of the NAACP, but perhaps it will persuade at least some—who read footnotes—that this essay is not written as an attack on the South.

5. "It Isn't the C—L War." Unsigned and undated pamphlet in my possession.

6. See, for example, John S. Tilley, *Facts the Historians Leave Out: A Confederate Primer* (Nashville, Tenn., 1951), p. 11.

7. Alfred H. Stone, "The Early Slave Laws of Mississippi," *Publications of the Mississippi Historical Society* 2 (1889): 143–44.

8. For examples, see William C. Davis, *"A Government of Our Own": The Making of the Confederacy* (New York, 1994), pp. 161, 190, 290, 332.

9. Janet Sharp Hermann, *The Pursuit of a Dream* (New York, 1981), pp. 40–41.

10. Roy P. Basler, comp., *The Collected Works of Abraham Lincoln* (New Brunswick, N.J., 1953), 1:438.

11. Ibid., 5:537.

Chapter Twelve. The Civil War and the Confederacy in Cinema

1. Randy Roberts and James S. Olson, *John Wayne, American* (New York, 1995), pp. 174–75.

2. Conversation with Andrew McLaglen, March 1982.

3. Robert B. Toplin, ed., *Ken Burns's The Civil War: Historians Respond* (New York, 1996). This book, like the series, is unfortunately flawed in scope and content and is just as likely to spawn controversies as to settle any.

Index

Adams, Daniel, 151
Adams, John Quincy, 6
Addey, Markenfield, 162
Alvarez Kelly, 195–96
Anderson, Richard, 55
Anderson, Robert, 54–55, 65, 70
Anderson, William ("Bloody Bill"), 82,
    86, 88–89, 90–91
Antietam, Battle of, x, 41, 49
    as turning point, 137–39
Appointment with Destiny, 198, 201
Atlanta, 140–41

Banks, Nathaniel P., 101, 105
Battery Wagner (siege of Charleston),
    61–64, 197
Baxter, Warner, 199
Baxter Springs, Kans., 89–90, 104
Beauregard, Pierre G. T., 13, 36, 40, 44, 49,
    155
    at Charleston, 55–57, 58, 62, 68, 151, 152
    and Davis, 15–34
    on Davis, 21, 25, 30, 32
    as general, 32–33
    portrait, 19
Benham, Henry, 59
Benjamin, Judah P., 5, 6, 11, 23, 24, 145, 155
Beresford-Hope, A. J., 172
Bickley, George, 133
Birth of a Nation, 193
Black participation, 77–78
Blue and Gray, The, 198, 200–201
Blue and the Gray, The, 198
Blunt, James G., 89
Bowers, John, 165
Bowie, James, 184
Boykin, Hamilton, on Johnston, 27
Bragg, Braxton, 6, 12, 16, 25, 28, 29, 30, 43,
    44, 48, 93, 99, 112, 113, 121, 152

Breckinridge, John C., x, 31, 145
    and Davis, 150–51
    and Lee, 150–51
    portrait, 149
    as secretary of war, 148–57
Breckinridge, William C. P., 156
Bridges, Lloyd, 193
Brown, John, 74, 187, 188
Bruce, Eli M., 150
Buchanan, James, 189
Buena Vista, Battle of, 8, 20
Bull Run, First Battle of (Manassas), 20,
    59
Burnett, Henry C., 158
Burns, Ken, 202–5
Burnside, Ambrose, 111
Burt, Armistead L., 55

Caine, Michael, 197
Calhoun, John C., 6, 180
Campbell, John A., 153
Caperton, Allen, 155
Centralia, Mo., massacre, 90–91, 104
Chambers, Lenoir, 165
Chancellorsville, Va., 42
Charleston, S.C., siege of, 53–70
    illus., 69
Chattanooga, Tenn., 44
Chesnut, James, 20
Chesnut, Mary B., 121, 157
Chivington, John M., 86
Churchill, Winston, 58
Cinema, Civil War in, 192–203
Civil War, names for, 178–79
Civil War, The, 202–5
Civil War Journal, 205
Civil War Times Illustrated, 177
Clay, Clement C., on Davis, 3, 32–33
Clay, Henry, 180

Index

Clement, Arch, 88
Cleveland, Henry, 131
Cobb, Howell, 151
Confederate States of America, mythology, 175–90
Connelley, Thomas L., 3
Cooke, John Esten, 162, 165–66, 168
Cooper, Samuel, 11, 16, 21, 22, 27, 37
Crane, Stephen, 195
Crist, Lynda, xi
Cronkite, Walter, 197
Curtis, Samuel, 81

Dabney, Robert L., 163–64
Dahlgren, John, 61, 63, 65
Dalton, Kit, 88
Dark Command, The, 194–95
Davis, Jefferson, ix, 55, 57, 77, 94, 95, 97, 100, 102, 104, 106, 107, 108, 120, 128, 130, 131–32, 134, 137, 148, 168, 188, 193
    and Beauregard, 13, 15–34
    on Samuel Davis, 5
    enigma of, 5–14
    on generalship, 32
    and Varina Howell, 9–10
    and independence, 145–46
    insecurity of, 13
    interference of with generals, 13, 28
    and Albert S. Johnston, 6
    and Joseph E. Johnston, 13, 15–34
    judgment, 6–7, 12–13
    and Lee, 35–50
    on Lee, 40, 50
    obstinacy, 12
    personality, 5–6
    portrait, 4
    and sycophants, 6
    and Sarah Taylor, 10–11
    on the war, 122
    work habits, 11–12
    youth, 35
Davis, Jefferson C., 54
Davis, Joseph, 5–6, 7, 9, 31, 48

Davis, Josiah, 218n4
Davis, Samuel E., 5, 7, 9
Davis, Sarah Taylor, 7, 9
Davis, Varina Howell, 8, 9–10, 40, 49, 207n10
Desertion, 114–15, 122
Disney, Walt, 196, 200
Dissent, 118–20
Divided Union, The, 202
Dixon, Thomas, 193
Douglas, Henry Kyd, 165–68
Drayton, Percival, 57, 61
Drayton, Thomas, 57
Dreyfuss, Richard, 201
Duke, Basil, on Breckinridge, 154
DuPont, Samuel F. I., 57–61, 214n5

Early, Jubal, 129, 130, 137, 166, 167
Echols, John, 151
Election of 1864, 127–47
Endfield, Cy, 197
Enlistments, 113–14
Evans, Nathan G., 59–60
Ewell, Richard, 174

Farragut, David G., 112, 137
Fifty-fourth Massachusetts Infantry, 62, 197
First Mississippi Rifles, 35
Ford, John, 196
Forrest, Nathan B., 82, 152
Fort Sumter, S.C., 54–55, 63–65
    illus., 63
Foster, John G., 65, 67, 69
Fox, Gustavus V., 60
Fredericksburg, Va., 42
Freeman, Douglas S., 165
Friendly Persuasion, 195

Gallagher, Gary, xi
Garnet, Richard, 170
General, The, 193–94
Gettysburg, Pa., 43, 49

Gettysburg (movie), 199–200, 201
Gillmore, Quincy, 61–62, 63–65, 69
Gist, Constitution, 60
Gist, Independence, 60
Gist, States Rights, 60
Glory, 197
Gone with the Wind, 194, 199, 200
Gore Vidal's Lincoln, 198
Grant, Chapman, 15, 208n1
Grant, Ulysses S., 15, 44, 50, 96, 100, 101,
    103, 104, 106, 112, 113, 128, 129, 140,
    146, 161, 173, 193
Gray Ghost, The, 197–98
Great Locomotive Chase, The, 196, 200
Greeley, Horace, 133
Green, Thomas, 83
Grierson, Benjamin, 196
Griffith, D. W., 193
Guerilla warfare, 71–92, 103–4

Hampton, Wade, 151, 195
Hardee, William J., 94
Harding, Warren G., 161
Harney, William S., 3
Havens, Benny, 9
Henderson, G. F. R., 164
Heston, Charlton, 201
Hill, A. P., 170
Hill, Benjamin, 127, 131
Hindman, Thomas C., 76, 77, 79–80, 87,
    91, 97–98, 100, 104
Hines, Thomas H., 136
Holbrook, Hal, 198
Holden, William, 196
Holmes, Theophilus H., 6, 12, 97–98, 99,
    100, 101, 102
Homefront, 116–21
Hood, John B., 6, 16, 30, 31, 45, 107, 131,
    137, 140–41, 145, 150
Hopley, Catherine C., 162
Horse Soldiers, The, 196
Hotchkiss, Jedediah, 164, 167, 172
Hough, Daniel, 54–55

Howell, Varina. *See* Davis, Varina Howell
How the West Was Won, 196
Hunley, Horace L., 66
Hunley (submarine), 66–67, 210n11
Hunter, David, 59, 69, 162
Hunter, R. M. T., 155
Huston, John, 195

Imboden, John D., 166
Indian participation, 78, 82, 84
Ironclads, 60–61, 65
Ironclads (movie), 199

Jackson, Andrew, 6
Jackson, Mary Anna, 163–64, 172
Jackson, Thomas J. ("Stonewall"), x, 41,
    45, 59, 111, 113, 197
  historiography, 161–74
  hypochondria, 167–68
  and Lee, 170–71
  portrait, 163
James, Frank, 91
James, Jesse, 91
Jefferson, Thomas, 184, 186
Jennison, Charles, 86
Johnson, Andrew, 156
Johnson, Waldo, 155
Johnston, Albert S., 16, 18, 21, 22, 24, 25,
    36, 37, 39, 43, 45, 49
  relationship with Davis, 6
Johnston, Joseph E., 13, 38, 39, 40, 43, 44,
    45, 48, 49, 131, 137, 140, 151, 152, 155,
    156
  and Davis, 15–34
  as general, 25–29, 30
  portrait, 17
Johnston, William Preston, 25, 157
  on Beauregard, 24
  on Lee, 40
Jones, Samuel, 68

Kantor, McKinlay, 205
Keach, Stacy, 201

Index

Keaton, Buster, 193
Kenner, Duncan, 146, 147
Klein, Frederick S., 217n6
Knights of the Golden Circle, 128, 132–33, 136, 137

Lafitte, Jean, 184
Lane, James, 77, 89
Lane, Walter P., 72–73, 76, 83
Lawrence, Kans., massacre, 84–88, 89, 104
Lee, Fitzhugh, 151
Lee, Robert E., 16, 21, 22, 26, 27, 30, 31, 32, 34, 68, 76, 78, 93, 111, 121, 129, 131, 138, 139, 142, 161, 168, 186–87, 189, 193
    on Breckinridge, 157
    at Charleston, 57–58
    and Davis, 35–50
    on Davis, 36, 47, 48
    portrait, 37
Letcher, John, 18, 36
Lincoln, Abraham, x, 33, 50, 58, 105, 112, 119, 120, 146, 161, 168, 197
    and Charleston, 56–57, 59
    and election of 1864, 127–47
    portrait, 128
Lincoln Conspiracy, The, 196–97
Longstreet, James, 43, 113, 131, 154, 170
Lopez, Narciso, 36
Lyon, Nathaniel, 95

McCarthy, Frank, 201
McClellan, George B., 26, 33, 38, 40, 43, 111, 139
    and election of 1864, 127–47
    portrait, 143
McCulloch, Ben, 95, 96
    portrait, 96
McCulloch, Hugh, 104
McIntosh, James, 82
McLaglen, Andrew, 196
Magruder, John B., 74, 98, 99, 100
Major Dundee, 196

Mallory, Stephen R.
    on Beauregard and Johnston, 24
    on Davis, 8, 12, 45, 155
Mansfield, Battle of, 72
Marmaduke, John S., 81, 98
Marshall, George, 50
Meade, George G., 44, 112
Meade, R. K., 55
Melton, Samuel, 115
Mexican involvement, 83–84
Minnegerode, Charles, 47
Montgomery, Isaac, 185
Morgan, John Hunt, 130, 134
Mosby, John S., 197–98
Mudd, Samuel, 199
Mulligan, James, 75

Napoleon III, 102–3
Nixon, Richard, 189
North and South, 198
Northrop, Lucius B., 11, 12, 150, 151
Northwest Conspiracy, 132–37

Oldham, Williamson, 123
O'Sullivan, Timothy, 192
Owsley, Frank, 124

Palmerston, Lord, 138
Patton, George S., 173
Pea Ridge, Ark., Battle of, 72, 76, 79, 86, 88, 96
Peck, Gregory, 201
Pemberton, John C., 12, 31, 58, 59, 60
Pendleton, Sandie, 167
Perfect Tribute, The, 199, 201
Pershing, John, 15
Phillips, William A., 84
Pickens, Francis, 38, 57, 58
Pierce, Franklin, 6, 8, 55
Pike, Albert, portrait, 85
Pleasonton, Alfred, 81
Polk, James K., 8, 39
Polk, Leonidas, 6

Porter, David D., 83
Port Royal, S.C., 56–57
Prairie Grove, Ark., Battle of, 76, 77,
    79–80, 91–92, 98
Presley, Elvis, 191
Preston, William, 157
Price, Sterling, 75, 90, 95, 137
    Missouri raid, 81, 105–6, 130
    portrait, 80
Prisoner of Shark Island, 199

Quantrill, William C., 84–85, 86, 87,
    89–90, 91, 104, 194

Raid, The, 194
Raintree County, 195
Randolph, George W., 150
Reagan, John H.
    on Davis, 12, 155
Red Badge of Courage, The, 195, 198
Red River Campaign, La., 72, 83–84, 105
    illus., 83
Rhett, Robert B., 181
Richmond, Va., illus., 123
Ripley, Roswell S., 55, 57, 58
Robards, Jason, 199, 201
Robertson, James I., 165, 171, 174, 217n7
Rommel, Erwin, 173
Roosevelt, Franklin D., 50, 187
Rosecrans, William S., 43, 81
Ross, John, 84
Russell, John, 138

St. John, Isaac M., 150, 151–52
Sandburg's Lincoln, 198
Schimmelfennig, Alexander, 67–68, 69
Scott, George C., 201
Scott, Winfield, 9, 39
Sears, Stephen, 138
Secession, 186–87
Secessionville, S.C., Battle of, 59, 60
Seddon, James, 101, 107

Semmes, Raphael, 176–77
    portrait, 176
Shaara, Michael, 199, 201
Shaw, Robert G., 62, 197
Sheen, Martin, 200
Shelby, Joseph O., 81, 85, 91
Shenandoah, 196
Sheridan, Philip H., 173
Sherman, William T., 32, 69–70, 106, 112,
    128, 140–41, 145, 146, 156, 173, 137
Shiloh, Tenn., Battle of, 112
Sibley, Henry H., 95, 96
Slavery, 181–85
Slidell, John, 102
Smith, Edmund Kirby, 16, 30, 78, 130, 155
    on guerrillas, 104
    portrait, 79
    in the Trans-Mississippi, 99–107
    on the Trans-Mississippi, 93
Smith, Gustavus, 22, 39, 40, 48, 98
Smith, William, 151
Stanwyck, Barbara, 199
State rights, 180–81, 182
Stephens, Alexander H., 9, 130, 134, 145,
    147, 178
    quoted, 127, 130–31
Stewart, James, 196
Stone fleet, 59
Stonewall, CSS, 172
Stonewall, USS, 172–73
Stonewall Jackson, USS, 173
Stuart, James E. B., 45, 161, 173
Submarines, 65–67
Sumner, Edwin V., 18

Tap Roots, 194
Tate, Allen, 164
Taylor, Elizabeth, 195
Taylor, Richard, 100, 101, 102, 105, 150
Taylor, Sarah Knox. *See* Davis, Sarah
    Taylor
Taylor, Zachary, 6, 8, 35, 39
Thomas, Richard, 198

Index

Thompson, Jacob, 132–37
Thurber, James, 161
Todd, George, 86, 90
Toombs, Robert, 5
Torn, Rip, 201
Towers, Constance, 196
Trans-Mississippi Department
    nature of fighting, 71–92
    war in, 92–108
Truman, Harry S., 179
Twiggs, David, 22

Vallandigham, Clement L., 119, 132, 133
Van Buren, Martin, 6
Vance, Zebulon, 151, 152, 155, 156
Vandiver, Frank, 3, 164–65
Van Dorn, Earl, 94–97
Vest, George G., 155
Villa, Pancho, 15

Walker, Leroy P., 157
Watie, Saladin, 86
Watie, Stand, 82, 83, 84, 85, 86
Watts, Thomas, on Davis, 12
Wayne, John, 196, 201
Weaver, Dennis, 199
Westport, Mo., Battle of, 81, 85, 105
Widmark, Richard, 196
Wigfall, Louis T., 155
Wiley, Bell I., 3
Will, Confederacy and loss of, 111–26
Winslow, John, 176
Wood, Ben, 172
Wyler, William, 195

Yancey, William L., 3
Young, Bennett, 135, 194

Zulu, 197